# Some
# Hustling
# This!

## TAKING JAZZ to the WORLD
### 1914 - 1929

OTHER BOOKS BY MARK MILLER

The Miller Companion to Jazz in Canada and Canadians in Jazz (2001)
Such Melodious Racket: The Lost History of Jazz in Canada, 1914-1949 (1997)
Cool Blues: Charlie Parker in Canada, 1953 (1989)
Boogie, Pete & The Senator: Canadian Musicians in Jazz, the Eighties (1987)
Jazz in Canada: Fourteen Lives (1982)

# Some
# Hustling
# This!

## TAKING JAZZ to the WORLD
## 1914 - 1929

# MARK MILLER

The Mercury Press

The publisher gratefully acknowledges the financial assistance of the Canada Council for the Arts, the Ontario Arts Council, and the Ontario Book Publishing Tax Credit Program. The publisher further acknowledges the financial support of the Government of Canada through the Department of Canadian Heritage's Book Publishing Industry Development Program (BPIDP) for our publishing activities.

Editor: Beverley Daurio
Cover, composition and page design: Beverley Daurio
Cover image: Photograph of Louis Mitchell, Mark Berresford Collection
Printed and bound in Canada
Printed on acid-free paper

1 2 3 4 5    09 08 07 06 05

Library and Archives Canada Cataloguing in Publication
Miller, Mark, 1951-
Some hustling this : taking jazz to the world, 1914-1929 / Mark Miller.
ISBN 1-55128-119-8
1. Mitchell, Louis, 1885-1957.  2. Jazz musicians--Biography.
3. Jazz--Europe--1911-1920--History and criticism.
4. Jazz--Europe--1921-1930--History and criticism.
I. Title.  II. Title: Taking jazz to the world, 1914-1929.

ML422.M552M64 2005     781.65'092     C2005-905298-8

The Mercury Press
Box 672, Station P, Toronto, Ontario  Canada  M5S 2Y4
www.themercurypress.ca

*Some Hustling This!*
*Taking Jazz to the World*
*1914 - 1929*
is dedicated to the memory of my mother,
Ruth Mary Miller

# Table of Contents

# Acknowledgments

*Some Hustling This!— Taking Jazz to the World, 1914-1929* is the result of four years of research and, latterly, writing; it is also the product of a much longer interest in the lost, the forgotten and the overlooked in jazz history, an interest that I have previously explored in my books about jazz in Canada, the first of which was published in 1982.

More specifically, *Some Hustling This!* is a direct extension of my fourth book, *Such Melodious Racket: The Lost History of Jazz in Canada, 1914-1949* (1997), which in part documents some of the earliest visits of American musicians. *Some Hustling This!* is also linked, at least in spirit, to my third book, *Cool Blues: Charlie Parker in Canada, 1953* (1989), which concerns the alto saxophonist's appearances in Montreal and Toronto two years before his death.

My interest more generally in the pioneering American figures who took jazz to the world has been fueled by the research and writings published under Laurie Wright's watchful editorial eye in the British journal *Storyville* between 1965 and 2003. That material, in many cases presented essentially as raw, chronologically organized data, has served as a basis for several of the sections in *Some Hustling This!* and has been a starting point for the research that supports many of the others.

Accordingly, I must respectfully acknowledge the work of Laurie Wright and several of his contributors, in particular Horst J.P. Bergmeier, Mark Berresford, Morton Clausen, Robert Pernet, Howard Rye and Rainer Lotz, for their diligence, resourcefulness and attention to detail. Chris Goddard's book, *Jazz away from Home* (1979), has also been valuable for its first-person accounts of jazz in Paris during the 1920s, as provided by musicians who were still alive in the 1970s.

As with my previous projects, I have further benefitted from the professional assistance of fellow writers and researchers and, equally, from the personal support of friends. I list them here, colleagues and friends both, with my thanks.

For their generosity in providing research assistance above and beyond the call: Mark Berresford in England; Lawrence Gushee, Robert Hegamin and Richard L. Mumma in the United States; Juan Carlos Lopes in Argentina; Janine Pernet-Van Esch in Belgium; Mike Sutcliffe in Australia; Erik van den Berg in The Netherlands; Colin Bray, Richard Green, Rob van der Bliek, John Wilby and Ross Wilby in Canada, and Theo Zwicky in Switzerland.

For various professional courtesies in response to specific inquiries and requests: Jerry D'Souza and John Norris in Canada; Barry Kernfeld, Floyd Levin,

Jim Loeffler, Mike Montgomery, Dan Morgenstern, Frank Powers, Bruce Vermazen and Kathleen Wyer Lane in the United States; Rainer Lotz in Germany; and Joe Moore, Howard Rye and Laurie Wright in England. My thanks also to the staffs of the interlibrary loan departments of the Toronto Reference Library and the Robarts Library, University of Toronto.

For assistance in translation: Marc Chénard, Kat Tancock and Lise van der Bliek.

More personally, for the interest and encouragement that sustained my work as it progressed: Kelly Baird and John Wilby, Mark Berresford, Stuart Broomer, Greg Buium, Geoff Chapman, Marc Chénard, Monika Croydon, Paula Fayerman and Doug Harkness, Richard Green, James Hale, Tiffany Knowles, Andrea Koziol, David Lancashire, Jack and Margaret Litchfield, Ken Little, Eugene Miller, Keith Miller, Ruth Miller, Lorne Nehring, Lewis Porter, Craig Storey, Ron Sweetman and Kevin Whitehead. Special thanks in this regard to Robin Elliott, Lawrence Gushee, David Stimpson, Sherrie Tucker and Rob van der Bliek.

Finally, I offer my sincere thanks to Beverley Daurio of The Mercury Press. *Some Hustling This!* is my third book for Mercury and, like the others, has benefitted greatly from her support, understanding and trust as a publisher, and her careful eye and keen intuition as an editor.

Work on *Some Hustling This!* was supported in part during early 2003 by a grant from the Writers' Reserve of the Ontario Arts Council.

*Mark Miller, Toronto,*
*August 2005*

# Preface

At this late date, it is entirely reasonable to suggest that jazz belongs to the world. This is not to deny its American — or, more correctly, African-American — origins, only to assert that it has been embraced and acculturated by many other countries.

Most of these countries have developed their own legend and lore with respect to their early exposure to, and contact with, American jazz musicians. The theoretical implications of these encounters — in Canada, England and France before 1920, and elsewhere in Europe, South America and the Far East during the 1920s — have become a popular subject for critical analysis, bringing together as they do the interrelated cultural and sociological themes of modernism, primitivism, exoticism, racism, identity and "otherness."

Missing from this body of writing, however, is a basic account of who went where, when, and did what. To that end, *Some Hustling This!*— *Taking Jazz to the World, 1914-1929* is a narrative of first encounters, notable events and significant figures in the internationalization of jazz.

The narrative is framed by Louis Mitchell's career abroad, beginning with his first trip as a drummer with the Southern Symphony Quintette to London in 1914 and concluding with his final attempt as an entrepreneur to operate a nightclub in Paris in 1929. True, other ragtime musicians travelled in vaudeville outside the United States as early as, or earlier than, Mitchell and his four fellow members of the Clef Club of New York; the Musical Spillers, the Six Brown Brothers and clarinetist Wilbur Sweatman had all appeared in Canada by 1911, for example, and Spillers and Browns in England by 1914. Mitchell alone, however, embraced the advent of jazz and adjusted the music that he played accordingly. For this and other initiatives he would become a central figure in the nightlife of Paris, the city that served as the *gare centrale* of jazz on the Continent during the 1920s.

The 15 years of Mitchell's European sojourn encompassed the Jazz Age, which has been dated from either the initial recordings of the Original Dixieland Jass (Jazz) Band in early 1917 or from the end of the First World War in November 1918, to the New York stock market crash of October 1929.

*Some Hustling This!* is not, however, the story of the Jazz Age as such. It is the story of the young men and women who took jazz in its formative stages to the world, both before and during this period: Mitchell, Billy Arnold, Sidney Bechet, Arthur Briggs, Jack Carter, Sonny Clay, James Reese Europe,

Earl Granstaff, William Hegamin, Jelly Roll Morton, Mazie Mullins, Tracy Mumma, Benny Peyton, Hughes Pollard, Danny Polo, Noble Sissle, Ada (Bricktop) Smith, Crickett Smith, Valada Snow, Jasper Taylor, E.E. Thompson, Dave Tough, Teddy Weatherford, Frank Withers, Sam Wooding, J. Paul Wyer and many others — pioneering figures who in most cases have been lost to jazz history simply by virtue of leaving the United States when they did, in many instances never to return, or to return only after their styles had long since fallen out of fashion.

It is a story of hope, escape and wanderlust, success, infamy and tragedy. For every Arthur Briggs, who went to England with Will Marion Cook's Southern Syncopated Orchestra at the age of 19 and spent virtually all of the next 72 years of his life in Europe, there were several musicians who died within a year or two of leaving home, among them George Watters in London, Mazie Mullins in Paris and Clinton Moorman in Shanghai. Illness, misadventure, murder and suicide all took their toll.

The experience of life outside the United States was nevertheless intoxicating, especially for African-American musicians unaccustomed to the freedoms that it offered. Sidney Bechet, for example, the Southern Syncopated Orchestra's star soloist in London in 1919, would spend many of the next dozen years travelling in Europe, undeterred by his deportation first from England and then from France on criminal matters. More obscurely, Cyril Mickens, who played trumpet with the Southern Syncopated Orchestra in London in 1920, found his way to Shanghai by 1926; the Los Angeles saxophonist James Carson, a veteran of Tijuana's thriving nightlife in 1923 and 1924, sailed in 1927 for the same Chinese city, there to remain through the 1930s. Bricktop's sojourn as a singer and dancer in Vancouver from 1919 to 1921, meanwhile, anticipated a much longer stay in Paris, where she surely would have encountered the clarinetist and saxophonist Horace Eubanks, who had also been in Vancouver at the turn of 1921.

Many travelling musicians sent back reports of their success professionally and, in the case of African-American musicians, of their acceptance personally, although the subtext of the latter's dispatches may also be interpreted in part as sly criticism of the country they had left behind; to suggest, as many African-Americans did, that life abroad was grand, implicitly condemned life at home as something rather less.

Encouraged by these and other accounts, many more jazz musicians ventured overseas during the 1930s, notably Louis Armstrong in 1932, Duke Ellington with his orchestra in 1933, Coleman Hawkins in 1934 and Benny Carter in 1935, all to Europe, and Buck Clayton in 1934, to China. Their places in jazz history have long since been assured, of course, as have those of the beboppers who moved to Europe after the Second World War and the avant-gardists of Chicago's Association for the Advancement of Creative Musicians (AACM) who followed in 1969, retracing the footsteps of their counterparts from New York's Clef Club 50 years earlier.

The pathfinders themselves, however, have been undeservedly forgotten, and with them an important chapter in the history of jazz and its significance to the world.

This is that chapter.

# "If we like it, we'll stay"

NEW YORK BAY, MAY 26, 1914. The *Vaderland* emerged from the Narrows between Brooklyn and Staten Island and turned slowly east to face the Atlantic Ocean. In her wake, the Statue of Liberty grew fainter against the glare of the noon-time sun, then disappeared from view. The temperature was in the unseasonably warm 80s, with winds blowing up pleasantly from the south. Louis Mitchell would not see land again for six days.

The *Vaderland* was a large, fast ship for her time, capable of 23-1/2 knots. In an era when the world found itself increasingly captivated by the newest of the new and the most modern of the modern, the *Vaderland*'s arrival at Hoboken, New Jersey, on her maiden voyage from Hamburg, had caused a sensation. Some 17,000 people paid 50 cents each to inspect the ship during her brief layover and several celebrities were among her 800 passengers for her return trip to Europe, including Britain's Earl and Countess Gray, Germany's Admiral Oscar van Truffel and at least two noted Americans, the diplomat Henry Morgenthau and the humorist Will Rogers.

The *Vaderland* made Southampton, England, on June 1. "We'll go over for a little while to see what's what," Louis Mitchell later recalled telling his fellow musicians in the Southern Symphony Quintette — bandolinist Jesse Hope, pianist Palmer Jones, banjo player Vance Lowry and cellist William Riley — before they left New York for London.

Mitchell, their drummer, was of course hoping to allay any apprehensions that his colleagues may have had about a trip that could take them away from home indefinitely, especially at a time when geopolitical tensions in Europe were building toward what in a few short months would become the First World War. Lowry, in fact, was travelling with his wife; Riley, with his wife and daughter. "If we like it, we'll stay," Mitchell told them, "If we don't, we can always make a go of it here [ie, New York]."[1]

Mitchell, at 28[2] handsome, athletic and demonstrably persuasive, knew all too well the uncertainty of a life in show business. Moreover, he was by nature a gambler, both figuratively and literally; his love of risk would cost him several small fortunes. Possessed of a particularly sweet tenor, he had been discovered some eight years earlier while singing with friends for spare change on 53rd Street in New York and soon began working professionally for the famed African-American songwriters Bob Cole and J. Rosamond Johnson, touring in their productions of *The Shoo-Fly Regiment* in 1906 and 1907 and

*The Red Moon* from 1908 to 1910. When his stage career faltered, though, he was forced to diversify, taking a managerial position briefly in 1911 at New York's Chelsea Theater and developing some facility as a drummer. Both skills — together with a love of baseball — would serve him well during his time abroad.

Once ashore at Dover[3], Mitchell and the other members of the Southern Symphony Quintette travelled on to London and presently entered into the employ of Prince's Restaurant, a popular Piccadilly establishment not unlike those in which the five musicians had sung and played ragtime for dancers during the previous two years in New York — the Taverne Louis, the Café des Beaux Arts and, lately, Reisenweber's, home three years hence to the Original Dixieland Jass [Jazz] Band.

In London, as in New York, Mitchell *et al.* were a hit. After Britain declared herself at war with Germany in August, however, they were forced to cancel their next booking at the New Supper Club and instead joined the general exodus of American entertainers leaving England and the Continent for home. Splitting up, they sailed from Liverpool in mid-September — Hope and Lowry on the *St. Paul* and Mitchell, Jones and Riley on the *Olympia*.

"If we like it, we'll stay," Mitchell had said, voicing a sentiment surely felt by many of the American jazz musicians, both black and white, who would follow him abroad, uncertain about the language, culture and even the weather that awaited them. Mitchell liked it well enough. War or not, he and Jesse Hope were back in London separately by April 1915. Vance Lowry followed in May 1916. Mitchell and Lowry, reunited as two of the Seven Spades, moved on to Paris in November 1917.

# "Absolute indifference... full accord"

WINNIPEG, CANADA, SEPTEMBER 21, 1914. Freddie Keppard looked out over a blaze of foot-lights into the darkness of the Pantages Theatre. At 24,[1] the cornetist was as recent to the vaudeville stage as most of the other musicians in the New Orleans Creole Ragtime Band — clarinetist George Baquet, trombonist Eddie Vincent, violinist James Palao, guitarist Norwood Williams and bassist Bill Johnson. Organized under Johnson's leadership in Los Angeles just weeks before, they were making their official Pantages debut with a matinee today — the same day that the *St. Paul*, with Jesse Hope and Vance Lowry, docked in New York — and they were making it at the bottom of a five-act bill some 1500 miles from home.

Keppard had been a familiar figure in New Orleans with his Olympia Orchestra; by 1918 he would be a popular attraction in Chicago nightclubs. For the moment — indeed for the next three years — he took his place in a 20-minute "plantation" skit that included song, dance and comedy. It was relatively lucrative work; the Creole Band had the distinction of being one of the few African-American acts on "Pan Time," as the Pantages circuit of 14 theatres in western U.S. and Canadian cities was known. But the band's success as "the latest specialty from the Pantages production department"[2] came at a price.

Keppard was a tall man, broad of shoulders, deep of chest; his distinguished bearing could only have been diminished by the attire that he and the other members of the Creole Band found themselves wearing in their guise as rustics from the American South, a purposely ill-fitting wardrobe of Civil War castoffs and rumpled work clothes, pant legs invariably riding high at the ankle. No less humbling for Keppard himself, surely, was the sight of unsuspecting patrons in retreat from the front rows of the theatre whenever he began to play, his cornet still ringing with the tremendous power that he had developed in the streets and drafty dance halls of New Orleans.

And there was more: the Creole Band had to share the spotlight with a singer and dancer, H. Morgan Prince, and with, by some accounts, a trained chicken. Prince, taking the role of an old man, cane in one hand and jug of corn liquor in the other, sang such favorites of the South as *Old Black Joe* and *My Old Kentucky Home*. He also led the musicians through various bits of comic business and danced spryly to the vivacious ragtime instrumentals that the band played on its own.

Ninety years after the Southern Symphony Quintette and the New Orleans Creole Ragtime Band returned home, the details of their respective travels are clearer than the specifics of their music. The British press allowed the quintet to come and go without appraisal, while a reviewer in Winnipeg could only suggest that the Creole Band "[played] some weird instruments in a wonderful way."[3] Commentary from the other Canadian stops on the band's first Pantages tour — Calgary, Edmonton, Vancouver and Victoria, each for a week — was no more enlightened.

The word "jazz" was not part of the musical vernacular in 1914; to the extent that it was in circulation at all, it had only salacious connotations. Not until the fall of 1916 did "jazz" and its early variants "jaz," "jas" and "jass" begin to appear in the show business columns of the African-American press.

For the time being, this evolving music was still known as "ragtime." Retrospectively, there is no single, identifiable point on the continuum between ragtime and jazz at which the former actually becomes the latter. Recordings from the 1910s are too random to stand as anything more than anecdotal evidence of the transformation. Indeed, according to legend, the Creole Band declined, at Freddie Keppard's insistence, to record at all, lest its ideas be "stolen" by other musicians — a prescient notion that, ironically, would prove central to the very evolution of jazz through the 20th century.

Clearly, though, the Creole Band, with Keppard's cornet, George Baquet's clarinet and Eddie Vincent's trombone, was more of a jazz band — as jazz bands would soon come to be recognized — than the Southern Symphony Quintette, whose bandolin, banjo and cello were typical of a politer ragtime style that flourished during the 1910s in and around New York — and in London and briefly Paris — but did not survive into the 1920s.

Significantly, when the Creole Band returned to Canadian theatres on the Pantages circuit during the summer of 1916 with "Big Eye" Louis Nelson in George Baquet's place, its performance in Victoria prompted this perceptive observation from an unidentified reviewer for the local *Daily Colonist*: "Nobody but six negro eccentric players could shatter so many rules of a well-integrated band and make it so enticing to an audience. The cornet, clarinet, violin, guitar, trombone and double bass are played by individuals with seemingly absolute indifference to what the other man was doing but they always managed to arrive at appointed places in full accord."[4]

Implicit in the apparent contradiction between "absolute indifference" and "full accord" is the casual polyphony that characterized the collective improvisation of New Orleans jazz at its earliest.

While the Creole Band was the first group to take jazz in its nascent form from New Orleans to national and indeed international audiences, the Southern Symphony Quintette was just the latest African-American ragtime ensemble to cross the Atlantic. Its significance lay instead in Louis Mitchell's presence and, to lesser degree, that of Vance Lowry and Palmer Jones; all three men would play a role in the popularization of jazz in Europe during the 1920s.

Even as these two bands heralded the future, however, they were tied to the past. Each retained some vestige of an older and ultimately discredited musical and theatrical tradition, that of minstrelsy, which was introduced in the early 1800s and had been heard on the world stage with some regularity since the 1870s.

Minstrelsy's origins were actually quite noble, specifically the "jubilees" mounted by African-American slaves on holidays and other festive occasions; these plantation celebrations included songs and dances, the latter often parodying the affected mannerisms of the celebrants' white owners. Ironically, these subtle acts of defiance were transformed by uncomprehending white performers — faces and hands blackened with burnt cork — into caricatures of African-American behaviour for theatrical exhibition, largely before white audiences. The same caricatures were only partly rehabilitated when blacks themselves moved into minstrelsy after the American Civil War; whatever their personal aversion to minstrelsy's demeaning stereotypes, they were bound by audience expectations to remain faithful to its conventions.

The popularity of minstrelsy was not limited to the United States. African-American companies travelled abroad at least as early as the summer of 1866 — just 14 months after the end of the Civil War — when the Slave Troupe Minstrels, under the direction of an Englishman, Sam Hague, went to England and made the St. James Theatre in Liverpool their base for several years.

Hundreds of other black entertainers and musicians toured in Canada, Europe, Australia and the Far East during the next 50 years — minstrel companies, vocal and instrumental ensembles, solo instrumentalists and, as "pickaninny" (or "piccaninny") acts, groups of children.[5] Together, they introduced a wide range of images and musical styles to audiences for whom the mere sight of black performers would have been a rare and often wonderful thing.

The Creole Band, for example, sustained minstrelsy's rural tableau and character types without particular qualification in its vaudeville performances. The Southern Symphony Quintette, on the other hand, provided a more urbane presentation of songs, dances and instrumental music for restaurants and nightclubs patronized by New York's social set. Still, the quintet held on to one of minstrelsy's staples, the banjo, and to some of its repertoire. Moreover, Louis Mitchell, like all novelty drummers of the day, drew at least obliquely on the tradition of minstrelsy's "Mr. Tambo," who played tambourine, and "Mr. Bones," who slapped pairs of small bones or sticks together with a roll of the wrist, as much to comic as rhythmic effect.

The Southern Symphony Quintette nevertheless represented a new order among African-American musicians. Mitchell, Jesse Hope, Palmer Jones, Vance Lowry and William Riley were all members of the Clef Club of New York, an organization established in 1910 as a trade union and booking agency for African-American singers and instrumentalists who had been excluded from local 310 of the American Federation of Musicians on the basis of their race.

The advent of the Clef Club coincided with the demise of at least three large African-American musical theatre companies — among them that of Bob Cole and J. Rosamond Johnson, in which Louis Mitchell had sung — and at the same time anticipated the rise of dancing as an acceptable, indeed fashionable, activity in elite white social circles. The dance craze, which was well underway by 1912, made international stars of Vernon and Irene Castle, whose versions of the "Turkey Trot," "Castle Walk" and other steps would be emulated by dancers of all social strata.

As the work available to black musicians in the theatre decreased, employment in dance orchestras increased. Calls for the Clef Club's services came from many quarters — whether for a single night's entertainment at private parties, or for extended engagements in cafes, restaurants and nightclubs. The Clef Club's founding president, James Reese Europe, also formerly with the Cole and Johnson company, became music director for Vernon and Irene Castle in 1913; Europe's Society Orchestra accompanied the pair at their school, Castle House, at their 42nd Street nightclub, Sans Souci, and in 1914 on a concert tour that took them as far afield as St. Louis and Omaha and, once, out of the country altogether — to Toronto in Canada. Europe's successor as Clef Club president, Dan Kildare, served another dancer, Joan Sawyer, in the same capacity for most of 1914, both at New York's Persian Garden and in vaudeville. Coincidentally, each man, Europe and Kildare, would find himself overseas before the decade was over, albeit in very different circumstances.

Under Europe's direction from 1910 to 1913, the Clef Club took a variety of steps to improve its members' professional standing. Demands were made for better working conditions and less exploitive terms of employment; black entertainers had often been hired as menials with the expectation that they would also perform merely for tips. Standards of conduct were also put in place, including a dress code that required tuxedos for engagements booked in advance, and at least a dark suit, white shirt and black bow tie for work taken on short notice.

Europe, moreover, was the driving force behind the Clef Club's own orchestral concerts, presented at the Manhattan Casino in Harlem and at Carnegie Hall downtown with a view to elevating the image of the African-American musician and his music in the public eye. While Europe's instrumentation was limited to mandolins, banjos, violins, harp guitars, pianos and percussion, his model was clearly the European symphony orchestra and all that such an august institution represented in terms of musical and social respectability.

Engagements abroad would have been similarly valued for their apparent prestige. Naturally, as the dance craze spread to Europe, British promoters — and soon enough their counterparts in France — looked to the Clef Club as a convenient contact for the ragtime ensembles, and later the jazz bands, that were so essential to the phenomenon. Rare in London and Paris before 1920 was an African-American musician not affiliated with the organization.

# "Fearsome means of discord"

**LONDON, MAY 16, 1915.** It was with evident satisfaction and some relief that Dan Kildare dashed off a quick letter home to New York from his new lodgings on High Street. Kildare, then 36, had been in London with his band for five weeks and in residence at Ciro's Supper Club for four;[1] he would remain associated with the Orange Street nightspot, near the National Gallery, until the summer of 1917, and was again in its employ at the time of his death in 1920.

"Friend Deacon," he began, addressing Deacon Johnson, his successor as president of the Clef Club, "I can safely say that the Clef Club aggregation [has] made good — in fact, more than made good. We have simply made a clean sweep, and it is more than gratifying to me, as the nervous strain as to how we would be received by the London populace worked on us some. And so I am thankful to state that our success has been beyond our imaginings. Seth Jones is the star, and he is fast making a spot for himself with the London 400."

Kildare's letter found its way into the New York *Age* of June 17, 1915,[2] and thus came to the attention of the city's other African-American musicians, including the pianist's fellow members of the Clef Club. His success in London, like that of the Southern Symphony Quintette before him, would have been seen as a credit to the organization. His "nervous strain" was certainly understandable, even though his drummer at Ciro's was the Quintette's Louis Mitchell, whose experiences at Prince's Restaurant in Piccadilly a year earlier should have been reassuring. And Kildare's reference to Seth Jones' popularity with "the London 400," likely as a singer and dancer, although he also played banjo, is revealing: from the very beginning, this new, syncopated music, not yet called jazz, was the plaything in Europe of the rich and the titled.

Mitchell and Jones aside, Kildare took four other Clef Club members into Ciro's: his younger brother Walter, a cellist, the banjo players George Watters and Joe Meyers, and the bassist John Ricks. Mitchell later claimed to have received $67.50 a week for his services;[3] a report in the London *Times,* on the occasion of court proceedings in December 1916 against the club for the illegal sale of liquor after-hours, set the band's weekly stipend at £100, or approximately $475.[4]

Once settled at the club, however, Kildare lost two of his musicians in fairly quick succession. Mitchell left by August — his replacement is not known, although surely there *was* a replacement, given the drummer's central role in bands of this sort — and Watters shot and killed himself early one Saturday evening in September, apparently by accident. News of Watters' death made the front page of the New York *Age*,[5] a sobering postscript to Kildare's enthusiastic letter home three months earlier.

Still, Kildare's stay at Ciro's was by all indications very much the success that he had described to Deacon Johnson. It soon led to invitations from members of the London elite to appear at charity and social events around the city, including at least one performance for convalescing soldiers and another attended by Edward, Prince of Wales, who was making his first acquaintance with the music that would so captivate his attention in the years to come.

Kildare, in fact, had his contract at Ciro's renewed for a second year in April 1916, at which time he returned briefly to New York in search of replacements for Joe Meyers and John Ricks, who had given notice, and presumably also for Louis Mitchell and George Watters. The new lineup was in place by June: the Kildare brothers, Seth Jones, banjo players Ferdinand (Ferdie) Allen and former Southern Symphony Quintette member Vance Lowry, bassist Sumner Edwards and — likely, though not conclusively — the drummer Harvey White.

Thus revitalized, the band began to double on most evenings between its regular engagement at Ciro's and "private" functions at after-hours clubs several blocks to the west on Grafton and Old Bond streets. Disturbances late at night outside both addresses drew the attention of local authorities; on the assumption that there was a connection between all three rooms beyond the musicians they appeared to share in common, London police raided Ciro's in October and found sufficient evidence that liquor was being sold illegally — that is, after the appointed hour of 9:30 p.m. — to warrant prosecution. (As reported by the London *Times*, the Chief Inspector testified tangentially and with some disdain that Kildare's music was "of a rather crude and riotous character," which prompted the prosecution to remark dryly that the officer "[did] not know ragtime music evidently."[6]) Ciro's was "struck from the register" in December, its liquor license suspended for a year.[7] Kildare and his musicians stayed on for a time but by the spring of 1917 only Kildare himself and Harvey White remained. Came summer, they too were gone.

Joe Jordan followed Dan Kildare to England in 1915 by 16 days. No stranger to transatlantic travel, the pianist and violinist — then 33[8] and another prominent member of the Clef Club — had made similar crossings at least twice before, once in 1905 with a vocal and instrumental ensemble, the Memphis Students, and again in 1910 with the dancers King and Bailey. Moreover, one of his musicians on this latest trip, Jesse Hope, had been in England only months earlier with Louis Mitchell and the Southern Symphony Quintette. Jordan nevertheless appears to have been unprepared for London audiences, and they for him; his Syncopated Orchestra did not even begin to match the Kildare band's success.

Instead, Jordan and company were unceremoniously dispatched to the hinterlands soon after they undertook a contracted eight-week run at London's Hippodrome with the revue *Push and Go*. (The title was a catch-phrase recently coined by future British prime minister David Lloyd George to describe the ideal candidate to take charge of munitions for the country's war effort — "a man of push and go.") According to a report in the New York entertainment newspaper *Variety*, the Jordan orchestra "failed to start anything at all."[9] The London newspapers, meanwhile, reserved what little comment they offered on the act for — in the words of the *Daily Chronicle* — "the remarkable drum turn of a coloured gentleman from Chicago, who most understandably goes by the name of Black Lightning."[10]

The revue, described by the *Daily News and Leader* as "distinctive amongst other revues in that it does not possess even the shadow of a plot,"[11] was simply the mildest of diversions from the concerns of war, not least the sinking — just three days before *Push and Go* opened — of the *Lusitania* by a German submarine off the southern coast of Ireland with a loss of 1200 civilian lives, many of them British subjects. In this sombre light, Jordan's act was perhaps not mild enough; unlike the Kildare ensemble, with its strings and percussion, the Jordan orchestra prefigured the jazz band of a few short years hence with the addition to its piano, banjos and drums of Russell Smith's cornet and John Mobley's trombone, no doubt to comparatively clamorous effect.

Whatever their successes or failures professionally in England, the musicians of both the Kildare and Jordan bands were, by their own accounts, well received personally. Attitudes on matters of race in England would soon harden in the years following the war, but for the moment remained relaxed.

"Words couldn't give you an idea of the way we are treated here," Kildare advised Deacon Johnson in his May 1915 letter. "Just imagine yourself in [Enrico] Caruso's place in New York, and you can have an idea how we are posing over here. Hallmen, chauffeurs, porters and employees in general of the different establishments all stand and salute you as you pass by. In other words, you are treated as a gentleman and an artist."[12]

Russell Smith, who would later spend 16 years with the Fletcher Henderson Orchestra in New York, remembered the Jordan band's travels on the Moss circuit of theatres outside of London in similar terms. "You were treated nice. You stayed in the best hotels — you thought you were someone else, like you was [sic] really American; you were just treated right." [13]

For Smith, however, and for most of Joe Jordan's other musicians, it was over all too soon: when the band's original contract expired in July, the cornetist — together with John Mobley, Jesse Hope, Earl Bumford, Joseph Grey and Nathan Sears — returned to New York. Only Jordan, "Black Lightning" and pianist William Dorsey remained behind.

It was Jordan who enticed Louis Mitchell away from Ciro's in the summer of 1915; Black Lightning may well have been Mitchell's replacement there, if only momentarily. Jordan and Mitchell worked together briefly as duo, their itinerary including a week in August at Manchester's Ardwick Green Empire Theatre as part of the variety half of a bill topped by a one-act play about family life in England during the war, J.M. Barrie's *The New Word*.

"It's a wonder we weren't booed off the stage," Mitchell mused years later. "We were the rottenest act of the lot."[14] His recollection is largely substantiated by the Manchester *Guardian*, whose reviewer suggested, "[I]f the making of great and various noises were a mark of talent the American entertainers Jordan and Louis Mitchell would rank high."[15]

Jordan, now twice party to a flop, sailed for home in October.

Black Lightning — J. Hughes Pollard, then 23[16]— was the son of John Pollard, who had served as a drummer with the 83rd Colored Infantry during the Civil War. The senior Pollard was also known in the regiment for his skill as a boxer. Each of his five sons was athletic; Fritz, two years younger than Hughes, would become one of the most celebrated African-American figures of his day in college and professional football.

Pollard's trip with Joe Jordan to London in 1915 was neither his first venture overseas nor his farthest. Three years earlier, as a member of the Hugo Brothers Minstrel Company, he had embarked on a world tour that stopped for several months in Australia where, according to family legend, he took an Australian wife. (Another member of the company, H. Morgan Prince, soon to join the Creole Band, also found love locally, marrying a Maori pianist, Ollie Fitzsimmons, who later worked in San Francisco, Seattle and Vancouver as Olive or Princess Bell[e].)

With Joe Jordan back in the United States, Pollard and William Dorsey continued to work in England "on the halls," as did Jordan's erstwhile partner, Louis Mitchell, joining several other African-American variety artists who had enjoyed considerable success in Britain over the previous 10 or more years.

The New Orleans singer Belle Davis, for one, first toured the country with her Piccaninnies in 1901 and was still active in London during the war years. So, too, were Louis Douglas, an "eccentric dancer" from Philadelphia who had made his British debut as a teenager in 1903, and the Four Black Diamonds, a vocal ensemble that had started its European career in Prussia in 1905.[17] The Versatile Four, meanwhile, a vocal and instrumental group affiliated with the Clef Club, began doubling at the Alhambra, Palladium and other London theatres not long after it entered — possibly as early as 1913 — into a lengthy engagement at Murray's, a popular Beak Street nightspot.[18]

One of the Four Black Diamonds, Norris Smith, contributed a news column, "Dear old Lunnon," intermittently to the Chicago *Defender* from 1916 to 1922 and made occasional references to the activities of Pollard, Dorsey and Mitchell, among many other African-American entertainers abroad. Whether or not Pollard replaced Mitchell at Ciro's in the summer of 1915, he could be found by the fall of that year drumming at an unidentified London theatre and later, according to Smith, toured with the revues *Watch Your Step* and *Special Mixture*. He also worked in 1917 with dancers Guy Magley and Mlle. Adore; references in ads for the Coliseum in the London *Times* and the *Daily Telegraph* to their "JAZZ BAND with Hughes Pollard, the Eccentric Drummer,"[19] stand as an early use of the word "jazz" to describe musicians active in Britain.

William Dorsey, who had spent several years as music director for the Monogram Theater in Chicago before sailing with Joe Jordan to England, resumed his stage work in London, writing music or playing for several productions between 1915 and 1918, including the revues *Darktown Jingles* and *Bing Boys from Broadway*. Latterly, he also led a band that included Hughes Pollard at Murray's, playing opposite the Versatile Four. The engagement appears to have continued until Dorsey, suffering from tuberculosis, returned to the United States in search of a cure late in 1919.[20]

Like Pollard, Louis Mitchell took theatrical work as a solo drummer — *Joyland* at London's Hippodrome late in 1915, *Follow the Flag* at Liverpool's Olympia Theatre in early 1917 — and led a band in support of a popular dance team, La Belle Leonora and Signor Valentino. He also took a few engagements in 1917 with his own Syncopating Sextette, completed by white musicians.

Showing a flair for publicity, Mitchell made a public request in Liverpool — with a £5 reward — for suggestions of sounds that he might use in his act. He received several surprisingly wistful responses, including the crackle of fire, the rustle of a bank note and the creak of "father creeping upstairs at 2 a.m.," as well as two rather more telling ideas in this time of war, the explosion of an eight-pound shell and the "Shout of Victory."[21]

If the British public was clearly still puzzled by Mitchell's intentions, it was by most accounts excited by his exertions — and by the Union Jack he had painted on the head of his bass drum, to be illuminated by a light inside the drum itself at climactic moments in his performances.[22] Critical response to his efforts, meanwhile, and to the bands in which he played, ranged from ambivalence to at least moderate indignation.

This, from the London *Times*, concerning his performance with La Belle Leonora at the Coliseum: "That never before have four human beings made so much noise we can readily believe, but the ear is less charmed than is the eye by the marvellous antics of Mr. Louis Mitchell, 'America's foremost trap drummer,' who with only two legs and two arms contrives to play at least a dozen instruments..."[23]

And this, from *The Stage*, with reference to the same act, now at the London Opera House: "The value of the dancing of La Belle Leonora and Signor Valentino is unnecessarily discounted... by the cacophony of an American ragtime band, with a trap drummer operating upon cow-bells, motor-horns, tramcar-gongs and other fearsome means of discord."[24]

Inevitably, given Mitchell's wont to upstage La Belle Leonora, his association with the dancer was relatively brief — at most, four months. It did, however, take him to Paris for the first time in November 1916.[25] His return with the Seven Spades almost exactly a year later would mark a new stage in the internationalization of jazz.

# "How's *that!*"

HAYES, MIDDLESEX, ENGLAND, FEBRUARY 3, 1916. The Versatile Four were on their fifth take of their first recording session at the Gramophone Company's studios west of London. Two of their four completed takes would be deemed worthy of commercial release on Gramophone's HMV label, *Circus Day in Dixie* and *Araby*, each with a vocal by A.A. (Gus) Haston; the other two would ultimately be rejected, among them the quartet's initial attempt to record the instrumental *Down Home Rag*.[1]

Wilbur Sweatman's spirited composition was a staple of ragtime and jazz repertoires in the 1910s. At least three versions had already been recorded, the earliest at this very same studio by the Gramophone Company's resident London Orchestra in 1913. James Reese Europe's Society Orchestra and the Six Brown Brothers had also completed versions for Victor in the United States, Europe later in 1913 and the Browns, a white saxophone sextet originally from Canada, in 1915. The composer himself, a popular African-American clarinetist and vaudevillian, would make his first recording of *Down Home Rag* in New York for Emerson before 1916 was out.

The Versatile Four's second attempt at the piece started somewhat unsteadily, with drummer Charlie Johnson scrambling to catch up to Haston and Anthony (Tony) Tuck, who were playing banjos or banjo-mandolins, and Charles Mills, who was at the piano. The quartet's chosen tempo was brisk and its rhythms staccato, exactly the way the dancers at Murray's in London liked them. Soon enough, Johnson edged slightly ahead of his fellow musicians; this new pull forward only added to the urgency of the performance.

*Down Home Rag* was ultimately Johnson's feature and, as such, a rare and revealing demonstration of a drummer's role in the evolution of ragtime into jazz. Equally, the recording captured some of the exuberance with which Johnson — no less than his countrymen Louis Mitchell and Hughes Pollard — had lately been startling London audiences.

Once fully underway this second time, Haston, Turk and Mills simply repeated the Sweatman melody with great enthusiasm as Johnson set out a snappy tattoo of single strokes and press rolls alternating between snare drum and wood blocks, with small gongs, bells and even a slide whistle added for extra emphasis or whimsical effect. (No bass drum here, though, nor any cymbals; the mechanics of the recording process in 1916 were far too delicate to accommodate loud, heavy or sudden sounds. Indeed, the quartet's first take of

*Down Home Rag* might well have fallen victim to a percussive disturbance that the Gramophone Company's recording technicians had not anticipated.) Significantly, some of what Johnson played was improvised, or at the very least responsive to the growing abandon of the performance, and it is precisely this immediacy that begins to move the music beyond ragtime to something closer in spirit, if not yet in style, to jazz.

Appropriately, the performance concluded with a triumphant "How's *that*!" from one of the musicians. Apparently, it was just fine; coupled with *Winter Nights*, take number six from this same session, *Down Home Rag* was issued by HMV as the second of the dozen 78s that the Versatile Four would make during its next four-and-a-half years in London.

# "Jaz band"

CALGARY, CANADA, SEPTEMBER 1, 1916. To travel to London, a city with more than seven million residents and a history measured in centuries, was one thing. To visit Calgary, a cattle town of about 55,000 established as an outpost by the North-West Mounted Police on the Canadian prairies in 1875, was surely quite another.

Nevertheless, George Weaver's Instrumental Four, with drummer Enzie Morgan, were in town from Chicago to inaugurate the Cabaret Garden, a basement room in the Grand Theatre Building on 1st Street West. The quartet's engagement would last through late November; Enzie Morgan returned to Calgary two months later and — in the spirit of Louis Mitchell's suggestion, "If we like it, we'll stay" — was still there in 1922.

Receipts from the Garden's opening night were promised to the Canadian Patriotic Fund; Canada's soldiers, who had been fighting in the fields of France and Belgium since January 1915, were never far from the thoughts of family and friends back home. The evening was a great success as a result, and the Instrumental Four with it.[1]

Like its Clef Club counterparts then in London — Dan Kildare's band at Ciro's and the Versatile Four at Murray's — the quartet featured stringed instruments, George Weaver's banjo and M.B. Vassar's mandolin. Weaver was also a cellist, and Vassar a violinist; Clarence Long was the quartet's pianist.[2] But jazz was on the ascendant in the fall of 1916, both as a descriptive term and as a style of music, and nowhere was its rise quicker than back in Chicago, where bands were arriving from New Orleans with some frequency, including the Original Dixieland Jazz Band, en route to New York. When Morgan returned to Calgary in February 1917 with his brother Lawrence, a pianist, they, too, had a "jaz" band, complete with a saxophonist.

The Cabaret Garden was renamed the Plaza by the summer of 1917, although the flowers and trellis work that decorated its bandstand remained in place. The Morgan brothers, meanwhile, continued at the Plaza through 1918, surviving Lawrence's arrest and conviction — with a fine of $50 — for living off the avails of prostitution.[3] Enzie stayed on in 1919 when the brothers' banjo player, Arthur Daniels, took over the band; Morgan was still at the Plaza with four white musicians in early 1921 and with another racially integrated band, the Plaza Jazz Fiends, in the summer of 1922.

By then, a few other African-American jazz musicians had settled in Calgary, or in Edmonton to the north, notably one of Morgan's fellow Jazz Fiends, saxophonist and dancer Robert Everleigh, and the pianist Shirley Oliver. Everleigh had a background in minstrel bands — those of the Rabbit Foot and Silas Green companies in particular — while Oliver had apparently played with Charles (Doc) Cook in Chicago before travelling to Edmonton around 1920.

Like Morgan, both men worked of necessity in Alberta with white bands; the province's black population, in the main refugee Oklahomans based mostly in and around Edmonton, was simply too small to supply the three Americans with the musicians they would have needed to fill out even the most modest of bands locally.[4] So it was that Everleigh moved back and forth between engagements in Calgary and Edmonton during the early 1920s and Oliver played from 1923 to 1929 with Edmonton's leading white dance band of the day, Tipp's Orchestra. It was a measure of Oliver's prosperity that he could make a summer trip home to Chicago in 1927 at the wheel of his Studebaker "Big Six" sedan.[5]

Whatever the attractions of the two Alberta cities, however, they were not enough to hold the three musicians indefinitely. Morgan was gone by 1923 and Everleigh by 1925, the latter settling in another Canadian city, Montreal, toward the end of the decade after travelling in vaudeville with Wilbur Sweatman and Ragtime Billy Tucker. Oliver, who had purchased a house in Edmonton for his family in 1922, stayed on for the better part of 10 years in total before he, too, returned to the United States.

# "Special privileges"

WASHINGTON, D.C., APRIL 6, 1917. America was now at war. For two-and-a-half years, President Woodrow Wilson had held firmly to a position of neutrality in the campaign waged by Britain, France and their allies against Germany and the other countries of the Central Powers. Indeed, Wilson's successful bid for re-election in November 1916 had as one of its slogans "He Kept Us out of the War." But the events of March 1917 — several German submarine attacks on American merchant ships crossing the Atlantic, together with the public disclosure of Germany's efforts to draw Mexico and Japan into an alliance against the United States — finally left him with no choice but to commit his country to the conflict.

His decision, announced on April 2 and endorsed by Congress four days later, changed the course of the war. It also had the effect of turning America's face to the world, to see and to be seen. Though historically inclined to iso-lationism, the country now began to exert itself internationally; its horizons grew accordingly, and with them, its influence — militarily, culturally and politically. Europe came to know Americans first-hand, and Americans, Europe. The attraction at a personal level, particularly in France, was mutual.

There were American soldiers in England by May 1917, among them several white university students from Cleveland and St. Louis, all musicians, who were immediately absorbed into the British army — whether as musi-cians or soldiers, their status is not known — only to emerge together after the war in Paris, where they recorded as the Scrap Iron Jazz Band and l'Orchestre Scrap Iron Jazzerinos.[1]

The first American troops in France, meanwhile, arrived in late June; by war's end, the American Expeditionary Force totalled some two million doughboys, roughly a tenth of them African-Americans. Most black soldiers overseas saw duty behind the lines of battle as labourers, however, their roles defined by the same segregationist policies that they had faced at home. Only a few black regiments, specifically those of the 92nd and 93rd divisions, were directly involved in combat.

Significantly, each regiment had its own band, often with an important New York orchestra leader as its director — James Reese Europe with the 15th New York Infantry, for example, Tim Brymn with the 350th Field Artillery, Egbert E. Thompson with the 367th Infantry, and Will H. Vodery with the 807th Pioneer Infantry. Many of their bandsmen were recruited —

or, later, drafted — from dance and theatre orchestras, vaudeville, circuses and minstrel shows.

James Reese Europe appealed in the New York *Age* to his colleagues' sense of patriotism on behalf of the 15th Infantry:

**ATTENTION!!!**
**Negro Musicians of America.**
**Last Call Golden Opportunity**
**If you want to do your DUTY in this present crisis...**[2]

A colonel with the 368th Infantry from Baltimore made a more pragmatic pitch in that city's *Afro-American*, advertising salaries of $30 to $48 a month, together with this promise in bold letters:

**NO TRENCH DIGGING, GUARD DUTY OR OTHER**
**LABORIOUS DUTIES TO PERFORM**
**SPECIAL PRIVILEGES ACCORDED TO BANDSMEN**[3]

The 15th Infantry would become the first black combat regiment to sail for France, its departure — December 13, 1917 on the *Pocahontas* — hastened by clashes between its members and the white residents of Spartanburg, South Carolina, where it trained briefly in October. In one such incident, the regiment's slim, bespectacled drum major, Noble Sissle, at 28[4] a successful singer and songwriter who had worked with James Reese Europe in civilian life, was assaulted in the lobby of a local hotel by the establishment's owner; only the intervention of Europe himself prevented other soldiers, both black and white, from retaliating. In order to avoid further such conflicts, the U.S. Army determined that the 15th Infantry should complete its training overseas.

Elsewhere during the difficult summer of 1917, a race riot in East St. Louis left at least 40 blacks dead, and a rampage in Houston saw 17 whites killed and 13 black soldiers subsequently hanged for their part in the violence. It was against these events at home that African-American troops measured their experiences abroad. In fact, France — both its army and its people — accorded the soldiers a level of respect that they had rarely known before and would not know again once they returned to the United States after the war.

# "(some hustling this!)"

SOUTHSEA, ENGLAND, APRIL 9, 1917. Louis Mitchell's new act, the Seven Spades, was essentially Dan Kildare's old band from Ciro's. Kildare and his drummer, Harvey White, were still momentarily in place at the London club, and would continue to work together elsewhere for at least two years more, but the rest of his musicians — Ferdie Allen, Sumner Edwards, Seth Jones, Walter Kildare and Vance Lowry — had been let go when Ciro's was placed off-limits in March 1917 to the lucrative patronage of military personnel.

Mitchell, ever the opportunist, moved quickly, trading up from his Syncopating Sextette, which closed at the Hippodrome in Portsmouth on April 7, to the Seven Spades, who opened at King's Theatre in nearby Southsea just two days later.[1] Only a couple of adjustments were necessary: Mitchell promoted Walter Kildare from cello to piano and added the "mad dancer" Fernando (Sonny) Jones, who had first visited England in 1901 at the age of seven as one of singer Belle Davis' Piccaninnies.

From Southsea, the Seven Spades returned to London, where their opening-night performance at the Empire Theatre in Finsbury Park drew a prediction of great things to come. "Each item, be it instrumental or vocal," noted a reporter from *The Encore*, "is given with lightning rapidity, particularly good being the popular selections on the banjo and Mitchell's trap-drumming (some hustling this!) and if Monday's reception (which was truly terrific) is any criterion, the act should feature on all the principal London halls."[2]

In fact, the Seven Spades performed successfully for the next seven months in halls throughout England — Empire theatres on the Moss circuit, mostly — and also visited Glasgow, Edinburgh and, in their final engagements before crossing the English Channel to France, Belfast and Dublin, where the Union Jack on Mitchell's bass drum caused no small offense to the Irish.

Meanwhile — in the matter of offense — the band's name appears to have given none at all. Whether "Seven Spades" was Mitchell's idea or a suggestion of the Moss organization, its racial inference was direct, unlike the subtler geographical allusion, for example, of "Southern Symphony Quintette." By later standards, of course, "Seven Spades" would be considered wholly demeaning; indeed, with the exception of Sam Wooding's Chocolate Kiddies Orchestra and Cofie's Colored Cracks, few black jazz bands working in Europe even in the 1920s announced their ethnicity so explicitly.

At this earlier date, though, "Seven Spades" may well have been chosen to *celebrate* the group's race as one of its defining attractions as a musical ensemble; the same premise might explain the Graphophone Company's use of "Ciro's Club Coon Orchestra" as the band name on more than a dozen "78s" made by several of these same musicians for the Columbia line in 1916 and 1917.[3] After all, three years had passed since the Southern Symphony Quintette first appeared in London; British audiences were becoming quite familiar with the novelty and skill of African-American ragtime musicians, be they Mitchell or Hughes Pollard as soloists or Dan Kildare's band and the Versatile Four as ensembles. Promoters — and perhaps the musicians them-selves — would have known a good selling point when they saw one.

Whatever Mitchell's personal thoughts on the matter, he handled its implications lightly. A poster promising "The Greatest Combination of Ragtime Instrumentalists, Singers & Dancers" used photos of each member of the group cropped in the shape of spade, as if on a playing card,[4] while a promotional shot of Mitchell in 1917 captured him sitting at his drums under a metal frame that carried a tambourine, a cymbal, cow-bells and — tied to one of the uprights — a garden shovel.

# "Everywhere at once"

HAMILTON, CANADA, SEPTEMBER 1, 1917. The "Grand Reopening" of the Royal Hotel on James Street called for a jazz band. Or so Ben Greenhood insisted. The hotel's manager had made inquiries of the Clef Club both by mail and by wire without success. Finally, he went to New York himself. "They are sending Jass bands to Europe and all parts of the continent," he told the Hamilton *Spectator* on his return, "and I consider myself lucky in being able to secure one."[1]

The Royal's "Dixieland Jass Band," as it was advertised at the outset of the five-week engagement,[2] was led by cellist Alexander Fenner and had previously appeared at Healey's in New York. Typically, its central attraction was its drummer. "If [this] individual had been made of India rubber," noted a Hamilton *Times* reporter on opening night, echoing the sentiments of reviewers in London, "he could not have encompassed such a large field of operations more easily. He could be accurately described as being everywhere at once."[3]

The drummer remained unidentified, but his example — and that of the band more generally — inspired five members of Hamilton's small black community to organize their own Whang Doodle Jazz Band. Its instrumentation, as noted in the Chicago *Defender* just weeks after the New York musicians' departure, had a familiar Clef Club look: banjoline, violin, piano, cymbals and drums.[4]

# "The usual darkey vim and vigor"

WINNIPEG, CANADA, NOVEMBER 5, 1917. H. Quali Clark and John Mobley were once again abroad, if only briefly. Clark, a cornetist and comedian, had travelled alongside Hughes Pollard and H. Morgan Prince to Australia and New Zealand with the Hugo Brothers Minstrel Company in 1913. Mobley, of course, was the trombonist in Joe Jordan's Syncopated Orchestra on its trip to London in 1915. Now, Clark and Mobley crossed into Canada on the Orpheum circuit as two of the seven musicians in the Tennessee Ten, a vaudeville act that — like its rival and likely inspiration before it, the Creole Band — was making its northerly debut in Winnipeg, with stops in Calgary and Vancouver to follow.

Mobley and Clark would ultimately be forgotten figures in jazz history, but other musicians with the Tennessee Ten played documented roles in the music's development during the 1920s, notably the bass player on this trip, Ed Garland, and possibly also the drummer, identified by the Chicago *Defender* as Kid or Young "Killaire," a name intriguingly close to that of Andrew Hilaire, who would have indeed been in his teens at the time.[1] Garland and Hilaire, both from New Orleans, subsequently participated in early and important jazz recording sessions, Garland with Kid Ory in Los Angeles at some point in 1921 or 1922 and Hilaire with Jelly Roll Morton's Red Hot Peppers in Chicago in 1926. Later personnel of the Tennessee Ten — the company continued to visit Canada intermittently until 1921, when it played Montreal, Toronto and Hamilton — also included several other musicians who appeared on record during the 1920s, including drummers Curtis Mosby and Paul Barbarin, clarinetist Jimmy O'Bryant and trumpeters Gus Aiken and Thomas Morris.

After the example of the Creole Band, the Tennessee Ten mixed music — song, dance and instrumental numbers — with comedy. This, in a "plantation" setting created by a painted backdrop that depicted the interior wall of a log cabin with George Washington hanging in portrait stage right and Abe Lincoln stage left.

The jazz band took its place down front with the eccentric dancer U.S. (Slow Kid) Thompson and two singers, Lulu Walton and Florence Mills, the latter a few short years away from international stardom in *Shuffle Along* and *The Plantation Revue*. Thompson, in the role of "dancing director," set up the grand finale of the act by making a great show of coaxing his musicians, mock recalcitrants all, to tune up. "The band would hit a terrible chord," he explained years later, "and I would do a front somersault, as if I was surprised out of my skin."[2]

Between Thompson's acrobatics and the jazz band's spirited music — played with "the usual darkey vim and vigor," in the words of the Vancouver *Daily Sun*[3] — the Tennessee Ten were well received in their Canadian appearances in 1917 and again in 1919, on each trip easily eclipsing the other acts on the bill, a typical Orpheum assortment of singers, comics, actors, musclemen, gymnasts, tight-wire artists and even a lariat expert. The Tennessee Ten's second visit, which included an additional stop in Victoria, was a particular success; by 1919, of course, the jazz craze was well underway in North America and jazz bands were increasingly a familiar sight in vaudeville.

In Winnipeg, reported the *Tribune* on the occasion of the company's return appearance, "the applause kept up until all the Ten could do was say they didn't have anything else to put on."[4] In Victoria, according to the *Daily Times*, "an overwhelming chorus of whistles, catcalls and loud applause continued for ten minutes as the audience strove to obtain an encore..."[5]

# "The biggest sensation that ever hit Paris"

PARIS, NOVEMBER 16, 1917. Louis Mitchell was not prepared for the response that greeted the Seven Spades' first performance in France. He knew, as he and his musicians made their way from the Theatre Royal in Dublin to the Alhambra in Paris, that the number of American soldiers in the country was growing quickly; there would be 300,000 troops on the ground by the end of the year. He knew, too, that some of those soldiers were in Paris, either on duty or on leave, and that they represented a new and potentially sizable audience for any theatre that would cater to their tastes with the latest in American entertainment. This included jazz, or something very like it; the startling sounds of the Original Dixieland Jazz Band, captured earlier in the year in New York on its recordings for Victor of *Livery Stable Blues* and *Dixie Jass Band One-Step*, were just beginning to sweep North America as the first troop ships sailed for France.

The Seven Spades, whose music was at least something very like jazz, would be an early test of this new market in Paris. Too early, in fact. It took time for the doughboys to come around, leaving Mitchell and his musicians to make their debut at the Alhambra before the local *citoyens* who filled the *rue* Malte theatre's 2,500 seats week in and week out.

"Even though we had been a sensation in England," he remembered, "much to my surprise, the French, knowing nothing about American jazz, booed us off the stage at our first performance. It broke my heart. I thought I was finished and I was all but ready to pack up and go home. But the manager came back stage [sic] and told me that I had the biggest sensation that had ever hit Paris. I perked up a bit and listened to his advice and revamped my act a bit."[1]

A bit, and quickly. Mitchell adjusted the Seven Spades' turn in time for their show that same evening, according to a short history of jazz in Paris written some years later by Edgar A. Wiggins for the Chicago *Defender*. Dating the Seven Spades' Paris debut improbably to "the second Sunday of November, 1917" — the 11th — Wiggins noted, that "after changing their program, for the benefit of these people who had never seen or heard anything like it before and couldn't understand it, to override the hissing and booing that resulted from their first matinee appearance, [they] created a sensation that night."[2]

Mitchell did not elaborate on either the reasons for the poor initial reception or the nature of the changes that he made in response; a later account of the event suggests that the matinee's shortcoming might have been as simple as Mitchell's unthinking decision to sing *Poor Butterfly* in English.[3] But the experience of a white drummer from New York, Murray Pilcer, whose "Sherbo American Band" with as many as seven banjos[4] opened at the Casino de Paris one month later, may be instructive.

Pilcer, then 25,[5] was the younger brother of dancer Harry Pilcer, in turn the partner of the Marseilles beauty Gaby Desyls in the Casino's new revue, *Laisse-les tomber*. (The title — literally "Let 'em fall" — may have been either an indifferent shrug to the imminent bombing of Paris by German airships or perhaps just an insouciant reference to the revue's celebrated ladder scene, "Les échelles lumineuses," in which chorus girls wearing only G-strings and high heels made an improbable 30-foot descent to the Casino stage — surely a sight for sore doughboy eyes.)

Harry Pilcer and Gaby Desyls teamed up in New York in 1911 and had been performing in England since 1916 — at times with Murray Pilcer's band — when they were engaged by the French producer Léon Volterra to reopen the Casino. The *rue* de Clichy establishment had previously been a white elephant among Paris theatres but henceforth stood at the centre of the city's reborn music-hall tradition with all of its new extravagances, American jazz musicians not least among them.

Murray Pilcer's band, in the words of *Variety*'s Paris correspondent E.G. Kendrew,"made good" at the Casino, "but rather frightened some gentle folk." Kendrew added that its "noisy antics" — including, by some accounts, the firing of blanks from revolvers — were thought "inappropriate in war time" and had to be "somewhat toned down."[6]

The French poet Jean Cocteau, who was enthralled by the band's performance, described it in different and rather poetic terms. He, after all, had borne witness to the premiere of Stravinsky's *Le Sacre du printemps* (*The Rite of Spring*) in Paris four years earlier; now as then, he revelled in the shock of the new. "To the right of the little group dressed in black," Cocteau noted, "there was a barman of noises under a gilt pergola laden with bells, rods, boards and motorcycle horns. From them, he made cocktails, adding from time to time a dash [*un zeste*] of cymbals, rising [from his seat], swaying and smiling beatifically."

The music, Cocteau continued, was a "hurricane of rhythms and drum[s]," to which Pilcer and Desyls danced "a kind of controlled catastrope [*catastrophe apprivoisée*] that left them completely dazed [*ivres et myopes*] in a shower of six anti-aircraft searchlights." Cocteau concluded by comparing what he had witnessed to the operas of Jacques Offenbach that had long been a staple of Paris theatres. This new spectacle was "a tank," he suggested, revealing a Frenchman's understandable preoccupation with the imagery of war at the time — a tank to Offenbach's "calèche of [18]70."[7]

The attack, as it were, was also developing on two other fronts in France at the turn of 1918. Dan and Harvey — or rather Dan *et* Harvey, Kildare and White — crossed the English Channel for two weeks at the Olympia in Paris, beginning December 28,[8] and the 15th New York Infantry's regimental band under James Reese Europe played its stirring arrangement of *La Marseillaise* for the first time in France when it arrived at Brest on New Year's Day.[9]

Significantly, both the Seven Spades and Murray Pilcer's band offered complimentary performances at the American Soldiers' and Sailors' Club on *rue* Royale in Paris, the Seven Spades as early as December 12. What was good for morale was also good for business; by the time the Seven Spades had moved to the Olympia in late January 1918, the promotional strategy clearly was working.

"The Olympia is drawing a big audience of American uniforms just now," reported the Paris edition of New York *Herald* after opening night. "The magnet is the Seven Spades, a dusky troupe which sings, ragtimes, lullabies and glees. They dance well, too, and their ragtime band, in which one of the troupe plays sixteen instruments, is a real joy. In the final melee it is hard to tell just how many instruments he is playing but, judging by the noise, he seems to have taken an offense against all of them."[10]

After a month at the Olympia, the Seven Spades joined Clara Faurens in *Ramasse-les donc!* ("Pick 'em up!") at the Théâtre Caumartin for their last engagement together under Louis Mitchell's leadership. By then — mid-March 1918 — Gaby Desyls and the Pilcers had also left the Casino de Paris, the dancers returning to England and the Pilcer band moving briefly to the Folies-Bergère. Their places in *Laisse-les tomber* were taken, respectively, by Mistinguett, Maurice Chevalier and an "extraordinaire orchestre américain" — one Bershad's Band.[11]

Ah, Mistinguett. Her name appears often in connection with American jazz bands abroad. She shared the stage with them in Paris, Brussels and — in 1923 — Buenos Aires, Montevideo and Rio de Janeiro. Curiously, their names do not in turn appear at all in her memoirs, *Mistinguett: Queen of the Paris Night*, which are devoted instead to her lovers, her rivals, her *costumiers* and her producers. Mistinguett, *née* Jeanne Bourgeois, was the toast of Paris during and after the war. Photographs of the day made much of her legs, but they also captured her eyes — sparkling yet somehow sad — and her smile — dazzling but rather shy. "They said I was not beautiful," she wrote in her memoirs, "but I had personality."[12]

Clara Faurens, the star and impresario of *Ramasse-les-donc!*, was one of many Parisian singers and actresses who worked in Mistinguett's shadow. She had taken over the small Théâtre Caumartin, a cabaret around the corner of the Boulevard des Capucines and *rue* Caumartin from the Olympia, in the hope of capitalizing on the new demand in Paris for American entertainment. To that end, she soon lured the Seven Spades away from Louis Mitchell, whose own entrepreneurial inclinations would be similarly revealed at various other addresses in nearby Montmartre during the 1920s.

The changes to the Seven Spades — and their embrace of jazz, at least nominally — seem to be reflected in the overlapping names that appeared in notices for the Caumartin in *Le Figaro*: first the Seven Spades and "les Joyeux nègres de New-York" in April 1918, then the latter interchangeably from June until November with "the Coloured Jazz Band of New York" and, for a time in July and August, with "l'orchestre américain de Johnson, roi du Banjo." (The King of the Banjo was identified elsewhere as Happy Johnson and may have been William A. Johnson, once a member of the Clef Club in New York and later the leader of an orchestra at the Hotel Ritz in Paris.[13])

The French writer Michel Leiris, who heard the band at this time, remembered Seth Jones as its new drummer and also noted the presence of Johnson — "said by some to be the brother of [boxer] Jack Johnson" — and Vance Lowry. The musicians were not a formal part of the program at the Caumartin, he recalled, but performed instead during the *entr'actes*. They were nevertheless presented strictly as a theatrical attraction; the audience did not dance to their music. In any event, he added without need of further explanation, Parisians did not dance very much during the war.[14]

The time for dancing would soon come.

# "The Fireworks"

NANTES, FRANCE, FEBRUARY 12, 1918.[1] Lieutenant James Reese Europe and the regimental band of the 15th New York Infantry were en route from their temporary base at St. Nazaire on the Atlantic Coast to Aix-les-Bains near the Swiss border when they stopped in Nantes for an evening concert at the local opera house. This would be their first performance in France for an audience largely of civilians; at the same time as the Seven Spades and Murray Pilcer's band were winning over Paris — the former now at the Olympia and the latter still at the Casino — Lieutenant Europe and his musicians were beginning to court favour with the rest of the country.

The 15th Infantry as a whole was in the sixth week of what would be a 13-month tour of duty overseas. As the only African-American combat regiment on the Continent to date, however, it had immediately slipped into military limbo as it awaited the arrival of other black units in strength enough to form a full division that could be sent to the front in northeast France. For the time being, the regiment remained more than 300 miles away at St. Nazaire, where it helped ready the port city's infrastructure to handle the influx of troops arriving, convoy by convoy, from the United States.

Even Jim Europe, at 37[2] older than many of his fellow members of the 15th Infantry, was obliged to do his fair share of manual labour. He had, after all, enlisted in New York 16 months earlier as a private and was assigned to the machine-gun company that he now commanded. He accepted the additional responsibilities of bandmaster reluctantly and only in response to the regiment's difficulties in recruiting volunteers and obtaining proper equipment; a good band, he was advised, would bring the 15th new and necessary prestige in the eyes of both the public and the military.

At that, Europe agreed to the assignment on the conditions that he be given 44 musicians, 16 more than army regulations stipulated for a regimental band, and that the section leaders among his bandsmen have their salaries augmented in order to attract the quality of players he desired. With private funding, including $10,000 from a sympathetic New York industrialist, Europe was also able to hire 13 reed players from Puerto Rico.

By the time the 15th Infantry had reached France — after postings at Camps Whitman and Upton in New York, Camp Dix in New Jersey and Camp Wadsworth in unwelcoming South Carolina — Europe and his assistant, Lieutenant F. Eugene Mikell, had a band thought by those fortunate enough to have heard it to be the best in the army. Such was its reputation that it soon found itself seconded from the regiment proper to play for soldiers on leave at a new recreation centre established by the American army at Aix-les-Bains, a resort town on Lac du Bourget in the Alps.

The trip from St. Nazaire took three days by train, with whistlestops along the way for performances at railway stations and civic squares whenever time allowed. These concerts were necessarily brief, but in Nantes the band offered a full evening's program in the presence of an American general and his staff for the entertainment of the local populace.

Sergeant Noble Sissle, Europe's friend and the band's drum major, set the scene in a vivid letter published later in 1918 back home.[3] "I am sure," he wrote, "that the greater part of the crowd had never seen or heard an American band and I know it had never heard a Negro band play a 'Ragtime' piece, so what happened can be taken as a test of the success of our music in this country, where all is sorrow and sadness."

Sissle itemized the concert's program as a French march, a few overtures and some selections by the band's vocal quartet, followed after an intermission by *The Stars and Stripes Forever* and an arrangement of "Plantation melodies." It closed with what he described as "the Fireworks" — a version of W.C. Handy's popular tune, *The Memphis Blues*.[4]

Came time for the last, Sissle wrote, "Lieut. Europe, before raising his baton, began to twitch his shoulder, apparently to be sure his tight-fitting military coat would stand the strain." And so it began — the cornetists with their "most harmonious discordant jazzy shrieks that even Broadway would have shivered to have heard," the clarinetists with their "bewitched wooden whistles," and the drummers, who "when they struck their stride their shoulders were trying to keep up with their bobbing heads, which in turn were jerking in time to the syncopated raps of their drum-sticks."

Sissle continued: "Then it seemed the whole audience began to sway: dignified French officers began to pat their feet in time with the American general, who temporarily lost his style and grace. Lieut. Europe was not the Lieut. Europe he was a few moments before; he was once more Jim Europe, who a few months before had rocked New York with his syncopated baton. His body swayed in willowy motions and his head was bopping as it did in the days when terpsichorean festivities reigned supreme: he turned to the trombones who sat impatiently waiting for their cue to have a 'Jazz Spasm.' At the signal, in perfect unison, the whole section threw their slides to the extremity and jerked them back with an ear-splitting crack... and the audience could not stand the strain any longer: the 'Jazz germ' hit them..."

Sissle went on to note that the band's reception in Nantes was not an isolated incident. "All through France," he wrote, "the same thing happened wherever we played." *The Memphis Blues* was just one of the jazzy pieces in the band's repertoire, which also included *The Army Blues*, *Bugle Blues* and *Shim-Me-Sha-Wabble*, the last still a few years away from becoming a standard item in the jazz repertoire.[5]

As Sissle's letter makes clear, however, the 15th Infantry band played music in a wide variety of styles and traditions. To what extent Lieutenant Europe adapted this material is not known, although his arrangement of *La Marseillaise* was said to have a rhythmic vitality that took his French listeners by surprise; many failed at first to recognize their national anthem, so vivaciously had it been transformed. That this should have been the work of African-American musicians, hitherto neither seen nor heard in the hinterlands, could only have added to the element of surprise. Indeed, such was the response to the band's music that Lieutenant Europe found himself carried triumphantly aloft on French shoulders after a performance in Lyons.[6]

The musicians arrived in Aix-les-Bains on February 15, in time to greet the first contingent of furloughed soldiers at the railway station with *Hail, Hail, The Gang's All Here* and then march with the "gang" circuitously through town to the strains of *La Marseillaise* and *The Memphis Blues*. Here — back again among his countrymen — Lieutenant Europe found that his reputation in New York had preceded him. "If you ever danced all night to the music of Europe's players," a representative on the scene from the New York *Herald* suggested, "you will not wonder that the soldiers marched untiringly a good part of the morning." The reporter added a punning afterthought. "There's one thing certain: even if Aix-les-Bains is not the musical centre of Europe, Europe is the musical centre of Aix from this morning on."[7]

The band stayed for two weeks as originally directed, then two weeks more, giving concerts at the Casino and in a local park, as well as accompanying religious services and travelling to the nearby cathedral city of Chambéry, at every opportunity proving themselves able and willing ambassadors for the African-American in France. On one occasion — described by an officer with the 15th, Arthur Little[8] — Jim Europe noticed a young Chambéry orphan mimicking his conducting gestures; to the audience's delight, he brought his young admirer onstage and, after directing his musicians to play a relatively uncomplicated piece — *Dixie*, by one account[9] —

allowed the boy to lead the band. At many other concerts, he programmed music proffered or requested by local citizens, music that he himself would have had to arrange before it could be performed.

Even as the band was winning a place for itself in French hearts, its regiment found a new home under French command. In the continuing absence of any opportunity to move to the front with other American units, the 15th Infantry's officers accepted a transfer to the 16th Division of the 4th French Army. On April 20, 1918, with Jim Europe returned to combat duty and F. Eugene Mikell given charge of the band, the 15th — now re-designated the 369th — took up a defensive position in the Argonne Forest, some 100 miles east of Paris.

# "A sort of khaki"

CAMP DIX, WRIGHTSTOWN, NEW JERSEY, JULY 12, 1918. Earl Granstaff was known to write a good letter. The young trombonist had a sense of humour, a way with words and a keen enough grasp of show business to understand the value of keeping the Indianapolis *Freeman* and Chicago *Defender* apprised of his successes; the publicity, which was of course free, complemented the favourable notices that he garnered as he travelled around the United States, into Canada and, for the last five years of his relatively short life, in Europe.

"Granstaff gets more downright satisfaction out of a trombone than any player that has appeared in Indianapolis," observed a reviewer for the *Freeman* late in 1914. "There may have been better ones, but they have not made the old trombone contribute all that was in it. This lad does this. Then he puts on such tantalizing blues."[1]

"This lad," 20 at the time,[2] had recently graduated to vaudeville from P.G. Lowrey's Concert Band and Minstrel Show, and was working with another former Lowrey musician, cornetist Leslie Davis. The team of Granstaff and Davis stayed on the road together for another four years — until Uncle Sam intervened in the summer of 1918.

"The two boys open playing cornet and trombone behind the scenes [ie, offstage]," wrote Seymour James, the *Freeman*'s Baltimore columnist, describing one of their last shows together. "The talk [ie, patter] is all new stuff. Davis plays two cornets at the same time, he being the only one of the Race doing this. Grandstaff [sic] plays a jazz number, doing steps [ie, dancing] at the same time. Closing the act was the Blues. This is where they stop the show. Five bows and [they] come back with the *Livery Stable Blues*. The two boys like to stop shows."[3]

Now, however, the show was over. Granstaff found himself posted with the 350th Field Artillery Band to Camp Dix, where elements of the 15th New York Infantry had been stationed less than a year earlier. The 15th — as the 369th — was then into its third month on the front lines in the Argonne Forest; the heroism of privates Needham Roberts and Henry Johnson in face of a German attack on May 14 had won them the French *Croix de guerre* and brought their regiment a nickname — "Hellfighters."

As Granstaff sat down to develop a lighthearted metaphor for his experiences in boot camp to amuse readers of the Chicago *Defender*, Lieutenant James Reese Europe was recuperating behind the lines from the effects of a gas attack on his machine-gun position in late June and the other members of 369th at the front awaited a rumoured German offensive that in fact began on July 14, and that — once repelled — led to a turning point in the war, the Battle of the Marne.

"Well," Granstaff wrote from Camp Dix, "I am booked for the longest engagement I ever had in my career, and incidentally the longest single jump. Although I always wanted to play across the pond [ie, in Europe], this was rather sudden... The money isn't so big, but it's on a play-or-pay basis. I do three full acts a day in the mess hall, with bows and encores a plenty [sic]. We have a three-piece orchestra — knife, fork and spoon — but they clean up on my music, especially on the dance. Between shows I do a lot of rehearsing, going over old steps and learning new ones. The stage manager is a pretty good fellow, but he likes to have his way and is always telling me how I should do my stuff... But boy, the biggest surprise to me was the property man; he is a prince; he looked at my wardrobe and saw how worn out it was and told me if I didn't mind he would present me with a brand new and complete outfit. Naturally I hated to hurt his feelings, so I accepted it. It is all one color, a sort of khaki..."[4]

# "Stealing money"

PARIS, AUGUST 21, 1918. The Seven Spades were now history as such, but Louis Mitchell was still using their letterhead, with excerpts from glowing reviews of the group in London, Birmingham, Bradford and Glasgow printed in a single column down the left side of the page. Mitchell typed in his current Montmartre address in the upper right corner — 69, *rue* [de] Clichy, a few short blocks north of the Casino de Paris at number 16 — and added the salutation "Dear friend Hubie."[1]

"Hubie" was the Baltimore pianist and songwriter Eubie Blake, at the time based in New York and a partner with James Reese Europe and Noble Sissle in the Tempo Club, an organization that Europe had established in 1914 upon his resignation as president from — and as a friendly rival to — the Clef Club.[2] With Europe and Sissle overseas, Blake was left to manage its business affairs, even as work for its orchestras was declining; the war had distracted New York's social set and, in any event, many of the city's black dance-band musicians were now in the service, Blake's partners not least among them.

In Paris Louis Mitchell had seen Europe and Sissle with the 369th and learned from Europe of Blake's interest in joining them there. Coincidentally, Mitchell was in need of at least 15 players to fill the growing demand for his music. In their absence, he was leading a band of Frenchmen, adopting the same strategy that he had previously employed when he formed the Syncopating Sextette with London musicians.

"I am teaching them to play rags," he wrote to Blake of his *protégés parisiens*, "and they are getting along fine[,] better than I thought they would." He had them playing at "one of the best Theatres here in Paris" — possibly the Casino de Paris, which introduced its Casino Jazz Band in late June 1918 — but wanted to replace them there with "a band of coulard [sic] boys."

To that end, he offered Blake a contract for either six months or a year at $75 a week. He also inquired about four other musicians, the mandolin player Seth Weeks among them, to whom he was prepared to pay lesser, unspecified salaries. The engagement, Mitchell noted, would also have non-monetary enticements.

"Hubie," he wrote, "this is the finest Country in the world and if you once get over here you will never want to go back to N.Y. again. I intend to stay here the rest of my life, as you can go where you want too [sic] and have the time of your life... I have seen all the fellows in Jim's [369th] band and they all want to stay here after the war if possible, I have all ready singed [signed] some of them up for after the war..."

After encouraging Blake to reply "at once," he resumed his pitch. "The work that we do over here now is different than the work in the States and not half so hard, we never work over two hours a day at most, [and] where I am now and where I want you and the fellows to come, we only work fifteen minutes a day and thrity [sic] minutes on the days that we have Matenees [sic], so you can see it is like stealing money, and you are treated white wherever you go as they like spades here and these Yanks can't teach these French people any different..."

Indeed, try as they might, "these Yanks" — first and foremost the U.S. army — could not prejudice the French against the African-Africans now in their midst. *Au contraire*, the relationship between the two was only growing warmer.

Eubie Blake nevertheless remained in New York where, two months later, he received another letter from France, this time from Noble Sissle, who had recently passed through Paris. Sissle alluded to Blake's exchange with Mitchell, and to the pianist's decision to stay put — at least for the time being. "I saw Mitchell," Sissle noted. "He said you wrote him. Well old boy hang on then we will be able to knock them cold after the war. It will be over soon. Jim [Europe] and I have P_____ by the balls in a bigger way than anyone you know."[3]

"Anyone" might well have included Mitchell, who still lacked the musicians he needed to consolidate his own "hold" on the city. So it was that he went in person to New York in January 1919, travelling on behalf of the Casino de Paris, where he had lately been a featured member of the theatre's otherwise all-French orchestra.[4] He left for five weeks with a mandate from the Casino's producer, Léon Volterra, to bring back as many as 50 players.

"I returned to America enthusiastic," Mitchell remembered in 1940, "for it seemed to me that this was a chance of a lifetime for colored musicians. I wanted to share my luck with them. I also had it in the back of my mind to choose an orchestra which would be able to play operatic selections as well as jazz numbers, with a view of displaying the versatility of the Negro artist."[5]

It was not quite to be. When Mitchell sailed again belatedly for France on the *S.S. Hudson* in late May, he had just five men in his employ, cornetist Crickett Smith, trombonist Frank Withers, saxophonist James Shaw, pianist Dan Parrish and banjo player Joe Meyers. The Jazz Kings, Mitchell called them, and they reigned over Paris for the next six years.

# "A very affectionate people"

RETHONDES, COMPIÈGNE FOREST, FRANCE, NOVEMBER 11, 1918. At the 11th hour on the eleventh day of the 11th month, the fighting stopped. German representatives agreed formally to the Allies' terms for an armistice at a meeting held in a railway car parked on a siding in a glade near the Aisne River, not 50 miles north of Paris.

News of the armistice reached the 369th Infantry at its new position in the Vosges Mountains, some 200 miles east of the capital, in a relatively quiet sector of Alsace that had offered the regiment a respite from the horrors of the Meuse-Argonne campaign in which it had won its *nom de guerre* as Hellfighters.

Lieutenant James Reese Europe and his band had recently rejoined the regiment there after two months of concerts in Paris for military leaders, political dignitaries, convalescing and furloughed soldiers, and local citizens. At one such public performance, amid the lime and chestnut trees of the 17th-century Jardin des Tuileries on the banks of the Seine, the band took its place with its illustrious counterparts from the French Republican Guard, the British Grenadier Guards and what Jim Europe described as a "Royal Italian" regiment.

"My band, of course, could not compare with any of these," he mused a few months later, "yet the crowd, and it was such a crowd as I never saw anywhere else in the world, deserted them for us."

What followed, as he remembered it, was an early and revealing encounter between the nascent African-American jazz tradition and the longstanding French musical establishment. While France in general embraced the new sounds without hesitation, at least some of its musicians remained skeptical. Accordingly, the conductor from the Republican Guard asked to borrow one of Europe's jazz scores; he wanted the French band to play it. He returned the following day quite perplexed, having failed to elicit from his musicians the effects that he had heard Europe's men produce. Would Europe himself attend a rehearsal? In character, yes Europe would.

"The great band played the composition superbly," he recalled, "but [the Guard's conductor] was right: the jazz effects were missing. I took an instrument and showed him how it could be done, and he told me that his own musicians felt sure that my band had used special instruments."

Clearly, Europe's "jazz effects" were tonal and textural colours — slurs, growls and such — achieved through techniques that would have been considered unorthodox to musicians trained in the classical tradition, as the French bandsmen undoubtedly were. "Indeed," Europe added, "some of them, afterward attending one of my rehearsals, did not believe what I had said until after they had examined the instruments used by my men."[1]

Their doubters duly assuaged, Europe and the band left Paris in time to catch up in October with the 369th en route to its new position in the Vosges and then, in the days after November 11, moved forward with the regiment into Germany. The 369th stopped at the west bank of the Rhine River, where for three weeks it occupied ground evacuated by the German army in accordance with the terms of the armistice. Europe continued to mix jazz pieces with more traditional military fare as the regiment marched through the towns and villages of Alsace, now giving the Germans there their first, brief exposure — however unfavourable the circumstances — to the music that had so captivated the French.

Jim Europe and his musicians may have been the first African-Americans in uniform to play some semblance of jazz in France, but they were not the last. New York's 350th Field Artillery (Black Devils) and the 367th Infantry (Buffalos), with bandmasters Tim Brymn and E. E. Thompson, respectively, arrived in France during the summer of 1918. The 807th Pioneer Infantry, with Will H. Vodery and his musicians, followed in the fall. Other black regiments — among them the 365th and 370th from Chicago and the 368th from Baltimore — also had bands on the ground in France, each with a few jazz musicians in its ranks and a jazz tune or two in its repertoire.

The drummer Jasper Taylor, already a veteran at 24[2] of W.C. Handy's orchestra and later active on the Chicago scene of the 1920s, was with the 365th. "Our band is in fine playing condition regardless to circumstances," he informed the Indianapolis *Freeman* late in the summer of 1918. "We manage to give the boys just what they want, plenty of *Literary* [sic; *Livery*] *Stable Blues*, love songs and a few standard selections."[3]

Meanwhile, the New York pianist Willie Smith, 21,[4] was with the 350th Field Infantry band, serving Tim Brymn as a drum major. "But when we were resting someplace," Smith explained in his autobiography *Music on My Mind*, "I would play the piano, if one could be found, and some of the horns from the band would join me in a sort of early jam session."[5] Russell Smith (no relation), who had been overseas with Joe Jordan in 1915, was one those horns, along with his brother Luke and their fellow cornetist Addington

Major; the last was subsequently a member in August 1920 of the New York band that Willie Smith led in support of singer Mamie Smith (also no relation) on the historic recording session that produced *Crazy Blues*, whose unprecedented success established the market for "race records" by African-American blues and jazz artists.

Willie Smith also saw combat in France with the 350th; by his own account, his prowess as a gunner brought him a sobriquet, "The Lion," that he would carry throughout the rest of his career as a musician. After 49 days under fire near Metz in the Meuse-Argonne campaign, he received a three-week furlough at Aix-les-Bains, where he recalled "playing a lot of piano for the French natives,"[6] no doubt in the rollicking, post-ragtime "stride" style that he, James P. Johnson, Luckey Roberts and others had so recently introduced to New York cabarets. Indeed, Smith's performances in Aix-les-Bains, however informal, were the first in Europe by a musician destined to become a significant figure in the history of jazz; clarinetist Sidney Bechet's appearances in London with the Southern Syncopated Orchestra remained the better part of a year away.

Like Bechet in due course, Smith found the French to his liking — "a very affectionate people," he remembered. "They move you. They kept our canteens full of cognac, which helped a lot; the water was full of poison." And there was something else, something that the experience of segregation at home made all the more enticing. "I became very fond of the French girls with the red cheeks and the bicycles."

No matter that fraternization of any sort between African-American troops and local citizens was actively discouraged by the army. Neither Smith and his fellow soldiers, nor their French lovers, were deterred. "One of our big problems was sneaking away from our camp at night and getting back on time in the morning. That was where those bikes came in handy — [the girls] would meet us with their bikes. In the dawn there was always a weird parade of soldiers wheeling toward camp with chicks on the handle bars."[7]

Smith's fellow pianist Sam Wooding, 23,[8] was also in the Meuse-Argonne campaign with the 807th Pioneer Infantry band, which subsequently won the honour of serving as the Post Band of the First Army Corps in competition with four of its counterparts from white regiments. Naturally, Wooding's experience as a pianist in Atlantic City — like Smith's in New York — was of little practical value to a military band in the field. Instead, he took up baritone horn and played in the 807th's brass section with trombonist Earl Granstaff, who had transferred from the 350th, cornetist Elmer Chambers and others.

Their repertoire was mostly marches, Wooding remembered, although the band did attempt *Bugle Blues* — later and more popularly known as *Bugle Call Rag* — after hearing it played by Jim Europe's musicians.[9] The 807th also drew on the skills of its bandmaster, Will Vodery, a veteran of both minstrelsy and Broadway productions, to produce entertainment designed to boost the morale of the troops. According to a letter sent to the New York *Age* after the armistice by one of his saxophonists, Charles L. Thorpe, Vodery created "two complete shows with music, which we use in the Y.M.C.A.'s, [sic] hospitals, Red Cross huts and aviators' quarters."[10]

As reviewed in the Paris edition of the New York *Herald* at Bar-sur-Aube in January 1919, one of those shows comprised the comedy sketches "Fun in a Parisian Hotel" and "Black Justice," separated by an interlude that featured a saxophone quartet, a comedian and a song-and-dance routine by Opal Cooper and Sammy Richardson.[11] "If conditions permitted," Thorpe added in his letter, "there was as a rule a dance with Jazz Band playing."

Army morale after the armistice was not the concern that it had been before. Despite the flush of victory, though, American troops soon grew bored, and then impatient, as they awaited demobilization; black soldiers further endured unprovoked slights, insults and harsh discipline designed to crush any expectations that their service to their country might now see them treated as well at home as they had been in France.

So it was with Jim Europe and the men of the 369th, who sailed for New York from Brest on January 31, 1919, though not before the entire regiment had been threatened repeatedly with the loss of its place in the order of embarkation if any individual member's conduct was deemed insufficiently deferential. The 350th and 367th followed the 369th across the Atlantic within weeks, leaving American troops still in France to be entertained by the musicians and singers of the 807th and by at least two white groups, the Scrap Iron Jazz Band and the United States Army Ambulance Service Jazz Band.

Inevitably, some African-American soldiers attempted to stay on permanently in France after the war, challenging the army's demobilization procedures to do so. Others, several musicians among them, made their way back to Paris at the first opportunity.

The story of Opal Cooper and Sammy Richardson was typical. Cooper had served with the 807th as its drum major, Richardson as one of its saxophonists. They had returned with the regiment to New York by the summer of 1919, just in time to hear the latest Tin Pan Alley hit, *How Ya Gonna Keep 'em down on the Farm (After They've Seen Paree)*, and to learn of James Reese Europe's violent death during a triumphant homecoming tour with his

Hellfighters band; he had survived trench warfare in France only to be the victim of an unprovoked attack backstage at the Mechanics Hall in Boston by one of the musicians who had served with him in the 369th overseas.

Came January of 1920, Cooper and Richardson were back in Paris again, this time with pianist Elliot Carpenter and other musicians from the Clef Club. Carpenter later remembered the circumstances. "I went to them and said, 'Do you guys want to go to France?' And they said, 'My God, yes!' And they started to tell me about the beauties of Paris — what they did and didn't do. They raved, 'Yeah, man. Let's go back there!' So I said, 'Hey, wait a minute. I haven't said anything about money.' And they said, 'The hell with that. Let's just get back to Paris.'"[12]

# "One-stepping up and down the pavement"

ROME, JANUARY 2, 1919. Calvin Sims and the men of his 332nd Infantry band assembled in front of Red Cross headquarters to offer an impromptu concert for the wounded soldiers and their attendants inside. As the musicians took up formation in the cool morning air, "the Red Cross ladies," as Sims described them, sent out a request for "a little American music."

In the presence of President Woodrow Wilson and King Victor Emanuel of Italy at the American Ambassador's residence two days hence, the band would play the lightest of classics, including a waltz by Delibes, a minuet by Paderewski and operatic melodies by Donizetti and Victor Herbert. On the street, however, it responded to the nurses' wishes first with a march comprising three sentimental themes, *Maryland, My Maryland, Long Long Ago* and *Annie Laurie*, and then with a popular ragtime song.

"Having appealed to their hearts," Sims wrote a few days later in a letter to *The Metronome*, "we next 'moved' their feet with *Darktown Stutters' Ball* and scarcely a strain had been played [before] the swaying Red Cross girls and nervous doughboys were one-stepping up and down the pavement." This sudden levity apparently took the local citizenry by surprise. "Perhaps," Sims ventured, "the Romans were scandalized to find Americans who could sometimes stop making dollars to enjoy themselves."[1]

The 332nd was a white regiment. So, too, was the 158th, whose band under A.R. Eztweiler had recorded *The Darktown Stutters' Ball*, along with three other tunes, for Pathé in Paris in October of 1918. The ragtime repertoire was thus not unique to the army's black regimental bands. Nor were those jazz "effects" — which can be heard to varying degrees in the 158th's recordings of *Darktown Stutters' Ball, When Alexander Takes His Ragtime Band to France* (complete with flourishes from *Swanee River* and *La Marseillaise*), *The Story Book Ball* and especially *Muttering Fritz*. Of course, those "effects" may well be an indication of the extent to which Jim Europe's influence had spread throughout the army; how ironic, in that case, that the 158th band would be recorded, while Europe and his men — present in Paris during the same period — were not.

A second, smaller group of white American musicians followed the 158th into the Pathé studio in late February or early March of 1919.[2] The seven members of the Scrap Iron Jazz Band, or l'Orchestre Scrap Iron Jazzerinos, had been attached in some capacity to the British army since the summer of

56

1917; the fact that most, if not all, possessed a university education, either from Washington University in St. Louis or Western Reserve University in Cleveland, and that they were among the first Americans to cross the Atlantic after the United States joined the war, would suggest that theirs was something other than a combat role.

Whatever their function in the British army, they were apparently exposed to the latest developments in jazz, whether the African-American regimental bands in France or those few recordings of the Original Dixieland Jazz Band that found their way via unofficial channels to England and France during the war.

The Scrap Iron Jazz Band's own recordings — six titles for Pathé and another 10 in June 1919 for HMV — leaven the formality of the regimental bands with the freneticism of the ODJB. Its horn arrangements are largely, and blaringly, homophonic, with allowance for neither breaks nor improvisation. The musicians, however, are in high spirits, particularly drummer Arshat (or Arshar) Nushan of St. Louis, whose furious rattletrapping on wood blocks and cymbals — as well as the "iron scraps" that gave the band its name — frequently outpaces the efforts of his bandmates.[3] Their material, moreover, is popular fare — songs as recent as *How Ya Gonna Keep 'em down on the Farm (After They've Seen Paree)*, which the entire band sings with knowing exuberance.

Between the Pathé and HMV recording sessions, the Scrap Iron musicians travelled extensively in France, joining a similar group, Sergeant Charles W. Hamp's United States Army Ambulance Service Jazz Band, on the YMCA's circuit of "leave centers." The 10 members of the USAAS group, most of them string players, had been stationed during the war in Italy, and in the weeks immediately following the armistice appeared in many of that country's major cities; most memorably, their appearance in Venice found them performing from two large gondolas on the Grand Canal — a picturesque setting, certainly, but one in which the musicians would have indulged their penchant for physical comedy at some risk.[4]

Indeed, their antics were their "greatest entertainment feature," according to the Paris edition of the New York *Herald,* which took note of the band four months later on the eve of its departure for the Riviera via Bordeaux and Biarritz. "Instead of sitting calmly on the stage," the *Herald* report continued, "its members dance, roll over, embrace each other and do various acrobatic acts without missing a note, the whole effect being whimsical and full of surprise."[5] No similar account of the band's music has survived; nor apparently have the 17 recordings that it made in December 1918 for the Fonotipia

company in Milan. The preponderance of violins and banjos in its instrumentation is in any event less than promising, as is the list of pop tunes that
it recorded — *Darktown Strutters' Ball* aside.[6]

Both the USAAS and Scrap Iron bands were still in France when the
Treaty of Versailles was signed on June 28, 1919, signalling the close of long
and difficult negotiations among the Allies as to the terms that would be
imposed on Germany. Several of the USAAS musicians sailed from Brest for
New York just five days later.[7] Most of the Scrap Iron Jazz Band's members
followed within three weeks, leaving the future of jazz in Europe momentarily in the hands of Mitchell's Jazz Kings, who were just now all the rage at the
Casino de Paris.

# "Where the soil is moist"

WASHINGTON, D.C., JANUARY 29, 1919. The 18th Amendment to the American Constitution — in a word, prohibition — was now law. Its enabling legislation, the Volstead Act, would not be passed by the Senate for another nine months, and its ban on the manufacture, sale and transport of intoxicating beverages only took effect on January 16, 1920, but the writing was on the wall for those who liked their liquor or made their livelihood in establishments where it was sold.

Many a jazz musician could find reason for concern on both counts. Offers of work abroad hereafter had something more to recommend them than simply their appeal to a latent sense of adventure. The white pianist Arnold (William) Guldeman — professionally, Billy Arnold — responded by taking his Novelty Band to London in May 1919; according to a report several years later in *The Billboard*, "The Arnold organization left America soon after the war, believing, erroneously as it developed, that the passage of the 18th Amendment would kill the nation's night life."[1]

The teenaged drummer Eddie Gross Bart, who went overseas in January 1920 with another white band that would work in London and Paris as the American Five, described the thinking among New York's musicians at the time. "It was known that Prohibition was coming in, and things were getting a bit tough for all the musicians. Everybody was looking for jobs, because all of the places like Rector's, Churchill's, The Peking and The Tokyo that depended on booze couldn't exist without it, and a lot of them had to close. So that's why I scarpered, and got out of New York."[2]

The African-American drummer Charles (Buddy) Gilmore, who left New York for London in August 1919 and became the toast of Paris during the 1920s, took a similarly dim view of events at home; the Chicago *Defender's* London correspondent, Norris Smith, noted in late 1920 that Gilmore was "at Ciro's and from what I can hear he is stopping over the way [ie, staying in Europe] until America goes wet again."[3]

By then, the black pianist and songwriter James (Slap [or Slap Rags]) White had made a more modest move from Chicago to Montreal. "When prohibition went into force in the U.S.A.," Dave Peyton noted in the Chicago *Defender* some years after, "Slap picked up his duds and said 'Goodby Forever.'"[4] For White, who — in the words of a contemporary — "could write a song every day and sold them for almost nothing, being content to have a bottle and a cigarette,"[5] the motivation may well have been personal rather than professional.

Montreal attracted many American jazz musicians during this period, as did a second Canadian city, Vancouver. Both were located in provinces that had rejected prohibition — Quebec, in April 1919, and British Columbia, in October 1920 — by exercising the "local option" allowed by the Canada Temperance [or Scott] Act of 1878. Their specific status, and the perception more generally that Canada's liquor laws were comparatively lax by U.S. standards, drew several cryptically favourable comments from the *Defender's* Los Angeles correspondent, pianist Ragtime Billy Tucker.

Taking note of pianist Oscar Holden's success at the Patricia Hotel in Vancouver during the summer of 1920, Tucker added this qualification: "Then, too, that's a country where you can 'crook your elbow' and never be molested." [6] On the eve of his own trip north with the Georgia Minstrels the following year, Tucker enthused, "Canada! oh boy! That's where the soil is moist and naturally that's where I shine (also several other of the boys)."[7]

To the south, night life in Tia Juana (later Tijuana), across the Mexican border from San Diego, also flourished just beyond prohibition's reach. Tia Juana and Vancouver in fact stood at opposite ends of a Pacific Coast cabaret circuit that also included Los Angeles, San Francisco, Oakland, Tacoma, Portland and Seattle — a circuit travelled in its entirety between 1919 and 1921 by no one less than Jelly Roll Morton, the greatest of the many jazz musicians to leave the United States in this period.

# "Bloody Americans!"

**LONDON, APRIL 8, 1919.** The Original Dixieland Jazz Band was at liberty. After just one night in *Joy Bells* at the Hippodrome, the quintet had been fired, a victim of its own success. So enthusiastic was the response to its debut performance that one of the show's stars, George Robey, issued an ultimatum to its producer, Albert de Corville: either the band and its two dancers be dismissed immediately or he — Robey — would quit.

The British comedian's concern was not so much the ODJB's riotous music — although that, too, must surely have rankled — as it was the band's reception, compounded unforgivably by its nationality. "The Britisher is not backward in claiming no American artist will at any time share attention with him," reported *Variety* in New York later in 1919, when another American entertainer in *Joy Bells*, comedian Leon Errol, ran afoul of Robey's vindictive streak. "It is believed that Robey will never forget his sad fate in America when he essayed to gain a hearing here."[1]

And so it was that cornetist Nick LaRocca, clarinetist Larry Shields, trombonist Emile Christian, pianist J. Russel Robinson and drummer Tony Sbarbaro were for the moment out of work. Adding insult to injury, the satirical magazine *Punch* noted dryly a week later, "'The Original Dixie Land [sic] Jazz Band has arrived in London,' says an evening paper. We are grateful for the warning."[2]

By then, however, the ODJB had opened at the Palladium. Its fortnight there passed without incident and was followed through June 1920 by bookings at the Martan (or Dixie) Club on Old Bond Street for two months, at Rector's on Tottenham Court Road for four and at the Palais de danse on Brook Green Road in the southwest London borough of Hammersmith for seven. That each venue was larger than the one before, and each engagement longer, reflected the band's growing acceptance in the city. So, too, did its command performance at Buckingham Palace before King George V, and its presence at the Savoy Hotel in a "Victory Ball" that followed the signing of the Treaty of Versailles.

The Original Dixieland Jazz Band has been hailed as the first true jazz band to record, beginning in early 1917, and the first to travel to Europe. Both distinctions have been disputed; at the very least, the irony that they should be held by a group of white musicians should not go unremarked.

Heard in retrospect — that is, in light of the many developments in jazz over the next 85 years — the ODJB does sound more like a ragtime group than a jazz band, and as such was preceded on record by James Reese Europe's Society Orchestra in New York and by the Clef Club ensembles in London. Heard sequentially with those same groups, however, it represents a notable step forward.

As well it might. Four of the five musicians who boarded the *R.M.S Adriatic* for London on March 22, 1919 were originally from New Orleans, among them Emile Christian, who joined the band in New York after its original trombonist, Eddie Edwards, was drafted. The fifth musician, J. Russel Robinson of Indianapolis, signed on just weeks before the trip overseas when the ODJB's pianist, Henry Ragas, died of the Spanish influenza that was sweeping the world.

Thus, between LaRocca, Shields, Sbarbaro and now Christian, the ODJB had firsthand knowledge of the cultural milieu and musical traditions that directly shaped jazz in its nascency, however stylized the band's approach may have been in comparison to that of the other New Orleans players — Sidney Bechet, the Creole Band's Freddie Keppard, Jelly Roll Morton, King Oliver — who had also left the city by 1919. Few if any of the Clef Club's musicians could make the same claim. Moreover, the ODJB took its identity from its cornet, clarinet and trombone in the New Orleans tradition, unlike the New York ensembles whose banjos, mandolins and such had become so familiar to London audiences.

The ODJB was not, however, the first such American band with horns to visit England; Joe Jordan's Syncopated Orchestra, which included cornetist Russell Smith and trombonist John Mobley, had come and gone in 1915. Nor were Nick LaRocca *et al.* the first American musicians to use the word "jazz" itself in Britain. Two of Jordan's erstwhile band members, William Dorsey and Hughes Pollard, had already applied it to their own efforts in London clubs and theatres.

Similarly, drummer Murray Pilcer, lately returned from Paris, made two 78s with what he — or perhaps his record company, Edison Bell — chose to call a "Jazz Band" in January 1919, three months before the ODJB's arrival. Pilcer had a trumpeter, trombonist and clarinetist among his eight musicians,[3] but the results, including *That Moaning Trombone*, are the work of a jazz band in name only — a description that may well have applied equally to the Pollard and Dorsey groups, in each instance representing an attempt to capitalize on the curiosity aroused in England by the jazz craze that the ODJB had precipitated the United States.

At that, the ODJB's recordings — including its biggest hit, *Livery Stable* (or *Barnyard*) *Blues*, now two years old — were still scarce in England. Not until June 1919, two months *after* the band itself had arrived in the country, did HMV import any of its Victor titles from the United States. By then, the ODJB had recorded six new sides in London for Graphophone's Columbia line, each a reprise of a tune that the band had already cut in New York for either Victor or Aeolian Vocalion: *Barnyard Blues, At the Jazz Band Ball, Ostrich Walk, Sensation Rag, Look at 'em Doing It* and *Tiger Rag*.

A reprise, and a replication — effectively contradicting LaRocca's assertion to the Palais de danse's newsletter, *Dancing News,* that "our prodigious outbursts are seldom consistent, every number played by us eclipsing in originality and effect our previous performance."[4] In truth, the band's arrangements had not changed markedly in the interval between the New York and London sessions, nor had the contrapuntal interplay, the elaborations or the breaks that should have allowed the musicians to display whatever spontaneous ideas they had to offer. Even the two members new to the band for its British sojourn, Emile Christian and J. Russel Robinson, remained faithful to the roles — indeed the very lines — created by Eddie Edwards and Henry Ragas.

Whatever the six new recordings disclose of the ODJB's limitations with respect to one of the most fundamental principles in jazz, they do capture the musicians' cohesion and striving sense of purpose, qualities made all the more provocative to the British public by the band's willful, quasi-DaDa-ist irreverence, as manifest in the Teddy Bear taken by the musicians as their onstage mascot and in the pointed suggestion made by LaRocca to *Dancing News* that he would "even go as far as to confess we are musical anarchists."[5]

In total, the ODJB completed 17 recordings for Columbia in London, the last nine with Billy Jones in Robinson's place at the piano; Jones, an Englishman, had played in a tango band that alternated with the ODJB at the Martan Club. Coincidentally or not, these later titles found the band departing from its earlier, well-worn repertoire of rags and blues in favour of more sentimental fare, including *My Baby's Arms, I'm Forever Blowing Bubbles* and *Mammy o' Mine*.

Back in New York by mid-July 1920, the band continued to record pop songs but slowly worked its way full circle back to new versions of *Tiger Rag* and *Barnyard Blues*, its fourth of each, in April 1923. These final recordings of the "original" Original Dixieland Jazz Band — it would re-form in the mid-1930s — signalled the end of what was essentially a preamble to the history of jazz on record, coinciding to the month as they did with the first sides by the young Louis Armstrong as a member of King Oliver's Creole Jazz Band and predating by two months the recording debuts of Sidney Bechet and Jelly Roll Morton.

The ODJB's success in London inevitably led to a demand in 1919 for other white jazz groups from New York. The Louisiana Five, for example, were booked late that year to appear at a London restaurant in the popular Lyons & Co. chain. The band, which included two New Orleans musicians, drummer Anton Lada and clarinetist Alcide (Yellow) Nuñez, was the ODJB's chief rival on record at the time, with more than 35 titles for Emerson, Edison, Columbia and OKeh to its credit. The British Ministry of Labour was nevertheless unimpressed; in a portent of official policy toward American bands during the 1920s, it refused the musicians permission to enter the country, offering no reason for its decision.[6]

Nevertheless at least two other, more obscure white groups did join the ODJB in Britain. The first, pianist Billy Arnold's Novelty Band from Paterson, New Jersey,[7] followed the ODJB to London by just eight weeks and appears to have preceded Nick LaRocca and company briefly — and awkwardly — into Rector's.[8] "When we started on a short engagement in London," Arnold recalled in 1925, "folks used to stare and gape at us as tho [sic] we were exhibits in a zoo. Their reaction to Yankee rhythm was not immediate by any means..."[9]

The band fared better at the Hammersmith Palais de danse — Rector's and the Palais were affiliated operations — and eventually came to the attention of the Gramophone and Graphophone recording companies. Its efforts for Gramophone's Victor label in October 1920, including a version of W.C. Handy's *Beale Street Blues,* were deemed unworthy of sale, but its recordings of *Stop It* and *Left Alone again Blues* for Graphophone's Columbia line two months later were thought to merit commercial release.

In retrospect, Victor would seem to have shown the better judgment. The two Columbia performances are quite primitive in comparison both to the work of the ODJB in 1920 and to the Arnold band's next recordings, three years hence in Paris. *Stop It* has only trombonist Billy Trittle's confident tail-gating to recommend it; clarinetist Henry Arnold, the leader's younger brother, is also prominent but to little good effect, playing in a thin, nervous tone and contributing awkwardly elaborate lines whose premeditation is betrayed by their repetition.

*Left Alone again Blues* is a more interesting recording to the extent that it anticipates the future role of the soloist in jazz by framing a succession of individual statements with a rousing collective introduction and finale. The statements themselves, however, are simply the melody of *Swanee River*, played straight by alto saxophonist Harry Johnson and then paraphrased in turn by trumpeter Charles Kleiner, Henry Arnold and Billy Trittle.

Ironically, too, Arnold's "Yankee rhythm" was now in the hands of a British drummer. Just as the ODJB had looked locally to Billy Jones when it needed to replace J. Russel Robinson, Arnold hired another musician from the Martan Club's tango band, Chris Lee, upon the departure of his original trapsman, Charles Moore. "Dinty" Moore, as he was known, went on to play at the Palais de danse with the Ragpickers, the third band in London to boast an Anglo-American personnel during 1920, however briefly.

Moore in fact returned to New York in December of that year; Arnold, Lee and the other members of the Novelty Band left for France soon after, there to begin an association with casinos in Cannes on the Riviera and in Deauville on the English Channel — an association that would continue very profitably into the 1930s.

*Joy Bells*, with George Robey still in place, was nearing its first anniversary at the Hippodrome when Albert de Corville again tempted fate by adding an American jazz band to the bill in early 1920. In truth, de Corville had thought better of the idea, but his communiqué cancelling the engagement arrived just as the members of what *Variety* identified as Yanks Comedy Five[10] — the future American Five — were about to board the *S.S. Celtic* in New York. They made the trip anyway and forced the producer to put them to work.

Like the ODJB before them, pianist Babe Fuller, violinist Phil Romano, trombonist Eddie Lapp, banjo player Dave Wallace and drummer Eddie Gross Bart played for a pair of dancers and also had a spot to themselves. "Now, in those days," Gross Bart remembered, "they had a walkway in the Hippodrome running right up the centre of the stalls, and I used to sing a song called *I Ain't Gonna Give Nobody None of My Jellroll* whilst I walked up this walkway, playing on my drumsticks, and then back to the stage... We were a great big hit, and George Robey, the star of the show, hated our guts, and he came off the stage banging his stick shouting 'Bloody Americans!'"[11]

It took Robey a little longer this time — six weeks, according to Gross Bart — but once again he had the band dismissed.

# "This artist of genius"

**LIVERPOOL, JUNE 14, 1919.** The *S.S. Carmania* was the second of three ships bearing members of the Southern Syncopated Orchestra to dock at Liverpool, following the *S.S. Norland* by two days and preceding the *S.S. Lapland* by 15.[1] The SSO's musical director, Will Marion Cook, was among the *Carmania's* passengers, as was the orchestra's featured clarinetist, Sidney Bechet.

The two musicians could scarcely have been less alike and yet, by all accounts, each looked quite favourably on the other. Cook, 50,[2] had trained formally as violinist and composer — his teachers included the celebrated Czech composer Antonin Dvoràk in New York — but found as an African-American that his hopes for a career in the segregated world of classical music were unrealistic. Turning to the theatrical stage in the 1890s, he organized several ventures that celebrated his own African-American musical heritage, including the New York Syncopated Orchestra in 1918 and its successor, the SSO, in 1919. He led his musicians and singers not with a baton but merely with body language and facial expressions; such sensitivity was apparently accompanied by a fragile psyche, one that had led Cook to suffer a breakdown in anticipation of a similar, ultimately unrealized booking in London in 1915.[3]

Bechet, meanwhile, could not read music and, in keeping with his characteristically round, stubborn *visage*, resisted suggestions that he should learn. Instead, he played — much as he lived — by his wits, first in his native New Orleans, briefly on the road in vaudeville and most recently in Chicago cabarets. At 22[4], he was already a commanding improviser, possibly the first in jazz, given his seniority by four years over Louis Armstrong; he was also a man capable of great charm and, equally, of sudden and occasionally violent flashes of temper.

Cook, Bechet and the other SSO musicians aboard the *Carmania* were greeted on their arrival in Liverpool by news of the race riots that had rocked that British city — as well as the Welsh ports of Cardiff, Newport and Barry — while the ship was at sea. British soldiers lately returned to Liverpool from service in France and now facing unemployment had clashed with black immigrants who had found work in local factories — and in some cases companionship with local women — during the war. The London *Times* estimated the city's West Indian population at upwards of 5,000. "Many have married Liverpool women," the newspaper's report added, "and while it is admitted that some have made good husbands[,] the intermarriage of black men and white women, not to mention other relationships, has excited much feeling."[5]

One of the SSO musicians from the *Norland*, cornetist (later, trumpeter) Arthur Briggs, later recalled that his party required a police escort to get from the docks in Liverpool to the train station.[6] Briggs, however, also claimed that some of his fellow passengers had seen black bodies floating in the Mersey River; contemporary news reports make no mention of any deaths resulting from the riots.

In London, the SSO's ultimate destination, racially motivated incidents, though more sporadic, targetted Chinese as well as West Indian immigrants. Such was the uneasy climate in which the orchestra, with its full complement of 24 instrumentalists and 12 singers on hand, opened at Philharmonic Hall on July 4 in a program of "Old Folk Songs."[7]

Old African-American folk songs, of course — mixed with Will Marion Cook's own compositions in the same tradition, as well as *Humoresque* by his teacher Dvoràk, and a few instrumental features, notably *That Moaning Trombone* for John Forrester and *Characteristic Blues* for Sidney Bechet. The word "jazz" was noticeably absent both from Cook's program and from the critical response to it, although Bechet was surely offering the most advanced demonstration of this new music that London had yet heard — more advanced than anything already presented by either the Original Dixieland Jazz Band or Billy Arnold's Novelty Band, each of which had just preceded the SSO to the city.

Bechet's contribution, though atypical of the SSO program as a whole, was widely noted, and no more enthusiastically than by Ernest Ansermet, founder and conductor of the Orchestre Suisse Romande and an early champion of the modernism represented in classical music by Debussy, Ravel and Stravinsky. Writing in *La Revue Romande*, Ansermet offered a lengthy and discerning analysis in French, complete with musical illustrations of the songs and instrumentals that he heard the SSO perform. In closing, he turned his attention to the "extraordinary clarinet virtuoso who is, so it seems, the first of his race to have composed perfectly formed blues on the clarinet."

Ansermet's points of reference were, of course, entirely European and, as such, uninformed by any awareness of jazz as it was played by African-American musicians in New Orleans and Chicago. Still, his insights are valuable, making clear — for example — that Bechet's blues were not simply set-pieces of the sort with which the Original Dixieland Jazz Band had so excited London.

"I've heard two of them," Ansermet wrote, leaving Bechet unidentified by name for the moment, "which he had elaborated at great length then played to his companions so that they could make up an accompaniment. Extremely different, they are equally admirable for their richness of invention, force of accent, and daring in novelty and the unexpected. Already they gave the idea of a style, and their form was gripping, harsh, with a brusque and piti-less ending like that of Bach's second *Brandenberg Concerto*. I wish to set down the name of this artist of genius; as for myself I shall never forget it: it is Sidney Bechet."[8]

Ansermet made a point of talking both to Will Marion Cook and to Bechet backstage at Philharmonic Hall. "Many a time," Bechet noted in his autobiography *Treat It Gentle*, "he'd come over to where I was and he'd ask me all about how I was playing, what was I doing, was I singing into my instrument to make it sound that way? We talked a whole lot about the music... There was just no end to the questions he could think to ask about it."[9]

In light of these encounters, Ansermet's highly idealized praise took on an oddly patronizing tone. "When one has tried so often to rediscover in the past one of those figures to whom we owe the advent of our art — those men of the 17th and 18th centuries, for example, who made expres-sive works of dance airs, clearing the way for Haydn and Mozart who mark, not the starting point, but the first milestone — what a moving thing it is to meet this very black, fat boy with white teeth and that narrow fore-head, who is very glad one likes what he does, but who can say nothing of his art, save that he follows his 'own way,' and when one thinks that this 'own way' is perhaps the highway the whole world will swing along tomor-row."[10]

Bechet was able to follow his own way at length just once in any given SSO performance, although he presumably had more latitude when a small group from the orchestra played for King George V outdoors at Buckingham Palace in August 1919. "Once we got started, we had the whole royal family tapping their feet," Bechet wrote in *Treat It Gentle*. "And Will [Marion Cook] told me later that he'd asked them what it was they enjoyed most and the King said it was that blues, the *Characteristic Blues*."[11]

Despite the limitations of his role with the SSO, Bechet remained in the orchestra's employ for the entirety of its five-month engagement at Philharmonic Hall. When it departed at Christmas for an engagement at Kelvin Hall in Glasgow, however, he and at least five other members stayed behind in London. At that, they were not the first to leave; Will Marion Cook himself had already gone back to the United States, his place as music director taken in October by cornetist E.E. Thompson, formerly bandmaster of the 367th (Buffalos) Infantry.

The history of the SSO is in fact a litany of comings, goings, parallel initiatives and musicians' strikes, exacerbated by legal and financial wrangles involving its manager, George Lattimore, in conflict with Cook (who returned to London in January 1920), various impresarios and several of the orchestra's members. More than 110 instrumentalists and singers passed through the organization and its namesakes before it ceased operations in 1922;[12] replacements for the original 36 were summoned from New York, hired away from other black bands already in London or Paris and, increasingly, drawn from Britain's own West Indian and African communities.

In a pinch, even a few white musicians were taken on, among them a young trombonist, Ted Heath, who would be a popular British dance-band leader after the Second World War. Heath participated in the SSO's final venture, a trip to Austria in the summer of 1922. It was, in his words, "a dismal failure,"[13] although Heath benefitted personally from the insights into the mysteries of jazz offered him by drummer Buddy Gilmore, who had succeeded Bechet as the orchestra's featured soloist.

Whatever the effect of this turnover on the quality of the SSO's performances, it did inadvertently make the orchestra a staging ground for a new, post-war wave of black musicians in Europe. More than a dozen instrumentalists from the orchestra in its Philharmonic Hall period went on to play important roles in the spread of jazz internationally, fanning out first into London clubs and then moving on to the Continent and beyond — Bechet, E.E. Thompson, Arthur Briggs, Buddy Gilmore, cornetist and saxophonist Bobby Jones, trombonists John Forrester and Jacob Patrick, saxophonist Ferdinand (Fred) Coxito, clarinetist John Russell, violinist and clarinetist J. Paul Wyer, banjo player Joe Caulk, pianist Pierre de Caillaux and drummers Benny Peyton and George Hines.

Bechet was typical. His first stop after leaving the SSO was the Embassy Club on Old Bond Street, where he, Coxito, de Caillaux, violinist George Smith and banjo player Henry Saparo opened under Benny Peyton's name on New Year's Eve, 1919. By the end of 1921 Bechet had also appeared briefly with Mitchell's Jazz Kings at the Alhambra Theatre in Brussels and travelled with the Peyton band — now also known as the Jazz Kings — to the Apollo Theatre in Paris.[14]

In the interim, Peyton's Jazz Kings recorded two tunes, *High Society* and *Tiger Rag*, for Graphophone's Columbia label early in 1920 — both were rejected for release — and undertook extended engagements at the Palais de danse in Hammersmith and its affiliated, Rector's, later in the year. It was during this same period in London that Bechet began playing a straight soprano saxophone; finding it more expressive than the clarinet, he soon made it his instrument of choice.

Clarinet or soprano saxophone, Bechet was as much a sensation in the Jazz Kings as he had been in the Southern Syncopated Orchestra. The electrifying effect of his presence with the band would be remembered years later by the British writer Harvey Astley. "Always arriving late, with a bulge in his hip pocket," Astley wrote, "[Bechet] set the band alight as soon as the first few notes had fallen like rain drops from his magic clarinet. The King of Jazz had arrived. That was the signal for a number of dancers to gather round the band for the remainder of the evening and listen to the real New Orleans music in the raw."

Although Astley went on to suggest that "a great number of the Southern Syncopated Orchestra had made the journey all the way from the Crescent City," only Bechet and Saparo — among Peyton's musicians — were originally from New Orleans, and Saparo was soon replaced by Joe Caulk. "The bright spot of the evening," Astley continued, "was when Bechet sat down in the middle of the dance floor, legs crossed tailor-fashion, and proceeded to give us solos on his soprano sax, usually starting off with the Prologue to *I Pagliacci!*"[15]

Bechet remained a member of the Jazz Kings until an altercation with a British woman saw him sent in September 1922 to Brixton Prison and then, in November, deported. It wasn't his first brush with the law abroad; he had twice paid fines before in London for offences unknown.[16] It would not be his last.

# "The hit of the revue"

PARIS, JULY 4, 1919. America's 143rd birthday. In London, the Southern Syncopated Orchestra opened at Philharmonic Hall. In Paris, Mitchell's Jazz Kings were making their debut in the premiere of the revue *OUF!* at the Casino de Paris.

Louis Mitchell had spent four months in New York trying to recruit a large orchestra of African-American players for the Montmartre theatre. The task proved difficult, however, and the resulting delay forced the Casino's producer, Léon Volterra, to cancel the initiative just as Mitchell had at long last completed his arrangements. Contracts were signed, rehearsals undertaken at Lafayette Hall in Harlem, passports obtained and passages booked — all, to Mitchell's great embarrassment, for naught. Several of his musicians, including Sidney Bechet, crossed the Atlantic as members of the Southern Syncopated Orchestra instead.

So it was that Mitchell sailed for France in May 1919 with an ensemble not of 45, but of five. At that, he had been instructed to return to Paris alone; he took the others along on his own initiative. It was another gamble in a career that had so far flourished on risks taken.

Frank Withers, remembered as "a dark little fella, short and thin"[1] and now prematurely balding at 38[2], was likely the oldest of Mitchell's new Jazz Kings, a veteran of the vaudeville stage and of cabarets in San Francisco, Chicago and New York. He often worked in the company of his wife, the trombonist, saxophonist and pianist Mazie Mullins; both had been members earlier in 1919 of Will Marion Cook's New York Syncopated Orchestra, which billed Withers as the "Great Trombonist who Introduced 'The Blues' to N.Y."[3]

Withers had drawn praise as a member of a Clef Club orchestra the year before from the classical music critic of the Boston *Post*, Olin Downes, for "the quality of his tone, curiously like a voice, and more sensitive and full of a hundred shades of color and inflection than any one could dream the instrument capable of." Downes, whose comments anticipated by 14 months Ernst Ansermet's similarly effusive analysis of the Southern Syncopated Orchestra in London, also remarked on Withers' "repeated alliteration of a single note, and the instinct and unconventional manner in which, by emphasis, or pause, or an unexpected crescendo or decrescendo, he makes his trombone fairly speak."[4]

Withers was among the 45 players that Louis Mitchell had originally signed for his Casino de Paris orchestra, as were three other future Jazz Kings, cornetist Crickett Smith, banjo player Joe Meyers, and pianist Dan Parrish. The band was completed by one James Shaw, a saxophonist.

Smith, 35,[5] short and stout, with a soft, bullish face that belied what the Belgian historian Robert Goffin remembered as "an embouchure of steel,"[6] had spent three months in London at the turn of 1913 with the ragtime Musical Spillers, then six years into a run of more than 30 as a successful theatrical attraction in the United States and abroad.[7] Smith then worked and recorded in New York with orchestras led by Ford Dabney and James Reese Europe and in 1919 was a member of W.C. Handy's Memphis Blues Band.

Joe Meyers, 30,[8] was also familiar with travel abroad, having been in residence at Ciro's in London with Dan Kildare in 1915 and 1916. Dan Parrish, meanwhile, had worked in Chicago cabarets and — in the weeks before joining Louis Mitchell *et al.* on the *S.S. Hudson* — with clarinetist Wilbur Sweatman at theatres in and around New York.

Taken on by the Casino de Paris as an *entr'acte* and billed simply as "Les six musiciens nègres,"[9] Mitchell's Jazz Kings were promoted at the premiere of *OUF!* when one of the featured artists went missing at showtime. They played just three tunes, but their performance was more than enough to leave the reviewer from *Excelsior*, Charles Méré, quite dismayed.

Méré began by suggesting that "this cacophonic ensemble" would likely find favour with what he described as "the Kaffirs," an obscure though dismissively racist reference to Africans. "[What is] hard to believe," Méré continued, "is that it would have the same [success] with a Parisian audience. Here is where we are after five years of war! This impromptu was the hit of the revue."[10]

Parisians, in other words, should have known better. Parisians, however, were now increasingly accustomed — and indeed attracted — to the clamour of jazz, thanks to Mitchell's activities since 1917 in the city, and those more recently of the Seven Spades — in their various guises *sans* Mitchell — and of the Scrap Iron Jazz Band. And the clamour was key, here as in London — the clatter and clang of the drums especially.

"For the French people," noted trumpeter Arthur Briggs, "the jazz band *was* the drums. They called [the drums] the jazz band."[11] His assertion is substantiated by the French pianist Alain Romans, who remembered, "We had no idea what jazz was. To the public, the word simply meant the drums, which were the attraction of the first orchestras and which were set up for all to see at the front of the stage. The drummer had at his disposal an infinite variety of accessories, more picturesque or unusual than musical..."[12]

Jean Cocteau, who had already witnessed Murray Pilcer's debut at the Casino some 19 months earlier, saw in the Jazz Kings something more, specifically yet another manifestation of the emerging trend that would come to be known as modernism. In a long, rambling and highly figurative essay, "Jazz-Band," published in the newspaper *Paris-Midi* a month to the day after Mitchell and his musicians opened at the Casino, Cocteau enthusiastically endorsed the growing influence of American culture on Europe and compared its impact to that of Hannibal's tactics during the Punic Wars some 22 centuries earlier.

"Machines, skyscrapers, steamers [and] negroes were certainly the origin of a new, excellent direction," Cocteau wrote. "They marched on Capoue like an army of elephants." The invaders brought "a wilder confusion" [*un désordre plus brutal*] to the relative calm that the Old World had known. "The Jazz Band," he added, "can be considered the essence [*l'âme*] of these forces."[13]

Modernism was not new to Europe in 1919. Six years had now passed since the premiere in Paris of Stravinsky's *Le Sacre du printemps* at the Théâtre des Champs-Élysées, an event later identified by the cultural historian Modris Eksteins as "a milestone in the development of 'modernism,' modernism as above all a culture of the sensational event, through which art and life both become a matter of energy and are fused as one."[14] Eksteins' definition could easily apply as well to the Mitchell band's debut at the Casino de Paris.

Paradoxically, the Jazz Kings were also applauded by the Parisian *avant-garde* as exponents of primitivism, which celebrated the superiority of the primitive over the modern and, in that spirit, considered African tribal masks and statuary, for example, high art. Jean Cocteau, though clearly an admirer of Mitchell and his musicians, portrayed them in almost animalistic terms — as "brave Negroes [suspended] in the air, in a sort of cage, dancing, swaying, throwing to the crowd pieces of raw meat chopped by trumpet and 'cog' rattle [*morceaux de viande crué à coups de trompette et de crécelle*]."[15]

Thus modernism and its apparent opposite, primitivism, were oddly aligned in Paris. Each in its way had the potential to be sensational; an example of primitivism could become an exercise in modernism simply by being unduly provocative, as the African-American dancer Josephine Baker would discover to her great delight when her appearance in *La Revue Nègre* brought fresh scandal to the Théâtre des Champs-Élysées in 1925.

The Jazz Kings' success soon gave rise to a second dichotomy, one more practical than theoretical but no less freighted with racial overtones. The issue was outlined by Jean Cocteau's fellow columnist at *Paris-Midi*, Jacques Florange. "Do you know the fees received by these black 'artistes'...? Some get 50 francs a day, others 100 and sometimes even more, according to their skill and the establishments that employ them. When you think that in the cinemas there are graduates of the Conservatoire receiving fees of 11 or 12 francs, you begin to think that in Paris it is the whites who are the negroes."[16]

The Jazz Kings further added to the disparity in 1919 by playing for "Harry Pilcer's Dancing" at the Apollo Theatre, located next door to the Casino de Paris at 20 *rue* de Clichy. "Our salaries were doubled after the first night," boasted James Shaw in a letter to the Chicago *Defender*, "and we have been playing both engagements for the past seven months and are at present getting three times the salaries that we contracted for."[17]

The band's profitable pattern of dual employment continued in 1920 when it went to the Alhambra Theatre on the boulevard de la Seine[18] in Brussels, appearing at first in Léon Volterra's revival of *Laisse-les tomber* with Mistinguett and Maurice Chevalier — Sidney Bechet was briefly their guest during this period — and also performing each night for dancing in the theatre's bar. After working during the summer in Ostend, on the North Sea coast, the Jazz Kings continued at the Alhambra until March 1921.

Ironically, they were still in Brussels when the Casino de Paris mounted *Paris qui jazz,* which perversely featured an Hawaiian orchestra, much to the satisfaction of local critics. "Will jazz resist the furious assaults against it?" asked Jacques Florange in *Paris-Midi.* "Already in Paris, the establishment that had produced the first 'band' during the war [ie, the Casino de Paris] has repudiated its innovation by replacing it with a far more melodic Hawaiian orchestra."[19] One "Ch. M," probably the contentious Charles Méré, went a step further in the *Excelsior.* "If the Hawaiian orchestra that the Casino is revealing to us... could depose, through its popularity, the barbarian, the horrid jazz band, we say what progress for Paris!"[20]

In the event, Mitchell's Jazz Kings were back in the city, and at the Casino, by the end of March 1921. Mitchell, moreover, convinced Léon Volterra to follow the Alhambra's example in Brussels and convert an upstairs storeroom at the Casino into a small nightclub that would serve as the Kings' nightly base of operations. Le Perroquet (The Parrot), Mitchell called it — just one of several clubs in Montmartre to feature jazz bands in 1921, including Zelli's, with pianist Tom Waltham's white Ad Libs, on *rue* Fontaine, and the Sans-Souci and the nearby So-Different Club, each in turn with the African-

American singer Florence Jones and her accompanists, the International Five, on *rue* Caumartin.

The Jazz Kings remained at Le Perroquet until 1925 and also took their place in many — though not all — of the Casino's revues during that time, among them *Avec le sourire, Dans un fauteuil, Paris en l'air, En Douce, Ta Bouche, Y a qu' Paris, On dit ça..., Bonjour Paris* and *Paris en fête*. When fire severely damaged the interior of the theatre in May 1922, the band spent a rare summer outside of Paris in residence at the Hotel Bernascon in Aix-les-Bains, the town that James Reese Europe and Willie The Lion Smith had introduced to jazz four years before.[21]

Such was the Kings' success that they underwent surprisingly little change in personnel during their four-year history under Mitchell's leadership. When Frank Withers left in late 1919 to join the Southern Syncopated Orchestra, he was replaced by Walter Kildare, who had played cello with Dan Kildare's band at Ciro's in London and piano with the Seven Spades on tour; Kildare remained as the Jazz Kings' bassist when Withers rejoined the band in Brussels a few months later. Both men, Kildare and Withers, appeared on all of its recordings for Pathé — more than 55 titles in total, including one accompanying Mistinguett — between December 1921 and May 1923. Mitchell also augmented the Kings at most of these studio sessions with a second saxophonist and, in some instances, with a violinist and a second or even third trombonist.[22]

The first of Jazz Kings' recordings was a celebratory *Ain't We Got Fun* that seems relatively progressive for its time, featuring as it does Crickett Smith in an extended, rhythmically astute, though melodically limited improvisation that anticipates the much greater strides that Louis Armstrong and Sidney Bechet would make on record two years hence. But *Ain't We Got Fun* is also an anomaly among the band's recordings, which were rarely — if ever — as "jazzy" again.

Like the Original Dixieland Jazz Band, the Jazz Kings have often been derided retrospectively as a ragtime ensemble. Some of their own tunes on record did indeed fall loosely into that category, including *Hep!, Montmartre Rag* and *Crickett Rag*. Most of their recordings, however, were simply dance music, specifically American and French pop songs given straightforward arrangements coloured only occasionally by some jazz effect — the breaks of *Oh Me! Oh My!* (1921), for example, and the rather reserved "shout" choruses of *J'en ai marre* (1921) and *Machinalement* (1922). Indeed, the Jazz Kings' recordings are in total a puzzling legacy, one difficult to reconcile with the vehement reactions that the band so readily provoked in person.

The Jazz Kings' association with Pathé ended, coincidentally or not, at about the same time as Mitchell left the band in favour of a new career as the owner of, or frontman for, a succession of nightclubs and restaurants in and around Montmartre. Crickett Smith took over the leadership of what he now called the Real Jazz Kings, the added emphasis perhaps intended to distinguish the band from Benny Peyton's Jazz Kings in London.

As it happened, Peyton himself, together with one of his musicians, saxophonist Fred Coxito, crossed the English Channel in time to join the Real Jazz Kings for their final months at Le Perroquet and the Casino de Paris in the spring of 1925 and then moved on with Smith, Frank Withers and Dan Parrish to Moscow early in 1926.

# "Red coats and black trousers
# and red-topped shoes"

PARIS, FEBRUARY 13, 1920. For every jazz band in Paris, it seemed, there was a tango orchestra. Where there was the one, there would usually be the other, beginning as early as 1919 when "le célèbre orchestre argentin Sarrablo"[1] vied each night with Mitchell's Jazz Kings for the favour of the dancers at the Apollo in Montmartre.

Tango music, like jazz, lived by its rhythms and its sensuality, subtler though it surely was on both counts. Its origins, like those of jazz, lay in a late-19th-century synthesis of Old and New World musical cultures, both classical and folkloric, in a cosmopolitan New World setting; Buenos Aires was to the tango what New Orleans would be to jazz. Each of these new styles had the power to scandalize, although the tango's offense was a question of morality — the erotic narrative of its dances in particular, often described as the vertical expression of horizontal desires — rather than a matter of music. Argentine musicians and dancers had caused a stir in Paris before the war, much as jazz bands would in the years after. A second wave of tango musicians arrived during this later period, among them Célestino Ferrer and his partner Carlos Güerino Filipotto, Manuel Pizzaro and Francisco "Pirincho" Canaro, whose orchestras worked opposite American jazz bands at various points throughout the 1920s.

Sarrablo, meanwhile, remained in place at the Apollo when the hall introduced a series of late-afternoon *thés dansants* featuring the "Jazz-Band du Majestic Hotel de New York"[2] on Valentine's Eve, 1920. The Apollo's new attraction was yet another group of musicians from the Clef Club: pianist Elliot Carpenter, 25,[3] with banjo player Opal Cooper and saxophonist Sammy Richardson, both veterans of the 807th Infantry, as well as saxophonist Roscoe Burnett and drummer Creighton Thompson. By some accounts, the Clef Club's president, banjo player Seth Weeks, was their leader, although he figures only distantly in the events recounted by Carpenter years later.[4]

The Apollo's tea dances ran each evening until 7 p.m., leaving the musicians with two hours to make their way to their nightly engagement at Morgan's, a dance hall run by a former U.S. Army mess sergeant, Willis Morgan, on *rue* Saint-Didier, near Place Victor Hugo in the 16th *arrondissement*.[5] There they appeared in what was advertised as *A Night in Jazzland*, a billing belied by the absence of any recognizable jazz tunes in the show — at least as they were listed by the Paris edition of the New York *Herald* on the occasion of a dance sponsored by American Legion in mid-February.[6]

The program, which mentioned only Carpenter, Cooper, Richardson and Thompson by name, was evenly divided between vocal and instrumental numbers. Cooper and Thompson were both skilled singers, tenor and baritone respectively, who had performed together in vaudeville with Thompson's brother, DeKoven, before the war. Each now had a song to himself — Cooper, once touted as "The Black Caruso,"[7] sang an excerpt from *I Pagliacci* — and they joined the others in duos, trios and quartets, a *Ragtime Rigoletto* among them. In turn, their dance selections included one-steps, foxtrots, a waltz and — proving the musicians to be quick studies after scarcely a week in Paris — two tangos.

They remained at the Apollo at least until mid-April 1920, at which point the hall began to advertise "Le Weeks Jazz-Band de New York"[8] in local papers, pointing to a change in its attractions or possibly to a split in the original the Clef Club lineup; the Weeks band went on during the next three years to work in Brussels, Trouville, Nice and Rome.[9]

Carpenter *et al.* were still at Morgan's in mid-May 1920,[10] however, by which time they had acquired both a name and a new wardrobe. "I got red coats and black trousers and red-topped shoes," the pianist explained, "and I called us the Red Devils. I got that name from French air aces."[11]

The Red Devils moved on in the summer of 1920 to London, where they held a residency at Rector's through 1921, working initially opposite Benny Peyton's Jazz Kings. "Benny played for dancing," Carpenter remembered, "and we were the 'entertaining' band." Indeed, the Devils' early performances there brought them an endorsement from *The Dancing World* for their "versatility, effectiveness and appropriateness," qualities certainly consistent with the propriety of their earlier performances at Morgan's. "Mr. Carpenter," the newspaper noted, "has insisted on the preservation of the musical element, and he laments the fact that many so-called 'jazz bands' seem to make the creation of noise their chief consideration."[12]

The Gramophone Company was interested enough to take the Red Devils out to its studio at Hayes, Middlesex, in September 1920, but not sufficiently impressed by the resulting four recordings to release them — the same exercise in apparent futility that Graphophone had gone through earlier in 1920 with Benny Peyton's Jazz Kings and that Gramophone would repeat in October with Billy Arnold's Novelty Band.

Ironically, a third recording company, Edison Bell, had no such reservations about the Jazz Kings' replacement opposite the Red Devils at Rector's in the summer of 1921. The Southern Rag-A-Jazz Band, a white sextet from the University of Nebraska in Lincoln via the Fontenelle Hotel in Omaha, recorded six tunes during its stay at the club. Edison Bell released all six on its Winner label, including a spirited version of *Tiger Rag* that is striking for Harold Peterson's remarkably fluid soprano saxophone lead — he appears to have fallen under Sidney Bechet's spell in London — and for Bert Reed's punchy trombone counterlines.[13]

Even without similar exposure on record, however, the Red Devils proved extremely popular in London. Nevertheless, as Carpenter told it, they ultimately succumbed to their own success. "These boys were making money like they'd never seen before because you see we were doing nightclub work. Anyway, you know that money will tell on [ie, do to] you."

For one thing, rehearsals proved impossible; Carpenter's bandmates were too busy pursuing other interests. "They had a freedom you didn't get [in the United States]," he noted. "Over there you didn't have to hide away. So they were just out for fun. In a way they wasted themselves."[14] Roscoe Burnett played the ponies, for example, while Opal Cooper chased the ladies. Came time late in 1921 to pay the accumulated tax on their income from Rector's, Cooper and Creighton Thompson — each overextended financially — instead left for Paris.

Carpenter, Cooper and probably Sammy Richardson reassembled the Red Devils for an engagement in Alexandria, Egypt, during the spring of 1922, then returned to Paris. There they variously added other musicians, including saxophonist James Shaw from Mitchell's Jazz Kings and an actor-turned-drummer, Arthur (Dooley) Wilson,[15] for a succession of engagements in the city's cabarets and theatres — the Acacias, the Alhambra and the Abbaye de Thélème through 1922 and the Quistiti in 1923. At this last, located in the Théâtre Marigny overlooking the Champs Élysées, they found themselves again in the familiar company of a tango ensemble, this time "le célébre orchestre argentin Carlos-Arolas."[16]

Carpenter and Richardson signalled the end of the Red Devils when they returned to New York in July 1923. The pianist was back in London by 1925, however, now working with the tenor Ike Hatch as the team of Hatch and Carpenter. He remained abroad until 1937 and later made his way to Los Angeles where, in the summer of 1942, he was reunited with Dooley Wilson on the set of the film *Casablanca*.

Both men were auditioning to play "Sam," the singer and pianist at Rick's Café Américain. Wilson, who was ultimately chosen for the role, could sing

— he received his nickname for his rendition of an Irish ditty, *Mr. Dooley*, while a member of the Pekin Stock Company in Chicago during the 1910s — but had no facility at the piano. Instead, Carpenter played for him from an instrument placed just out of camera range but close enough by for Wilson to see and approximate the movement of his old friend's hands on the keyboard.[17]

# "And the women loved us"

QUEBEC CITY, AUGUST 28, 1920. The journey that took Charles Harris and Millard Thomas north to Quebec City for the first night of a nine-month engagement at the Princess Theatre started in Shreveport, Louisiana, three years earlier. The two musicians met in the Caddo Orchestra, named for the parish in which Shreveport is located; Harris, a saxophonist and cornetist from Kansas City,[1] had been a member of the orchestra at least as far back as 1914, while Thomas, a pianist from Collinsville, Indiana, by way of the University of Nebraska,[2] had joined the band not long before it arrived at the Deluxe Cafe in Chicago in June 1917.

The Caddo Orchestra stayed only briefly at the Deluxe — it gave way in August to a group led by the New Orleans clarinetist Lawrence Duhé, with former Tennessee Ten bassist Ed Garland, Chicago pianist Lil Hardin and others[3] — but Harris and Thomas would linger on in the city long enough to justify, if only in their own minds, the name of the group that they took, possibly as early as December 1918, to Montreal: the Famous Chicago Jazz Band.[4]

Harris and Thomas had no more claim to "Famous," of course, than they did to "Chicago." By the time they moved on to Quebec City in August 1920, after a summer residency at the Hotel Bureau in Bout de l'Île ("end of the island") at the eastern extreme of Montreal, their band had as its only musician of note the drummer and xylophone player Jasper Taylor, late of the 365th Infantry in France and of W.C. Handy's Memphis Blues Band in New York. Taylor, at least, had worked just before and just after the war at the Owl Theater in Chicago.

In any event, Montrealers would have been none the wiser about either the band's celebrity or its origins. Chicago musicians, real or nominal, were still a rarity in the city; other visiting bands to this point had arrived from the east — Ban-Joe Wallace's Orchestra, Tipaldi's Syncopated Sextette (soon renamed the Melody Kings) and Yerkes' Blue Bird Orchestra from New York, and [Charles] Prevoa's Colored Jazz Band from Boston.

Meanwhile, jazz musicians of any stripe would have been a curiosity in Quebec City, where Harris, Thomas, Taylor and two others — likely violinist Arthur Holiday and cornet and banjo player Daniel Smith — settled into the first of two winters at the Princess Theatre on *rue* St-Joseph. In due course under Thomas's direction, the Famous Chicago Jazz Band became the

Famous Chicago Novelty Orchestra, the adjustment in nomenclature perhaps reflecting the nature of its programs at the Princess, where jazz tunes of the day — *Get Hot*, for example, and *Spread Yo' Stuff* — were widely outnumbered by pop songs and light classical pieces.[5]

The repertorial balance remained much the same when the FCNO returned to Montreal in September 1922 to spend the winter at the Starland Theatre on the *boulevard* St-Laurent as part of a vaudeville company led by the French-Canadian comedian Tizoune.[6] The program was similarly eclectic the following June when the band, with Charles Gordon now in Jasper Taylor's place, played Dvoràk's *Humoresque* as well as *Yes! We Have No Bananas* and *Weary Blues* on radio station CKAC.[7] It was not until the summer of 1924 that Thomas finally gave his musicians over entirely to jazz in a series of "race records" for the Ajax label, newly established by the Montreal company Compo.

Ironically, the Ajax line, with its roster of black jazz and blues performers, was intended for African-American purchasers stateside; few of its recordings were ever made available in Montreal, notwithstanding the presence of a small black community of American and West Indian origins along and near *rue* St-Antoine.

Of the 10 titles deemed worthy of release by Ajax, eight by the FCNO and two by Thomas alone at the piano, only the latter, *Blue Ivories* and *Reckless Blues*, were also issued in Canada on Compo's domestic label, Apex. While Thomas's solos are fundamentally solid, the band's efforts are truly shaky, faltering on the limitations of the musicians, individually and collectively, and on their still rudimentary understanding of a style of music that was now evolving quickly. Thomas and his musicians in Montreal were just as isolated as their counterparts in Europe from the latest developments in jazz; the early classics of King Oliver's Creole Jazz Band for Gennett and OKeh in 1923, for example, were no more readily available in Canada than the FCNO's own, far less illustrious recordings for Ajax.

Once again, Montrealers would have been little the wiser about the FCNO's shortcomings, save perhaps instinctively, thus allowing Thomas to sustain the band into 1926, if not later.[8] Whatever Montrealers thought of its music, though, they — like their Parisian counterparts — were hospitable to its musicians. The saxophonist Randolph Whinfield, a British Guyanan who arrived in Montreal in 1922 and passed through the FCNO's ranks in its later years, remembered, of the city's general level of racial tolerance, "It was like coming home to your mother's arms. The white musicians wouldn't let anyone call us those names. And the women loved us — they spoiled us!"[9]

James (Slap Rags) White arrived in Montreal just as Millard Thomas, Charles Harris and Jasper Taylor were leaving in the summer of 1920 for Quebec City. Like Taylor, White was a musician of some repute, having worked in Chicago cabarets throughout the 1910s, a period in which he also recorded piano rolls of his compositions *My Favorite Rag* and *Morning, Noon and Night* for Rolla Artis and wrote more than a dozen other rags, songs and blues that were published commercially.

Circumstantially, he appears to have travelled to Montreal in the company of several fellow Chicago musicians, including trumpeter Eugene Hutt and two saxophonists, Clarence Miller and a teenaged Rudy Jackson.[10] The band may have been Miller's, and its destination the Blue Bird Cafe on Bleury Street, although White, Hutt, Jackson and drummer George Wright were all reported in November 1920 to be members of violinist E.L. Venable's Collerette Jazz Band.[11]

Rudy Jackson was not long for Montreal — he later worked with King Oliver in Chicago and Duke Ellington in New York before travelling extensively during the 1930s in Europe and the Far East — but White found the city to his liking, possibly for the reprieve that it offered from the restrictions that prohibition had placed in Chicago on his wont to take a drink. His career was in decline, however, perhaps for this very same reason, and his time in Montreal saw him drift further and further into obscurity; he is thought to have died in the city in 1933.[12]

White had worked with George Wright in 1915 at the Pompeii Cafe in Chicago[13] and was likely one of the drummer's eight Kings of Syncopation when they made their debut in Montreal at the Roseland on Phillips Place in March 1921. White's presence in the band could account for Wright's ability to entice the noted violinist Will Tyler from Chicago for appearances during the fall of 1921 at various halls around the city; White and Tyler had worked together at the Boulevard Cafe in Chicago five years earlier.[14]

With or without White, the Kings of Syncopation remained sporadically active in Montreal through 1923, taking their last engagement of record at an east-end hotel, the Chateau Dupère on *rue* Notre Dame; while the city may have welcomed black musicians it nevertheless kept its largest dance halls downtown the domain largely of white bands.

The Melody Kings, most notably, spent five years at the Jardin de danse on Bleury Street before moving into the Ritz-Carlton Hotel in 1925 for three more. Under the direction of the Tipaldi cousins — Andy, who played banjo, and John, a violinist — the Kings also recorded extensively for Apex and HMV. Only a few of their releases, however, show the musicians' affinity

for jazz, in particular *Limehouse Blues* from late 1923, which features improvised cornet and trombone solos of some skill, likely by two of the band's
Canadian members, Johnny Dixon and Al Gagnon, respectively. Dixon,
though born in Massachusetts, was raised in Montreal and, in an odd turn of
events, first heard some form of jazz at the Folies-Bergère in Paris — possibly Murray Pilcer's band — while serving overseas with the Canadian army
during the war.[15]

Other white American bands with similar or greater inclinations toward
jazz came and went freely during this period. Early in 1921, for example,
drummer Dinty Moore, just back from London, performed at the Dansant
Deluxe with a new version of his Ragpickers, while cornetist Phil Napoleon,
trombonist Miff Mole and pianist Frank Signorelli — core members of the
Original Memphis Five — visited the city under unknown circumstances.[16]

Late the following year, the California Ramblers, who rivalled the
Original Memphis Five as the most widely recorded white band of the 1920s,
appeared at the Mount Royal Hotel. Of course the Ramblers were no more
from California than the Five had been from Memphis; both were based in
New York, which was close enough to Montreal to make engagements of a
week or at most a month both practical and profitable. Few American bands
stayed longer in the mid-1920s and those that did — the orchestras of Joseph
C. Smith, Sleepy Hall, Jack Denny at the Mount Royal, Harlan Leonard's Red
Jackets at the Windsor Hotel — had little or no inclination toward jazz at all,
leaving the Famous Chicago Novelty Orchestra, if only by default, with a
corner on the market.

# "Swell-headed"

VANCOUVER, DECEMBER 16 and 17, 1920. The word was out. The Vancouver office of the American Federation of Musicians, would require Americans working in its jurisdiction to pay their dues locally for the first quarter of 1921. Several visiting jazz musicians turned over the $2.50 fee in mid-December,[1] including members of one band from Chicago in the employ of the Regent Hotel on East Hastings Street and of another from Oakland and Seattle that was set to open at the Lodge Cafe downtown on Seymour Street a few days hence.[2]

The most illustrious of these musicians, Ferdinand (Jelly Roll) Morton, 30,[3] had been in and out of Vancouver since the summer of 1919, when he worked at another East Hastings Street establishment, the Patricia Hotel. Never shy about putting himself at the centre of events, Morton later claimed the engagement at the Patricia as his own, one that he had taken as a respite from the run of bad luck he'd experienced while gambling in Seattle. "About the time I got down to my last dime," he told Alan Lomax in 1938, with his customary hyperbole, "Will Bowman asked me to bring a band into his cabaret in Vancouver, Canada."[4]

Morton, by his own account, summoned a mysterious trombonist from Oakland, one Padio[5], originally from Biloxi, Mississippi, and evidently a strong improviser. "Poor Padio," Morton told Lomax, "he's dead now, never got East so none of the critics ever heard him, but that boy, if he heard a tune, would just start making all kind of snakes around it nobody ever heard before."[6]

Morton also mentioned Oscar Holden, who was "no hot man, but played plenty [of] straight clarinet." Morton added, "I had good men, but somehow that cabaret didn't do so good."[7] In fact, contemporary sources in the African-American press clearly identify Holden — not Morton — as the bandleader at the Patricia from the outset.[8] Moreover, Holden, who also played piano, would remain there for at least 22 months, which would suggest that the cabaret did very well indeed.

Morton's departure in the fall of 1919 left Holden with Padio, saxophonist Frank Odel, banjo player Charles Davis, drummer William (or Billy) Hoy and two entertainers, Ada Smith — known as Bricktop for her red hair — and Lillian Rose.[9] Holden, then in his early 30s,[10] was a veteran of the Chicago scene, as were Bricktop and Rose; Hoy, from Indianapolis, had recently travelled with Harvey's Greater Minstrels.

Notwithstanding the Patricia's genteel name, its cabaret drew a boisterous crowd that, according to Bricktop, included Swedish lumberjacks with a propensity toward brawling after a few drinks. In Vancouver, as in Montreal, if nowhere else in Canada, liquor remained readily available; the fact that both cities had a thriving if volatile nightlife was surely not a coincidence.

Bricktop herself suffered a broken leg during a melee at the Patricia on Christmas Eve 1919, no small setback for an entertainer whose act was as much dance as it was song.[11] She remained with Holden at the Patricia through 1920, however — long enough to see Jelly Roll Morton return from his travels down the West Coast to take a band into the Regent Hotel.

This time Morton had among his musicians a drummer from Baltimore, L.O. (Doc) Hutchinson, and a clarinetist from East St. Louis, Horace Eubanks, who later worked in Europe and later still — back in East St. Louis by 1936 — gave a young Miles Davis his first, informal lessons on cornet and his first professional job as a musician.[12]

"The Regent did a hell of a business," Morton boasted to Alan Lomax, "and pretty soon other places started [b]ringing hot men in."[13] Although his assertion once again overlooks Oscar Holden's success at the Patricia, it is supported by the arrival at the Lodge Cafe in late December 1920 of saxophonist Frank Waldron, pianist Olive Bell and drummer Adolph Edwards from Seattle, together with trumpeter James (King) Porter, trombonist Baron Morehead from Oakland, and by the presence early in 1921 of two other Oakland musicians, pianist Henry Starr and saxophonist W.H. Henderson, elsewhere in Vancouver.[14]

By then, however, a restless Morton had left the city for points south — as far south, before the year was out, as Mexico. He would return to Canada just once, this time from Chicago in July 1927, for a week at Crystal Beach across from Buffalo on the Ontario side of Lake Erie; his band for the summer was the Alabamians, who were led by pianist Henry Crowder but renamed the Red Hot Peppers after the group with which Morton had so recently made several classic recordings for Victor.

"Everything going nicely at present," Crowder wrote to the Chicago *Defender* while on tour, adding a candid aside that would have brought a smile to all who had known Morton on the coast. "I find Jelly to be swell-headed but altogether a pretty good sort of a fellow."[15]

# "Hellish disharmony"

KRISTIANIA, NORWAY, JANUARY 25, 1921. Arthur Briggs, like Jelly Roll Morton, was a musician on the move. Originally from Grenada,[1] the diminutive trumpeter spent just 18 months in New York before sailing with Will Marion Cook and the Southern Syncopated Orchestra for London in the summer of 1919. After another year and a half there — latterly in a band at the Palais de danse in Hammersmith with clarinetist John Russell, trombonist Jacob Patrick, pianist George Clapham and drummer George (Bobo) Hines, all from the ranks of the SSO[2] — he continued on to Norway.

Kristiania was still three years away from being renamed Oslo when Briggs, Patrick and Hines, together with clarinetist Jean Paul Clinton (or Roger Jean Paul[3]) and a white pianist, A.C. Garratt, opened as the Five Jazzing Devils in the Mauriske [Moorish] Hall of the elegant, new Bristol Hotel. Inasmuch as Norwegians were unaccustomed to the sight of black entertainers — Kristiania was not on the circuit travelled by African-American variety artists in Europe during the late 19th and early 20th centuries — local newspaper accounts of the Devils' opening night were explicitly racist in their imagery, though likely more as a function of naive amazement than of malice. The musicians were described as being "black as coal" by the *Aftenposten*, and their performance inspired allusions to the jungle and to faraway African villages in *Nationen* and *Dagbladet*.

Little commentary was offered on the Devils' music, although "Le Solitaire" wrote in *Verdens Gang* of their "hellish disharmony" — a suitably diabolical metaphor — and made special note of "Mr. Bobo" and the effect of his drumming on the women at Mauriske Hall, who were apparently fascinated by the range of sounds at his disposal, and on the men, who were impressed by his tricks.[3]

Enthusiasm for the Devils soon waned, however, and the engagement, originally scheduled for three months, was curtailed after just two. A.C. Garrett — who, *Aftenposten* reported in all seriousness, had worn dark, horn-rimmed glasses with Briggs, Clinton, Hines and Patrick so as not to "stand out" — stayed on at the Bristol when a Canadian banjo player, Jack Harris, arrived with the Premier Syncopated Five, a white band from the Embassy in London.[4] Harris enjoyed a warmer welcome than the Devils before him; he remained in Kristiania until the spring of 1923.

For Arthur Briggs, Norway was just the first stop during the 1920s on a circuitous route through Europe that stopped occasionally in France but also took him to Belgium, Austria, Hungary, Turkey and Germany. He was not alone in his willingness to forgo the comforts and camaraderie of the small but growing African-American community in Paris; other black performers who, like Briggs, had arrived with bands from the United States, were now setting out across the Continent with groups of their own, often hiring European musicians with some skill at jazz — or at least some sympathy for it — to bring their new lineups up to strength.

In Brussels during the spring of 1922, for example, Briggs and Jacob Patrick joined former Red Devils saxophonist Roscoe Burnett and a Spanish or Italian pianist remembered only as Gabriel in the employ of Joe Jordan's old Black Lightning, drummer Hughes Pollard, at the Alhambra Theatre.[5] Pollard himself had spent some part of the previous year at the Reserve in Saint-Jean-de-Luz, on the Basque Coast of France and Spain, playing for dancers from nearby Biarritz, Bilbao and San Sebastian with a band completed by unidentified Swedish, Dutch and Spanish musicians; his own specialties in each night's entertainment there included singing and — like Mr. Bobo's performances with the Five Jazzing Devils — "improvised acrobatics in the most approved fashion."[6]

Pollard's band with Briggs et al. worked at the Alhambra for the dancer Mistinguett — she of the long legs, sad eyes and shy smile — then moved on its own to Maxim's in Ostend for an ill-fated summer in which both the drummer and Jacob Patrick fell victim to violence in the seaside town's demi-monde. Pollard's drunken encounter with an Ostend pimp bearing a broken bottle left him with a facial scar that he carried for the rest of his short life, while Patrick ran into trouble in a cabaret over the question of payment for champagne that he had not in fact ordered. According to Briggs, the trombonist was assaulted by the club's manager and then, when he was unable to make his plight understood in English, beaten again by a local policeman. He died of his injuries some months later in Paris.[7]

Briggs viewed his colleagues' fate with some detachment, echoing Elliot Carpenter's comments on the problems that the Red Devils — "just out for fun" — had encountered in London. "You see," Briggs noted many years later, "a lot of the boys that came over, they realized that they were going to have a good time from the first and some of them had too much of a good time. They mix all the good times together, dissipating and drinking as well as doing their work and it finally gets the better of them."[8]

Pollard, still recovering from the slash to his forehead, returned briefly to work in November 1922 with Mistinguett and her dance partner of the day, Earl Leslie, at the Alhambra in Paris.[9] The drummer subsequently led a band at Le Souper LaJunie on *rue* Pigalle in Montmartre; as l'Orchestre Pollard's Six it recorded two titles in June 1923 for Pathé, *I'm just Wild about Harry* and *You've Got to See Mama Ev'ry Night*. Pollard's contributions to the latter recording, once again limited by the studio technology of the day, neither substantiate nor contradict the assertion of the Belgian historian Robert Goffin — who had heard Pollard in Paris — that he was "the greatest drummer of the heroic age." The relatively smooth flow of the band's performance in general is consistent, however, with Goffin's recollection that Pollard "already possessed that wonderfully supple sobriety that only Chick Webb was later to equal" and that he was "the first and the only [drummer] to use a four-to-the-bar rhythm on the bass drum."[10]

While Pollard thrived in Paris, Arthur Briggs continued to work in Belgium, spending the winter of 1922 in Liège with his Creole Five and moving seasonally in 1923, 1924 and 1925 between Brussels and Ostend with his Savoy Syncops, so-named for one of the Brussels nightspots in which they performed. Reflecting the new and already changing face of jazz in Europe, and possibly also Briggs' own willingness as a Grenandian to look beyond expatriate Americans for his musicians, the trumpeter's bands variously included the Haitian flutist and saxophonist Bertin Depestre (Flusky) Salnave — like Briggs a former member of the Southern Syncopated Orchestra — as well as men from Belgium, England, Guadeloupe, Hungary, Italy and Trinidad.[11] The lone African-American in Briggs' employ during his Belgium sojourn was Albert Smith, a singer and banjo player who had previously worked with Seth Weeks in France and Italy to support his studies toward what would be a modest career as an artist in Paris during the 1930s.[12]

Briggs left Belgium with the Syncops in 1925, moving south and east through Europe: Vienna first, where he appeared at the Weihburg Bar, then Budapest and Constantinople (Istanbul), before doubling back by September 1926 for a long engagement at a converted Berlin opera house on Hardenbergstrasse, the Barbarina, with its mirrored walls and red plush carpeting. In Turkey, where he probably appeared at the Maxim Jardin Taxim (Maxim's Dance Garden), his Syncops again included but a single African-American musician, trombonist Earl Granstaff, who had returned to live in Europe in 1924.

Remarkably, even as Briggs ventured further and further afield in Europe and fell increasingly out of touch with his American contemporaries, Granstaff aside, he remained as aware of new developments in New York and Chicago as any of his colleagues abroad. It was, after all, only good business: the very appeal of jazz to Europeans lay in its modernity, and Briggs had to compete in that respect with musicians who were arriving on a regular basis from the United States with all of the latest tunes and techniques.

"As a musician I managed to keep up with what was going on in the States," he later explained, "because I made arrangements with recording stores in all the countries where I worked, and I would go by at least once a week to listen to the new things. I'd get stuff from all over the world because they had good things in England too. You could sometimes get the race records from America. We used to get OKehs and stuff like that. And I'd listen to these and buy the stuff that was good. I had most of Fletcher Henderson's [recordings] and also the Wolverines and Frankie Trumbauer."[13]

As a relatively young musician, moreover — almost 16 years younger than Crickett Smith, for example — Briggs had matured under the influence of jazz, rather than ragtime, and thus was adaptable to the quickening pace of its advances. And indeed his own recordings, beginning with a flurry of sessions with the Savoy Syncops and others in 1927 for Vox and Deutsche Grammophon in Berlin, and continuing during the 1930s with pianist Freddy Johnson, tenor saxophonist Coleman Hawkins and others for various companies in Paris, capture the blossoming of his playing — and of jazz trumpet more generally — after the example of Louis Armstrong.

Certainly Briggs' fellow trumpeter Adolphus (Doc) Cheatham, fresh from New York in 1928, was impressed when he heard the Grenadian for the first time, probably in Paris. "He had originality and style," Cheatham recalled. "He was a stylist. He had a lot of technique — very clean and a good jazz swing man. He was one of the best over there at that time."[14]

# "The city of wine, women and song"

SAN DIEGO, OCTOBER 7, 1921. It was a dapper Jelly Roll Morton — driving cap, narrow tie, stickpin, white shirt, vest, jacket with wide lapels — who looked out intently from the small photograph affixed to the visa newly issued by the Mexican Consulate in San Diego.[1] In the nine months since the pianist left the Regent Hotel in Vancouver, he had played in Casper, Wyoming, as well as Denver, Los Angeles and San Diego. His next stop on this wide, southerly route would be Tijuana, but not before he had obtained the permit necessary to work below the Mexico-U.S. border.

As had been the case when Morton went to Vancouver, he was simply following his gambler's instincts. "The horses," he told Alan Lomax, "had taken me to a little place called Tia Juana on the borders [sic] of Mexico, where I got a job in a place called the Kansas City Bar. Tips ran as high as forty and fifty dollars a night. An old friend, a Negro millionaire out of Oklahoma, owned the place and I [had] taken a fancy to him [and] wrote a tune and named it after his bar — The Kansas City Stomps."[2]

Morton's engagement at the Kansas City Bar was probably brief — brief enough that he may well have commuted nightly from nearby San Diego. Another African-American musician who was working at the time in Mexico, the pianist and drummer Sonny Clay, remembered once catching a ride north from Tijuana in Morton's touring sedan.[3] Morton himself gave a Sixth Street hotel in San Diego as his mailing address in late October or early November when he contacted the Chicago *Defender* to disclaim the rumours of his death said to be circulating — as the newpaper so dryly put it — "throughout the civilized world and the South."[4]

Whatever his logistical arrangements in the fall of 1921, Morton was just one of a growing number of African-American musicians and entertainers who found work in Tijuana — and in Mexicali, another border town 100 miles to the east — during the early 1920s.

Ragtime Billy Tucker, who often visited Tijuana, "the city of wine, women and song,"[5] set the scene in one of his regular reports to the Chicago *Defender*. "Before the days of Prohibition," he wrote, "Tijuana was a typical, dusty Mexican town, sprawling and sleeping in the bright sunlight. Now, as the most convenient wet spot in southern California, it has awakened a roaring activity that has entirely changed its complexion. Situated 150 miles south of Los Angeles, and but 17 from San Diego, it is the mecca for all who wish to cast off restraint and kick up their heels."

Its clientele, in other words, was largely American, both white and black. Tucker went on to describe Tijuana as "a settlement of wide, dusty streets and narrow wooden sidewalks — a frontier town where the limit is the sky, and the air is so clear you can see a long way up. There are blocks of buildings where every space is occupied by a saloon."[6]

The Kansas City Bar was one such establishment. The Main Event, owned briefly in 1920 by boxer Jack Johnson, was another, and the Newport Bar and Cafe a third. The Kansas City and the Newport were run in 1922 by Sylvester Stewart who, as Ragtime Billy Tucker frequently noted in his column, was the only "Race Man" [ie, African-American] on the Tijuana board of trade.[7] After both clubs were destroyed in a fire that ravaged much of Tijuana, Stewart rebuilt the Newport and in 1924 added the Iona Inn and the Chicago Bar to his Mexican empire, in each case installing a jazz band.

Stewart hired most of his musicians from Los Angeles — the saxophonist James Carson in 1922, for example, and the pianist Frank (Dr. Jazz) Shiver in 1924 — but also looked as far north as Portland to find drummer Sam (Cream Puff) McDaniels and his Original New Orleans Jazz Band in 1923.[8] McDaniels, later a character actor in many Hollywood films, remained in Mexico for the better part of three years, working at the Newport, the Chicago and — over in Mexicali — the Black Cat Cafe.

By the end of 1925, however, the welcome that African-Americans enjoyed in Tijuana had cooled. Two years later, in a letter to the Chicago *Defender* from San Diego, the entertainer Buddy Brown blamed the increasingly racist attitudes of whites in the California city for the change. "The 'cracker' has such a foothold here," Brown wrote, "that he has spread his insidious propaganda over into Mexico. Result, no race entertainers or musicians are allowed to work in Tia Juana."[9]

# "She laughed... as one breathes"

NEUILLY-SUR-SCÈNE, PARIS, OCTOBER 14, 1921. Mazie Mullins lay dead at the American Hospital. She was 33,[1] a resident of Paris with her husband, Frank Withers of Mitchell's Jazz Kings, for the past two years.

This was not the first time that tragedy had struck an American jazz artist abroad. Several musicians had died in Great Britain since the banjo player George Watters accidentally shot and killed himself while working in 1915 with Dan Kildare at Ciro's in London. Kildare in turn, despondent in June 1920 over the breakup of his marriage to a London woman, murdered both his estranged wife and her sister, then committed suicide; he had only recently returned to Ciro's after an absence of almost three years, much of it spent working with drummer Harvey White in Dan and Harvey's Jazz Band. And just five days before Mullins's death, several members of the Southern Syncopated Orchestra drowned while en route from Glasgow to Dublin when their ship, the *S.S. Rowan*, was struck twice off the coast of Scotland, first by an American steamer and then by the British liner that came to the *Rowan*'s assistance. The deceased included two Americans, drummer Pete Robinson and singer Walter Williams.

Mazie Mullins's death, however, was a particular loss to the early history of jazz. There were few women instrumentalists in the field during this period and fewer still in Europe, just pianist Mattie Gilmore and saxophonist Sadie Crawford who, like Mullins, had left New York with their husbands — drummer Buddy Gilmore and saxophonist Adolf Crawford, respectively. An African-American woman travelling alone, much less working unescorted in Montmartre cabarets, remained beyond the pale in Parisian society. It would be another three years before the singer and dancer Ada (Bricktop) Smith arrived in the city by herself, and another eight before the singer, dancer and trumpet player Valada Snow followed.

Mullins, originally from Denver, was a notably accomplished musician by any standard in jazz of the day, although she has been remembered, if at all, only for her role as mentor to a young Fats Waller at the Lincoln Theater in Harlem. Mullins accompanied silent films there during the mid-1910s and occasionally allowed Waller to take her place at the piano; by the time she left for Europe, her protégé, now 15, had acquired the job for himself.

Concurrently, Mullins also played trombone in a "ladies orchestra" led by Marie Lucas at the Lafayette Theater, where an impressed reviewer from the

Indianapolis *Freeman* took note of "the address, verve and virility of the true masculine gender in [Mullins's] manipulation of this elusive instrument." He continued: "Her tone, ringing and triumphant in heroic phrases, nevertheless is tender and velvety in the purely melodic. Miss Mullins is the possessor of that most difficult of all trombone effects — the true legato."[2]

Elsewhere, Mullins played saxophone with the New York Syncopated Orchestra under Will Marion Cook on an American tour early in 1919 and with the Southern Syncopated Orchestra under E.E. Thompson in Scotland and England at the turn of 1920, taking Sidney Bechet's place — though perhaps not his featured role — in the latter organization.

Her brief affiliation with the SSO aside, few details of Mullins's two years in Europe have survived. Most concern her involvement in 1921 with the Tempo Club, a semi-private enterprise that she and Joe Boyd, a singer, drummer and gambler from Vicksburg, Mississippi, opened upstairs from Zelli's at 16 *rue* Fontaine — conveniently around the corner in Montmartre from the residence she and Frank Withers shared at 41 *rue* Pigalle.

According to the Paris edition of the New York *Herald*, the Tempo Club began as "a social retreat for the many negro jazz artists in Paris," Withers and the other members of Mitchell's Jazz Kings among them. Under Boyd's management, however, it soon came to enjoy — again in the *Herald*'s words — "a wide reputation among devotees of African golf [ie, craps], as the Paris temple of that exalted pastime, where the tuneful saxophone and traps, so conspicuously active in the front room, were only an accompaniment to the more subtle melodies of rattling 'bones' in the inner shrine."[3]

At the time of her death Mullins was working in the front room with two other former members of the Southern Syncopated Orchestra, cornetist and saxophonist Bobby Jones and singer (and likely pianist) Joseph Hall, as well as drummer Dooley Wilson.[4] The French writer Philippe Soupault later immortalized Mullins as "Mily" in an essay about his visits to the club; Mily, he wrote, "was noted not only for her virtuosity, not only for her love of alcohol, but especially for her gaiety. She laughed — one could write — as one breathes."[5] Soupault attributed her death to her drinking; news reports in African-American newspapers of the day, based on letters sent from Paris by Frank Withers, stated that she succumbed to complications from an appendectomy.[6]

The Tempo Club continued under Joe Boyd's direction until it was closed by the police in April 1922. Ironically, Boyd was responsible for his own downfall when he called the police after his wife was assaulted during a raid on the club by a group of armed robbers. Thus inadvertently apprised of the club's own criminal activities, the authorities staged a raid of their own a few days later.

"The negro's romantic career in Paris," moralized the *Herald*'s anonymous correspondent, "was thus oddly brought to an end through his righteous zeal in trying to bring wrong-doing to justice."

Boyd's wife, an Englishwoman, died of her injuries.[7]

# "A really sterling Jazz Band"

**PARIS, DECEMBER 6, 1921.** Darius Milhaud liked jazz. Or at least he liked Billy Arnold's Novelty Band, which was making an unprecedented appearance at the Salle des Agriculteurs in a program of modern concert music organized by Milhaud's friend, the pianist Jean Wiéner. The program also included a new Milhaud sonata for piano and winds with the composer himself at the keyboard, as well as excerpts of *Le Sacre du printemps* as prepared by Igor Stravinsky for a mechanical piano.

Milhaud, perhaps the most inquisitive member of the informal group of venturesome Paris composers known as Les Six, had first heard the Arnold band at the Hammersmith Palais de danse during a visit to London in the summer of 1920. He was especially taken with the rhythmic and timbral qualities of Arnold's jazz — qualities that he thought might be effective in his own chamber works.

Milhaud also enjoyed the music that Jean Wiéner had been playing at the fashionable Bar Gaya on *rue* Duphot in the shadow of l'Église Ste-Madeleine with the African-American banjo player — and, lately, saxophonist — Vance Lowry, formerly associated with Louis Mitchell and Dan Kildare. Duly inspired, Milhaud wrote what he called a "shimmy," *Caramel Mou*, for clarinet, saxophone, trumpet, trombone and percussion, and saw it danced in May 1921 by "the negro Graton"[1] — possibly Johnny Gratton, originally of New York and now based in Copenhagen[2] — during an evening of avant-garde works that also included three plays, two with music by other members of Les Six, Georges Auric and Francis Poulenc, and the third with both script and score by Erik Satie.[3]

As it happened, Auric, Poulenc and Satie had also been known to frequent the Gaya, as had — for that matter — Maurice Chevalier, René Clair, Jean Cocteau (who would sit in on drums), Serge Diaghilev, André Gide, Mistinguett, Pablo Picasso, Maurice Ravel, Artur Rubinstein and many other figures in Parisian arts and letters. Auric and Satie had already dabbled as composers with ragtime — Auric in his *Adieu New York* and Satie in his ballet *Parade* — and Poulenc, Ravel and Milhaud would incorporate elements of jazz in their works, Milhaud most notably in his score for his ballet *Le Création du Monde* (1923).

Indeed, it was inevitable at a time when the spirit of modernism and the sound of jazz were both sweeping Paris that French composers would find the two in some ways compatible, however selectively they adapted the latter's particulars and however cautiously they embraced its broader significance. Milhaud, for one, had presumed by 1924 to establish his own esthetic for jazz, one in which he went as far as to decry unnamed "drummers without taste, who fancied [that] they enriched their scope by adding false elements, like automobile horns, sirens, 'claxons,' etc."

Milhaud directed his readers' attention instead to "a really sterling Jazz Band, like that of Billy Arnold or Paul Whiteman." The latter's New York orchestra was in fact as polite as the Original Dixieland Jazz Band had been provocative, but its first recordings, *Whispering* and *Japanese Sandman* from 1920, were no less successful than the ODJB's initial efforts and thus presented jazz with its first counter-paradigm of many to come.

"Nothing is left to chance," Milhaud's characterization of the Arnold and Whiteman styles continued, quite missing the essence of jazz. "Everything is done with perfect tact and is uniformly distributed, which immediately testifies to the taste of a musician who is wonderfully familiar with the possibilities of each instrument."[4]

Milhaud had many chances to hear "*les Billy Arnolds*," as the Arnold band was sometimes billed *en français*, after they arrived in Paris from London, via Cannes, during the spring of 1921. They had gone "from strength to strength" in the interim, Milhaud remembered years later in his autobiography *Notes without Music*, and the audience at the Salle des Agriculteurs, though "indignant at first that anyone should dare to play dance music or restaurant music in a hall which had been graced by the presence of so many distinguished virtuosos," was gradually won over by the "languorous charm of the 'blues' and the exciting clamour of rag-time, and the intoxicating freedom of the melodic lines."[5]

In retrospect, however, Milhaud could not help but add that "the quality of the music was often questionable." Nevertheless, implicit in the Arnolds' mere presence at the Salle des Agriculteurs was the endorsement of France's cultural intelligentsia, or at least the modernists among its members — whatever their reservations might have been after the fact.

Of course, there was little profit in playing for the intelligentsia. Shrewd bandleader that Billy Arnold was, he looked instead to another elite for its patronage; as he and his musicians moved during the 1920s between the Restaurant des Ambassadeurs in Cannes and the Casino in Deauville, they found a prominent place among the many and various diversions enjoyed by the idle European and American rich. Together with a succession of dancers — Nina Payne, Harry Pilcer and the Dolly Sisters among them — the

Arnolds served as an evening's option in the daily social swirl of gambling, badminton and tennis matches, flower and horse shows, horse and boat races, golf, weddings, fox hunts and informal audiences with royalty.

Kings and queens, princes, princesses and pretenders, lords and ladies, shahs and sheiks, millionaires and military men all followed the seasons from resort to resort — to Cannes, Monte Carlo and Nice on the Riviera in the winter and Deauville, Trouville and Le Touquet on the English Channel in the summer. And still farther afield — to Aix-les-Bains and Evian-les-Bains in the Alps, to Pau in the Pyrenees and to nearby Biarritz and San Sebastian on the Basque Coast of France and Spain, respectively, to Naples, Rome and San Remo in Italy and, across the Mediterranean, to Alexandria, Cairo and Luxor in Egypt.

The Arnolds were not alone in these lofty circles. Nor were those circles restricted to white musicians. The Pelican Jazz Band with Vance Lowry, Seth Jones and other former members of the Seven Spades, was also popular through the mid-1920s along the Riviera. Such was the Arnolds' particular success, though, that a correspondent for *Variety* could suggest in 1924 that "the Arnold boys probably know a more extended group of social and wealthy cosmopolites than any other band combination in the world."

The writer offered a telling anecdote from Deauville as proof. "While Arnold's salary is large, the side money is tremendous. The other evening a foreign party sent a 100-franc note to Arnold to ask if he knew a woman in the room. Arnold replied yes. Came another note with 300 francs in it, asking Billy [for] her name."[6]

When the Arnolds weren't appearing in Cannes or Deauville, they travelled to San Sebastian in 1922 and to Biarritz in 1924 — as well as to Budapest in 1925 and Barcelona in 1929. They also spent some part of each year in Paris, where in June and July of 1923 they recorded a dozen tunes for the Pathé label.

The French company was especially active during this period, taking Mitchell's Jazz Kings into the studio for the eighth and last time while — in what was perhaps a related move — recording the Arnolds, l'Orchestre Pollard's Six and drummer Gordon Stretton's Orchestre Syncopated Six for the first. As it turned out, the Arnolds were easily the most progressive of the four bands. Their transformation in the two-and-a-half years since they had made *Stop It* and *Left Alone again Blues* for Columbia in London clearly supported Darius Milhaud's assertion that they had gone "from strength to strength," while belying his notion that "nothing [was] left to chance."

Their arrangements, complete with breaks and chase choruses, were intricate, their execution vivacious yet disciplined. Of particular note, two members had developed into confident improvisers, Henry Arnold on soprano saxophone and Charles Kleiner on trumpet. Each is heard on the band's finest jazz sides, *Louisville Lou* and *Running Wild,* in fluent if not yet flamboyant solos conceived with due regard for the changing harmonies of each tune, a breakthrough that members of neither the Jazz Kings nor the Pollard and Stretton "Sixes" had yet made, at least on record. Moreover, Henry Arnold, like the Southern Rag-A-Jazz Band's Harold Peterson, had obviously studied — perhaps even studied *with* — Sidney Bechet in London. Bechet's influence is especially apparent in the rich vibrato that animates Arnold's work on *Louisville Lou.*

To this point in its history, the Arnold band had undergone only one change since its arrival in France, with Victor Abbs replacing Harry Johnson as its second saxophonist.[7] By 1925, however, trombonist Billy Trittle was working under his own name in Paris,[8] and in the spring of 1927 the Arnolds expanded to 15 men, among them several French musicians.

The new band saw itself billed with suitable deference as "the best orchestra in the world after Paul Whiteman,"[9] a point of comparison that was both revealing and timely. Revealing — as an indication that Darius Milhaud's esthetic had prevailed after all. Timely — inasmuch the Whiteman orchestra, 30 strong and purveyors now of "symphonic jazz," had appeared at the Théatre des Champs Élysées in Paris during a successful European tour just the summer before.

# "Lord love a duck"

**CAIRO, JANUARY 1, 1922.** Billy Brooks and George Duncan apparently were amused to find themselves leading a jazz band, one whose particulars they itemized in a long and colourful New Year's Day letter, just the latest of several that they would send to the Chicago *Defender* about life in the Middle East during the early 1920s.

"We have a big concert grand piano with double forte pedals on it," they wrote, "big drum, small drum, two dud drums, two tambourines, bones, whistles, bells, motor claxons, motor horn, castagnets, a screecher, short-neck banjo, trombone, a whiss-a-wass, and to make things more binding we've a big tin tambourine with 20 jinks in it, each jink double the size of a trade dollar. This instrument is manipulated by being banged on the side of a chair. If you could only hear us when we get down or up to do our extemporaneous stuff, you would have to say, 'Lord love a duck.'"[1]

Brooks, from Washington, D.C., and Duncan, from Lynchburg, Virginia,[2] were oldtimers — two African-American entertainers who had left the United States in 1878 with a minstrel company and remained abroad on their own almost 45 years later, the past eight spent in what they called "the land of the Pharaohs."

Brooks and Duncan were nothing if not adaptable. After all, they had sustained themselves as a successful attraction through the fourth quarter of the 19th century and well into the first quarter of the 20th. Now that jazz was suddenly in demand in Egypt, as it was almost everywhere else in the civilized world, they readily complied. For their readiness, they had found work with four Greek musicians as the Devil's Jazz Band.

At that, they were not the first in Cairo to answer to call. "Billy Farrell is responsible for all this jazz stuff," they suggested, giving credit where credit was due locally. Farrell, another veteran of African-American minstrelsy, had spent recent years singing and dancing "on the halls" in England and Scotland before reinventing himself as a drummer and taking a band into Shepheard's, an internationally renowned hotel on Cairo's Opera Square, late in 1920.[3] "Before [Farrell] struck Egypt we only read about jazz," Brooks and Duncan continued. "Now cafes and all dances have caught on. You have only to get a couple of drums, a bit of wood to bang on and a penny whistle and there you are... [a] Jazz Band."[4]

By the time Brooks and Duncan had taken up the cause and its accoutrements for themselves toward the end of 1921, Farrell was working both at Shepheard's and at its rival among Cairo hotels, the Semiramis, which overlooked the Nile.[5] Farrell would remain the toast of the city for two, or possibly three years — "more popular," according to Brooks and Duncan, "than any musician who has ever been in Egypt handling dance stuff."[6]

The Devils, in turn, were employed in a "dancing palace," although this, too, seemed to amuse Brooks and Duncan. "Why it was first called a palace, as it is in a back yard of a garden, we don't know," they admitted. "What we do know is that it is on its way to [becoming] a palace and will surely be some[day] if all the plans are carried out. It has lately been covered up. Up to a short time ago it was in the open air. It was a grand sight to see the moon shining through the branches of green trees 80 feet high for a background."[7]

Such was the Devils' popularity under the palms that they were offered a summer season at Grand Café Français in Beirut — "the first place of the town," Brooks and Duncan boasted in a letter to the *Defender* in March 1922, "with a restaurant, cabaret, dancing salle and concert hall, run by an American company with the American consul at its head... It must be some place to have 42 waiters engaged." But, they added, "things are a little bit unsettled up that way right now,"[8] no doubt a reference to the violent reaction of Arab nationalists to the French trusteeship imposed on Lebanon by the reorganization of the Middle East that followed the First World War.

Egypt, a monarchy and British protectorate both, was momentarily quieter in this respect. "The Egyptians reign," the two entertainers wrote, "the English rule and everyone does pretty much just as they like."[9] The Devils thus advisedly declined the Beirut engagement, which was taken instead by an unidentified "Colored jazz band" that had been working in Alexandria; the band's replacement there may have been the Red Devils, who had arrived on the Mediterranean coast from Paris by April 1922.

Brooks and Duncan were still in place in late 1923, and their musicians now a motley crew of Greeks, Russians and Poles, when another jazz band from Paris — described by a correspondent to the New York *Herald* as "the best ever heard" in Cairo[10] — opened at Shepheard's. Circumstantially, this appears to have been a white group; in another of their long letters to the *Defender*, Brooks and Duncan identified only two other black performers in the city at this time, one of whom, Seth Jones from the Seven Spades and Pelican Jazz Band, was working as the music director for the new Cairo franchise in the Ciro's chain.[11] When Brooks alone wrote again to the *Defender* to report his partner's death in June 1924, he noted that Jones was still on hand.[12]

Shepheard's, meanwhile, remained a fixture of the city's nightlife for many years, although its bands were increasingly multinational, as two other African-Americans, clarinetist Albert Nicholas and guitarist Frank Etheridge, discovered while working their way west from China to France in 1927 en route back to the United States. After appearing in two Cairo nightspots, the Flamingo and the Fantasio, they were approached by the Italian bandleader from Shepheard's who thought their experience might have a salutary effect on the musicians already in his employ.

"They were playing stock arrangements, popular tunes," Nicholas later recalled, "but [they were playing them] just the way they were written. We went in there and we start[ed], just one, two people, [to make] the whole band sound different. The public wanted us right away...We [had] the best sounding band in Egypt."

After six months at Shepheard's, Nicholas and Etheridge went with the band to San Stefano Casino in Alexandria. Etheridge soon left for Germany, but Nicholas stayed until the end of 1928. "I enjoyed Alexandria," he remembered, painting an idyllic picture of the life a musician could enjoy in Egypt. "The weather was beautiful... the ocean and breeze, swim every day, live in the hotel, room and board paid for, eat in the main dining room — it was a beautiful atmosphere."[13]

# "Flogged"

MIAMI, JANUARY 25, 1922. Two cars, a Hudson and a Cadillac, waited outside the Halcyon Hotel at midnight to pick up Howard's Whispering Orchestra of Gold. With its evening's work finished, the Columbus, Ohio, band was off to play at a private party north of Miami. Or so the six African-American musicians believed. Their leader, banjo player Chauncey Lee, had agreed to the job by telephone earlier in the evening; the fee was set at $150, with transportation to be furnished by their host.

Once in the country, however, they found themselves driven down a dark, overgrown lane, pulled from the two cars and set upon by some 75 whites armed with guns, blackjacks and fence pickets. The musicians were severely beaten — "flogged" was the word used by the Miami *Herald* that same morning[1] and by the Chicago *Defender* 10 days later[2], freighted as it was with the history of race relations in the South — and their instruments were smashed beyond repair. Advised under threat of further harm to leave Miami immediately, they complied later the same day.

The *Defender* accused the city's white musicians of sponsoring the attack, noting that they had already made an unsuccessful effort through the American Federation of Musicians to have the Whispering Orchestra of Gold ousted from the Halcyon. "Too," the paper's report added, "there was a decided dislike among the rabble element in [Miami] against the men because they were from the North and evinced none of the humility and obsequiousness common to the native citizens of the town. It was complained that the men walked on the sidewalks, that they stood on corners and looked at white women, and that once they even went so far as to sit down in a public park."[3]

The details offered by the Miami *Herald* were more specific. After the musicians had attempted to dance at the Elser Pier, only to be turned out into the evening, "they walked along Flagler street arm-in-arm and ogled white girls..."[4]

The *Defender* gave the incident even greater play three weeks later in a full-page dramatization headlined "Florida mob's atrocities put 'Huns' to shame."[5] For African-Americans abroad, where copies of the *Defender* forwarded by friends and family from home were read widely, the story was a cautionary tale, one that offered the expatriates further encouragement — should any be needed — to keep an ocean between themselves and the country they had left behind. In due course, they were joined by the Whispering Orchestra of Gold's drummer and xylophone player, Jack Carter, who made the Pacific his ocean of choice in 1924 when he left on what would be a five-year odyssey in the Far East.

# "Half a dozen cacophonists..."

BUENOS AIRES, JUNE 7, 1923. Little could the Pensacola Kid have known that his debut at the Casino with Gordon Stretton's Syncopated Six in this Argentine city would change the course of his life. Then in his early 30s,[1] the Pensacola Kid had always been a man on the move, as witness his route from Florida to Buenos Aires, which was as circuitous as it was colourful — north via minstrelsy to Chicago by 1913, back on the road with W.C. Handy's Memphis Blues Band at mid-decade, across the Atlantic to London with Will Marion Cook's Southern Syncopated Orchestra in 1919 and on to Paris by 1923.

The Pensacola Kid — J. (John) Paul Wyer — played clarinet, violin and pool. He did all three very well, especially the third. His friend Jelly Roll Morton, who fancied himself something of a pool shark as well, boasted of beating Wyer once at the Astoria Hotel in New Orleans — "somehow all the breaks were with me that day"[2] — as though the victory was entirely improbable. The Kid, he told Alan Lomax, "later came to be the champion pool player of the world,"[3] which of course made Morton's lone triumph all the more noteworthy.

Once in England, according to family legend, Wyer was known to sustain his fellow members of the SSO from one missed payday to the next by taking what little money they had left between them and using it as a stake with which hustle unsuspecting pool players in London parlours.[4] Indeed his prowess with a cue was undoubtedly far more lucrative than his skill as a clarinetist, bringing him a reported $85,000 in winnings by the spring of 1921.[5] He was similarly successful at the track and in craps. Like Morton, he loved diamonds; unlike Morton, he enjoyed the sort of luck that allowed him to keep the gems once he had bought — or won — them. Even when he put the SSO behind him at the turn of 1920, though, he continued to work as a musician, playing with drummer Buddy Gilmore at the Savoy in London's West End, and leading his own band in 1921 at Moody's near Regent's Park.

At some point, whether in London or in Paris, he made the acquaintance of the drummer and singer Gordon Stretton, born William Masters of part-African ancestry, in Liverpool. Wyer was on hand in Paris with saxophonist Sadie Crawford, pianist George Clapham and others[6] when Stretton's Orchestre Syncopated Six recorded seven tunes, including *Tu verras Montmartre* and *Lovin' Sam*, for Pathé in May 1923.

*Tu verras Montmartre* ("You Will See Montmartre") and *Lovin' Sam* are both curios among early jazz recordings, if only for Stretton's vaguely operatic manner of singing; he had studied voice in Paris with one of Enrico Caruso's teachers, one Professor Balbis.[7] *Montmartre*, a march of sorts, and *Lovin' Sam,* more conventionally a pop song, receive rousing performances characterized by the fervency of Stretton's vocals and the congested support of his musicians. There are no solos as such, but Wyer moves occasionally near the fore in the collective passages, bringing with him the sound of New Orleans jazz that he surely would have heard early in his travels and later, while with the SSO, from Sidney Bechet.

Scarcely had Stretton completed his Pathé recordings than he, Wyer, probably former SSO trombonist John Forrester, and three other musicians, sailed for Buenos Aires, stopping in the Canary Islands long enough for Wyer, "having the time of his life," to send a postcard to the Chicago *Defender.*[8]

In due course, the musicians opened at the Buenos Aires Opera House in *C'est la Miss...!,* a review produced by Madame Rasimi of the Ba-Ta-Clan Theatre in Paris with Mistinguett as its star and Earl Leslie, the Tiller Girls and the African-American dance team of Louis Douglas and former Seven Spade Sonny Jones in its cast. In the meantime — with Mistinguett and Leslie still en route from Paris via Lisbon — the Stretton band appeared at the Casino and on June 10 began a month-long engagement opposite pianist Roberto Firpo's popular tango orchestra at the Royal Pigall Dancing on *avenida* Corrientes.[9]

When, finally, *C'est la Miss...!* premiered on June 22, Mistinguett and, secondarily, Earl Leslie, naturally drew most of the acclaim. Stretton's musicians, who accompanied Leslie in his featured spots (as Hughes Pollard's band had done in Brussels and Paris), nevertheless received a favourable notice in one of Buenos Aires' two English-language newspapers, the *Herald.*

"Just a word about the Gordon Stretton Syncopated Six," wrote "H.G." whose "word" was as notable for what it left unremarked as for what it acknowledged. "In spite of its name, it is a jazz band of the jazziest order," the reviewer continued. "Half a dozen cacophonists who manage to produce music under trying circumstances. For it is not given to everyone to sling a wicked oboe [sic] and dance at the same time. Yet this is what one member [presumably Wyer] did, while the lad at the piano couldn't keep in his seat — though he never missed a beat. And the thin gentleman with the trombone literally zipped his way to fame."[10]

Absent, though, was any mention of Stretton's own contribution; European reviewers had generally found a jazz band's drummer hard to ignore. And no reference was made to the musicians' colour, or to that of Louis Douglas and Sonny Jones, perhaps reflecting Argentina's own racial heterogeneity.

After three weeks in Buenos Aires, the Ba-Ta-Clan company crossed the Rio de la Plata for a fortnight in Uruguay at the Solis Theatre in Montevideo, where Stretton and his musicians "proved to be a complete novelty… and were forced to give many encores."[11] The band also appeared on its own at the Royal Theatre and Parque Hotel before continuing north in August with Mistinguett *et al.* for their final engagement together at the Lyric Theatre in Rio de Janeiro.[12]

The tour complete, Stretton, Wyer and Forrester made their way back to Buenos Aires and spent the Argentine summer of 1923-4 working further south at Mar del Plata on the Atlantic Coast. Forrester eventually returned to Europe, but Stretton and Wyer both remained in Buenos Aires — Wyer until his death in 1959.[13]

His career there peaked in the late 1930s when he was co-leader of a popular dance orchestra, the Dixy Pals, with the Argentine pianist Adolfo Ortiz. But even the years immediately following his arrival in Buenos Aires found him prospering, as another American musician, saxophonist Garvin Bushell, discovered while visiting the city with Sam Wooding's orchestra in 1927.

"I met the Pensacola Kid, the great clarinet player from Florida," Bushell later wrote. "He took me around his ranch in a car. He had so much land down there, I never did get to see it all. He'd bought it for two dollars an acre."[14]

# "Filthy lucre"

COPENHAGEN, DECEMBER 18, 1923. E.E. Thompson, Gay Bafunke Martins and William (Billy) Taylor — respectively, an American of Sierra Leonean birth, a Nigerian and an Englishman of African ancestry — had all been members of the Southern Syncopated Orchestra in one of its final incarnations. Thompson was in fact the SSO's music director of longest standing, succeeding Will Marion Cook in October 1919. Martins played banjo with the orchestra in 1921, and Taylor, bones.

Now, as Thompson's Jazz Band — with Thompson playing cornet and saxophone, Taylor at the drums and two other American musicians added, trombonist O'Connor Holmes and a white pianist, Carleton Kennicott — they were making their Danish debut at Riddersalen (Knight's Hall), a theatre in the Frederiksberg section of Copenhagen.[1]

The engagement, which continued until the end of June 1924 and saw Jean de Grace replace Holmes by March, also called for nightly performances at Riddersalen's sister operation, the Frederiksberg ballroom Guldaldersalen (Golden Age Hall); management of the two halls further reserved the right to hire the band out to other establishments, among them in February and March 1924 the Palehaven (Palm Garden) of the tony Hotel d'Angleterre in the heart of the city.

By then, Thompson and his musicians were the sensation of Copenhagen. Critical response to their performances echoed that accorded the Five Jazzing Devils in Oslo almost three years earlier. While Denmark was not as isolated as Norway on the circuit travelled by black entertainers during the late 19th and early 20th centuries, the local press made many of the same simplistic allusions to race, "jungle music" and African village life in its descriptions of the Thompson band's efforts.[2] One witness, however, the Danish novelist Jørgen Bast, took the music's measure with a couple of decidedly American references when he noted the band's ability to "make more noise than Niagara on a moonlit night" and to generate "a dance rhythm that can make your heart hammer like a Ford engine on its way up [Copenhagen's] Geels Hill."[3]

Whatever the terms involved, judgements in Copenhagen newspapers were at first favourable. Moreover, the band soon enjoyed the patronage at the Hotel d'Angleterre of the city's social elite, including members of Danish royalty. In March 1924, however, Thompson came under attack in *Folkets Avis* for his appearance at a benefit concert as the guest conductor of a 50-piece wind orchestra augmented by the members of his own band. Thompson's offense, according the newspaper, was ostensibly that he had performed in the capacity of a musician when his entry permit from Danish authorities in fact limited him to work only as a variety artist. Here, though, the pointedly racist rhetoric employed by *Folkets Avis* betrayed an editorial sentiment far less noble than any concern about the loss of employment suffered by the Danes whom Thompson and his musicians had displaced on this one occasion.[4]

Ironically, it was Thompson's very desire to be recognized for his musicianship that had led him to take the assignment, one which found him directing the orchestra in classical and near-classical works — or excerpts thereof — by George Frederick Handel, Otto Karl Nicolai, Coleridge Taylor, Francis Thomé and Carl Weber.

Much as Billy Brooks and George Duncan had in their way adapted to the demand for jazz in Cairo, so too did Thompson in Paris and now Copenhagen. No matter that he had trained at Britain's Royal Military School of Music, Kneller Hall, near London, and at the Institute of Musical Art in New York. Nor that he had preceded James Reese Europe in 1916 as bandmaster of the 15th New York Infantry and served in the same capacity during the war with the 367th Infantry (Buffalos) before taking over the SSO in 1919. Now he was playing jazz and clearly, as far as the Danish public was concerned, he had made the transition successfully. But not, apparently, without some cost to his self-respect.

A preview of the concert published in *Københaven*, presumably based on an interview with Thompson himself, stated the matter plainly, if circuitously: "He can't completely forget the time of war when he was the leader of a big military band in the French Army, and to give him[self] a chance to prove that he can do more than yell 'I love you' over dancing couples — so they sense the howlings from Africa's kraals and the strange sounds of the deep jungle — is among the reasons for arranging this concert."[5]

Thompson was not alone in his aspirations. At least two other African-American musicians who were playing with jazz bands in Europe felt a similar calling. The saxophonist and clarinetist Edmund Thornton Jenkins, a graduate of the Royal Academy of Music in London, completed an operetta, *Afram*, and a symphonic work, *Charlestonia*, among other solo pieces and folk rhapsodies, during the early 1920s, while the pianist Leon Crutcher, though apparently unschooled as a musician, composed the score for an operetta, *L'École des Gigolos,* in 1925. Jenkins, who was playing with the International

Five in Paris when *Charlestonia* was performed at the Kursaal in Ostend, Belgium, in 1925, did not hide his unhappiness about the direction that his career had taken, believing — in the words of a friend — that "he had betrayed his artist's conscience when the need of or desire for filthy lucre turned him into a dance band player."[6]

By tragic coincidence, both men died in Paris in 1926. Crutcher, working at the time in a duo with drummer George Evans at the Abbaye de Thélème on Place Pigalle, was shot to death by his French wife during an early morning quarrel at their Montmartre hotel in February.[7] Jenkins entered a Paris hospital for an appendectomy in July and died there in September.[8]

E.E. Thompson lived just a year longer. He left Copenhagen with his band in July 1924 but returned the following spring for another month at Riddersalen. After an interlude in Germany, where he and his musicians appeared in the film *Vergnügungen in Münich*, they took engagements in Montmartre at the Chateau Caucasien on *rue* Pigalle in November 1926 and at the Abbaye de Thélème in April 1927, the latter coupled with a run at the nearby Folies-Bergère. By then, however, Thompson was ill — whether or not he was aware that he had cancer — and would have been increasingly less able to work; Billy Taylor thus switched to saxophone and Bert Marshall, another member of the Southern Syncopated Orchestra five years earlier, was brought in at the Abbaye de Thélème and the Folies-Bergère to play drums in Taylor's place.

Surprisingly — in view of the standards that Thompson surely would have tried to exact on his musicians as a matter of both personal and professional pride — Marshall later remembered the band as "pretty lousy." So lousy, he continued, "that when we went onstage [at the Folies-Bergère] we had to pretend to play while the pit orchestra played for us and we just mimed to it."[9] The band was still at the Abbaye when Thompson died in August 1927 at the age of 44;[10] it continued under his name, and Taylor's direction, at least until 1929, when it appeared in Oslo and Copenhagen early in the year and at the French resort town of La Baule on the Atlantic coast during the summer.[11]

Whatever the band's shortcomings, however, and whatever Thompson's misgivings about his career, he had at least one consolation: he had lived comparatively well, and responsibly, by music. "Of all the musicians who have died in Paris," reported the New York *Age* in 1929, "it is said that only three, among them the late Lieut. E.E. Thompson, left enough francs to bury them[selves]. All the others have had [to have] a subscription raised for their interment."[12]

# "A strong pro-Negro prejudice"

PARIS, FEBRUARY 9, 1924. Kiley's, at 6 *rue* Fontaine, was just the latest establishment in Montmartre to feature American jazz musicians, following in the tradition established in 1918 by the Apollo and the Casino de Paris on *rue* de Clichy. The Crackerjacks and drummer Buddy Gilmore were among the entertainers for opening night;[1] the Crackerjacks — trumpeter Bobby Jones and banjo player Joe Caulk from the Southern Syncopated Orchestra, pianist William (Kid) Cole, drummer George Archer and others — remained in residence there seasonally for the next five years, through the renaming of Kiley's to Shanley's later in 1924 and of Shanley's to the Palermo in the fall of 1925.

The streets of Montmartre — or more specifically the streets of the Pigalle district where so many clubs, cafés and cabarets flourished, below and to the south and west of Montmartre's heights — were a maze of odd angles in which anyone seeking the pleasures of the evening could get happily lost. As described by Ada (Bricktop) Smith, who arrived in May 1924 from New York to sing at the Grand Duc, a late-night *boîte* that had opened five months earlier at 52 *rue* Pigalle, Montmartre was "a tumbledown little place, with red and yellow one-story buildings lining its narrow, twisting streets, and as many cafés and dance halls and bordellos as on State Street in Chicago."[2]

Bricktop remembered the Grand Duc itself as being anything but grand, just a "tiny" room with a dozen tables and a bar "that would feel crowded with six pairs of elbows leaning on it."[3] There was just space enough for a small band and, beginning later in 1924, for the drums and other paraphernalia that Buddy Gilmore used in his novelty act.[4] Bricktop, then 29,[5] could do nothing but cry when she first saw the room; the scarcity at first of any elbows at all on the bar made her no happier. In time, however, the customers came, and Bricktop would stay in Paris for 15 years, four of them at the Grand Duc and several more at succession of her own Bricktop's along *rue* Pigalle.

Her popularity at the Grand Duc, like the success of any performer in Montmartre, depended less on the patronage of Parisians than on the whims of the wealthy Americans and other foreigners of means or measure who flocked to the city in the years after the war. Indeed Bricktop's fortunes began to rise in 1925 only after she attracted the attention of Fannie Ward, an American silent-film star who was vying with another expatriate American,

Elsa Maxwell, for the distinction of being the doyen of the international set in Paris. Heretofore, Ward and her husband, the actor Jack Dean, had apparently favoured Florence Jones, who had been a fixture since 1921 in Montmartre with the International Five.

When Ward, Dean and their entourage inevitably tired of Bricktop, as they had of Jones, they were succeeded at the Grand Duc by writers and artists from Montmartre's Left Bank counterpart, Montparnasse, notably F. Scott Fitzgerald, who was living the very Jazz Age life that he evoked in his fiction. When the Montparnasse crowd in turn lost interest, Bricktop found new champions in songwriter Cole Porter and — through Porter — Elsa Maxwell, who was famous in Paris for throwing parties attended by the rich and the royal. Bricktop herself was soon in demand at such events, not least to teach members of the social elite the latest dances from Harlem, including the Charleston in 1925 and the Black Bottom in 1926. She claimed the Aga Khan and the Prince of Wales among her pupils.

Significantly, each of her benefactors at the Grand Duc — Ward, Fitzgerald and Porter — was American, reflecting the extent to which her countrymen and countrywomen were a presence in the Montmartre establishments that featured jazz musicians. When *Variety* sent its London correspondent to Paris for a night on the town in October 1924, he reported that Zelli's, which had been in business on *rue* Fontaine since 1921 with the Ad Libs, was "the rendezvous of every Yankee in Paris." At Shanley's, a few doors south of Zelli's, he noted, "the gang... consists of bootleggers from the land of the free." Around the corner at Mitchell's, opened by former Jazz King Louis Mitchell at 36 *rue* Pigalle in September 1924 with Florence Jones as its featured attraction, he reported, "You never hear much French spoken... [the] clientele is 99 per cent American."[6]

American, and of course white — creating a hierarchical dynamic between patron and performer that was pointedly evident in Buddy Gilmore's billing at the Grand Duc in 1925 as "The Mascot of Society."[7] Gilmore had led his "Orchestre Jazz Buddie" at the Ritz during the previous summer and was a popular attraction at Zelli's with his wife Mattie throughout the mid-1920s; he, too, could call the Prince of Wales one of his pupils if he so desired; he had given Britain's heir apparent a few drum lessons in London some years earlier.

Whatever the complexities of the relationship between white and black Americans in Paris, local — that is, Parisian — attitudes toward race generally prevailed, to the point where one Montmartre restaurant lost its license in 1923 when it chose to eject two Dahomeyan princes, one a lawyer and the other a physician, in deference to its American customers, who might have been prepared to accept blacks as entertainers but not as equals.

"Certainly," observed the Paris edition of the New York *Herald* in its front page report on the incident, "there is little hope of reconciling American visitors to the sight of seeing blacks, even though 'of native royal blood,' dancing with white girls and inviting American women to jazz and tango with them, as is customary in French dance-halls."[8]

Bricktop later identified "a strong pro-Negro prejudice" in the city, which she attributed to the favourable impression made by African-American soldiers during the war, an impression that the views of at least some white American tourists could not diminish in French eyes. "If there had been a lot of average Americans around," she wrote, "*they* might have influenced the Parisians, but there weren't. White Americans in Paris who were not rich and sophisticated and well traveled were pretty rare."[9]

Bricktop's rival in the mid-1920s, Florence Jones, also drew a cultured crowd to Mitchell's, which in short order was renamed Chez Florence — "the leading place of its kind in Montmartre, where only first-class clients can be found,"[10] according to a letter written to the Chicago *Defender* in March 1925 by Eugene Bullard, until recently manager of the Grand Duc.

Bullard's description was substantiated by a report in the Baltimore *Afro-American* four months later. "Many of the most fashionable Americans who at some time or other have been featured in front page stories in the papers are visitors," the newspaper noted, mentioning several of Chez Florence's customers by name, including the Vanderbilts, and identifying others as "playwrights, Russian princes and ostentatious members of America's alimony sisterhood." The story suggested further that Jones "owes her vogue to the fact that the Prince of Wales visited her establishment three times, thrilling to the plantation melodies."[11]

Unlike Bricktop, who moved to Paris on her own, Florence Jones had arrived with her husband, Palmer Jones, the pianist with the Southern Symphony Quintette when it visited London in 1914 and the leader now of the International Five. Florence and Palmer Jones were in Montmartre with the Five by the fall of 1921; she was then 28 and he was 33.[12] They appeared in quick succession at the Sans-Souci and the So-Different Club, on *rue* Caumartin. After a year at the So-Different, they returned to the Sans-Souci, which in the interim had become the Jardin de Ma Soeur and would soon be renamed the Embassy, their base until 1925 — latterly overlapping with their appearances at Chez Florence.

The International Five and the Crackerjacks both gave Montmartre's habitués an alternative to the Real Jazz Kings, who continued until the summer of 1925 under Crickett's Smith's leadership at Le Perroquet on *rue* de Clichy, roughly halfway between *rue* Pigalle to the north and *rue* Caumartin further south. While the Jazz Kings were strictly instrumentalists, the International Five and the Crackerjacks — like the Red Devils before them — featured singers prominently.

Indeed, an early version of the International Five — from 1921 to 1923 — included former Red Devils singer and drummer Creighton Thompson, as well as Palmer Jones, violinist Ralph (Shrimp) Jones, saxophonist Nelson Kincaid and the banjo player Usher Watts. With Thompson's departure in 1923, soon followed by Watts' death of a cerebral hemorrhage and Shrimp Jones' return to the United States, Palmer Jones added another singing drummer, Dan Kildare's old partner Harvey White, as well as a second Red Devil, Opal Cooper, and a new violinist, Louis Vaughan Jones.

A third Red Devil, Sammy Richardson, took Kincaid's place in 1924 and several other musicians moved through the band as it expanded from five to as many as nine musicians and in 1927 moved with Chez Florence to 61 *rue* Blanche.[13] Palmer Jones, Cooper, Richardson and White remained constant until Jones' death in 1928, also of a cerebral hemorrhage, at which point Opal Cooper sustained the band for several years more at Chez Florence with a succession of singers — Edith Wilson, Zadee Jackson, Alberta Hunter — in Florence Jones' place.[14]

The Crackerjacks, meanwhile, were relatively more stable, with Bobby Jones and Joe Caulk as the band's central figures and Caulk's singing as one of its primary attractions.[15] As heard in weekly radio broadcasts on the Petit Parisien station from December 1927 through March 1928, its repertoire comprised pop songs of the day rather than jazz tunes. The program for their first show, for example, included *Blue Skies, Bye Bye Blackbird, Mary Lou, Me and My Shadow* and *My Blue Heaven*,[16] all of which had been hits in the United States within the previous year and thus familiar to the American tourists who frequented the Palermo.

While the Crackerjacks — and the Real Jazz Kings — stayed relatively close to Montmartre during the 1920s, the International Five gave a command performance in Madrid before the King and Queen of Spain in 1924 and played in Rome for the Italian Red Cross at the behest of Princess di San Fautino in 1925.

A fourth African-American band active in Paris at this time, though initially not in Montmartre, was drawn even further afield by its admirers in

Europe's social and political elite. The Palm Beach Five arrived from New York in April 1924 for an engagement at Rector's, on *rue* des Acacias near the Arc de Triomphe, and in the summer of 1925 — after stops in Biarritz, Budapest and Madrid, as well changes in personnel that took the band from five musicians to seven[17] — accepted an invitation to appear in Constantinople from Mustafa Kemal, founder in 1923 and president of the republic of Turkey. Kemal, better known as Atatürk, would be celebrated for opening his country to the western and secular influences that had been shunned under Islamic rule; what could have been more symbolic of such changes — and in just the second year of the new regime — than the presence of an American jazz band?

According to pianist Leslie Hutchinson, who joined the Palm Beach Seven for the trip, Kemal had heard the band during a visit to Paris. He met the musicians personally on their arrival in Turkey and had them play for him both privately and publicly before they began to work in Constantinople;[18] their ultimate destination may have been the Maxim Jardin Taxim, which was owned by an expatriate African-American, Frederick Thomas.[19]

The Palm Beach Seven's subsequent travels also took them to Bern, and back to Biarritz and Madrid but not on to London; as was increasingly the case with American musicians, it was denied the necessary permits to work at the Piccadilly Hotel there in the fall of 1926.[20] Instead, it wintered in Madrid and joined the Crackerjacks and the International Five, as well as Thompson's Jazz Band, in Paris, playing its final engagement during the summer of 1927 at the Florida — formerly the Apollo Theatre — in Montmartre.

# "Jazz team"

PARIS, MAY 10, 1924. They called themselves the Clef Club, and one or two of them had indeed been members of the organization that James Reese Europe founded in New York in 1910. Here, however, they were playing baseball, not music, and they were making their debut in the Paris International Baseball League at the Stade Èlisabeth, Porte d'Orléans, in the south of the city, against a team of fellow amateurs known as the American Students.

"There are scores of American negro musicians playing in Paris music-halls and cafés," reported the Paris edition of the New York *Herald* when the prospect of a "jazz team" was first raised, "and many of them can swing a wicked bat with just as much success as they can coax syncopated notes out of a moanin' saxophone... They declare that, although the gyrations required by modern syncopation provide a certain amount of exercise, they feel the need of outdoor sport, and baseball just comes natural to a jazz-band player [and] they hope to waltz off with the pennant."[1]

Louis Mitchell, the Clef Club's captain, was scheduled to pitch this first game, with fellow drummer Hughes Pollard as his catcher; trumpeter Bobby Jones was set at short stop and trombonist Earl Granstaff in right field. Other expatriate African-Americans, including the activist and future scholar Rayford Logan, completed the side.[2] Came game time, however, a fellow named Pulliam was on the mound, with Bobby Jones in relief. Neither pitch-er could check the opposition's bats, which left the Clef Club on the losing end of the final score, 27 to 5.[3]

Mitchell did pitch the next game and struck out nine, enough to carry the team to victory over the Bedford Eco Club, 16 to 5. And so it went, with the Clef Club winning about as many as it lost against the other teams — American, French and Japanese — that made up the league. By mid-July, though, Paris nightclubs had closed for the season and enough of the Clef Club's ballplayers in their employ departed for summer engagements else-where on the Continent that the team was forced to forfeit the remainder of its schedule.

The Clef Club returned in May of 1925 with Mitchell, Bobby Jones, drummers Seth Jones and Billy Taylor, saxophonist Greeley Franklin, and banjo players Joe Caulk and Albert Smith among the musicians on its roster. The American Ambassador to France threw out the first pitch of the season, a 25-piece jazz band played, and the team narrowly defeated Bedford-Eco, 13 to 12.[4] This time, however, it started to miss games in early June and once again failed to finish the season — or to field a team at all in 1926, despite Mitchell's best efforts.

Such, nevertheless, was the size, spirit and sense of identity of the African-American community in Montmartre that its members would be comfortable asserting themselves more broadly in Parisian society, even if their new roles as athletes, like their accustomed roles of entertainers, complemented rather than challenged the stereotypes to which they had long been held both at home and abroad.

# "Squirmy cerulean harmony"

LONDON, APRIL 13, 1925. Not since the appearance of the Original Dixieland Jazz Band almost exactly six years earlier, had London borne witness to the latest sensation in jazz so quickly. The Mound City Blue Blowers, whose 1924 recording of *Arkansas Blues* rivalled the ODJB's *Livery Stable Blues* in sales, were making their British debut with a matinee at the Stratford Empire Theatre and opening a two-month engagement at the Piccadilly Hotel later in the evening.[1]

In the years following the ODJB's return to New York in 1920 and the departure of Billy Arnold's American Novelty Orchestra and the American Five for Paris in 1921, several other white bands had crossed the Atlantic for sojourns of varying duration in London.

The Southern Rag-A-Jazz Band, for example, which recorded for Edison Bell while working opposite the Red Devils at Rector's in 1921, went home to Lincoln, Nebraska, after less than a year abroad. Similarly, Art Hickman's New York London Five — of whom Hickman himself, a popular orchestra leader originally from San Francisco, was not one[2] — spent much of the same year at the Criterion in Piccadilly; the band, which made 10 dance recordings released by HMV, would be remembered for its versatility, its five-octave marimba, its bass saxophone and its undisguised disdain for Britons, this last leading its members on one occasion into a brawl at the Hotel Cecil with the resident orchestra.[3]

Antipathy in turn among British musicians toward their American counterparts also ran high, although more for professional than personal reasons. In London, as in Paris, visiting bands routinely usurped local musicians and — adding insult to injury — usually at higher rates of remuneration. The Hickman band received more than £250 (nearly $1000) a week, according to Bernard Tipping, a Londoner who replaced its original trombonist late in 1921. "The salary they paid me was pretty good," Tipping noted, "but I can assure you that it was not to be compared with the amount they were receiving. You see, I was English, and this fact alone did not entitle me to receive the same amount as the Americans."[4]

Efforts were made unsuccessfully to have the issue of foreign musicians in England brought before Parliament in November 1922, supported by accusations that Americans in particular were evading Britain's Alien Restriction

Act by presenting themselves on entry as tourists, all the while carrying contracts for restaurant or cabaret work in the country.[5]

Concerns were also raised in January 1923 about the pending arrival of an African-American revue, *Plantation Days*, to be offered as part of a larger production, *The Rainbow*, at the Empire Theatre. The British Musicians' Union lamented its members' loss of work to Americans, who in this instance included the pioneering New York stride pianist James P. Johnson, cornetist Addington Major (formerly of the 350th Field Infantry), violin and saxophone player Darnell Howard and bassist Wellman Braud, even though these surely were musicians — Johnson in particular — for whom no comparable British replacements could reasonably have been found.

The Actors' Association and Variety Artists Federation also made their objections known in view of the revue's theatrical nature, and questions were once more raised in Parliament. The entire controversy was further fueled by reservations expressed in the popular press about the desirability of allowing African-American performers into the country at all.[6] It was no coincidence in such a climate that most of the original members of the Southern Syncopated Orchestra had long since left England either for home or for the Continent.

*Plantation Days* did in fact fulfill its Empire Theatre engagement from April into May 1923, however, and another African-American production, *The Plantation Revue*, was mounted at the London Pavilion through the summer, also as part of a larger revue, *From Dixie to Dover*. This second show, directed by former 807th Pioneer Infantry bandmaster Will Vodery, starred Florence Mills and U.S. (Slow Kid) Thompson from the Tennessee Ten, Shelton Brooks and others, and travelled with an orchestra that included trombonist Earl Granstaff and trumpeter Johnny Dunn, both of whom would cross the Atlantic again and live out the rest of their lives, albeit not in England but on the Continent.

Granstaff in fact returned early in 1924, working with the International Five in Paris, the Palm Beach Five in Budapest, Arthur Briggs in Constantinople and on his own in Marseilles before his death in 1929. Dunn's second trip overseas found him in London and Paris as a member of the Plantation Orchestra with a new revue starring Florence Mills, *Blackbirds of 1926*; after his third trip, as a member of an orchestra led by Noble Sissle in 1929, he stayed on permanently, appearing in Paris and several Dutch cities during the remaining eight years of his life.

The welcome accorded white American musicians in England during the mid-1920s, meanwhile, was not clouded by racial considerations, of course, but remained unpredictable. The legendary Original Capitol Orchestra spent almost all of 1923 at Rector's without apparent incident, and Paul Specht's Georgians with trumpeter Frank Guarante had a similarly uneventful, though shorter run at the Corner House that year. On the other hand, Guarante himself was refused entry when he returned alone to England on Specht's behalf in the summer of 1924.[7] Deported to France, he took the Georgians into the Claridge Hotel in Paris until problems with work permits there forced the band further afield — to Brussels, Ostend, Amsterdam, Berlin and, in 1926, Geneva and Zurich. Guarante then returned to England — successfully — in 1927, his stay in London overlapping with the sojourns there of two other American trumpeters, Sylvester Ahola and Chelsea Quealey, who took their place among the city's first-call musicians during the late 1920s.

Paul Specht, meanwhile, and another of the many dance bands that visited England under his aegis, saxophonist Hal Kemp's Carolina Club Orchestra from the University of North Carolina, were held on board the S.S. Berengaria for two days at Southampton in July 1924 for want of the work permits required by the musicians to appear at the Piccadilly Hotel; only the intervention of one of the Berengaria's other passengers, U.S. Secretary of State Charles Evan Hughes, allowed the Carolinians to enter the country. Once ashore, they spent a month at the Piccadilly and also recorded a half-dozen tunes for Columbia before making a quick return on the Berengaria to New York.[8]

The Original Capitol Orchestra, which ultimately spent two years abroad, took its name from one of the steam boats that the fabled Streckfus company ran on the Mississippi River each summer. For some part of the season, the Capitol docked at Davenport, Iowa, birthplace of the legendary cornetist Bix Beiderbecke, who in fact played for Albert (Doc) Wrixon in the boat's orchestra briefly in 1921, alongside alto saxophonist George Byron Webb, pianist I.V. (Bud) Shepherd and others.[9] Beiderbecke's replacement was Victor Sells from Donelson, Iowa;[10] Sells, Webb, Shepherd, the banjo player Les Russuck and Sells' brother William, a drummer — all of whom presumably worked on the Capitol in 1922 — left for London at the turn of 1923.

As depicted in a caricature published by The Dancing World in February 1923 to announce their presence at Rector's, they had added four other musicians to the band, including violinist Leon van Straten. Soon after, they sent for another riverboat musician, clarinetist and alto saxophonist Tracy Mumma of East Moline, Illinois, across the Mississippi from Davenport; Mumma, who would turn 24 in London,[11] arrived in time to appear on the first of the two dozen recordings that the OCO made in the course of seven sessions for Gramophone's Zonophone label — recordings that would have been much less interesting, in terms of their jazz content, without him. By the measure of recordings made to date in England, they were very interesting indeed.

While Victor Sells provided a direct, if somewhat choppy cornet lead, making effective use of mutes, it was Mumma whose clarinet playing pointed to the direction in which the jazz soloist's art was developing. Heard to particular advantage on *I Wish I Could Shimmy like My Sister Kate*, *Tiger Rag* and several blues, Mumma's work reflects in its melodic fluency and tonal colouring the example of the New Orleans clarinetist Leon Roppolo, who — as it happened — had spent some part of 1921 in Davenport, likely offering Mumma a preview of the style that he, Roppolo, would reveal on record the following year with the New Orleans Rhythm Kings in Chicago.

Two weeks after the OCO's final recording session for Zonophone in February 1924, the band's American members — Mumma, Russuck, the Sells brothers and Webb — sailed from Southampton for Cherbourg. They appeared at first on the Continent under Webb's leadership at L'Hermitage on Avenue des Champs-Élysées in Paris[12] and for a time during the summer were engaged in Ostend in Belgium; work in Europe proved no less lucrative than it had been in England, with Mumma — for one — drawing a salary of $105 a week from Webb through September,[13] at which time he took over the band himself.

Mumma kept Victor Sells, and possibly his brother, while summoning two more musicians from Moline, Illinois — saxophonist Omer Speybroeck and banjo player Fred Flick,[14] — and hiring the French trombonist Leo Vauchant locally. He called the new lineup the Chicago Hot Spots and returned to l'Hermitage in November 1924[15] for an engagement that likely ran into 1925. According to Vauchant, they played "real dixieland" — *Sensation Rag*, *Panama* and other "tunes that were known in that [ie, dixieland] style." Vauchant was not particularly impressed by the band's arrangements, but noted that its solos "were the hottest thing in town."[16]

So too, back in London come the spring of 1925, were the Mound City Blue Blowers, two of whom did indeed blow — William (Red) McKenzie, 25,[17] through a comb wrapped in tissue paper to muted-trumpet-like effect, and Dick Slevin into a kazoo. Banjo player Jack Bland and guitarist Eddie Lang provided steady accompaniment and Lang, 22,[18] added judiciously bluesy solos of the sort that would make him the second American musician in England, after Sidney Bechet, to become a major figure in jazz history.

McKenzie, Slevin and Bland were from the Mound City — to wit, St. Louis — while Lang, who joined the group in the summer of 1924, was a Philadelphian. Just as jazz was flourishing abroad, it was spreading at home, as reflected as well in the origins of the Southern Rag-A-Jazz Band, the Original Capitol Orchestra and the Carolina Club Orchestra.

Though the Blue Blowers conceived their music in emulation of jazz, and fondly so, they quickly transcended their own novelty and briefly rivalled the object of their affection in mass popularity. Their success did not turn their heads, however, as a reviewer for *Variety* noted after seeing their 13-minute act at the Palace Theatre in New York.

"The work is unassuming in method, with few bids for vaudeville sensationalism outside the effective excellence of the novelty playing itself. No jockeying for bows at the end at all. One encore and off, though the applause would have tempted some acts to steal bows and bows, and at least two more pieces 'by popular demand.'"[19]

The Blue Blowers' reception on opening night at the Stratford Empire in London was not nearly as enthusiastic. "We played the first number real fast — *Tiger Rag*," wrote Bland 20 years later. "Nobody clapped or understood or anything...We finally got through the first show and we wanted to cancel the whole thing, but the agent said, 'All you have to do is play *Red Hot Mama* and [the audience] will learn and sing it with you and everything will be O.K.' So we played *Red Hot Mama* the rest of the week."[20]

The response at the Piccadilly Hotel was much different. While the Blowers "did only fairly" on their first day at the Empire, according to *Variety*, they were "a riot" that night at the hotel.[21] Indeed, the newspaper's London correspondent described the Blowers in a later review as "four American youths who emit squirmy cerulean harmony with such effect that the audience rise as one and yell 'Attaboy.'"[22]

# "A steady, joyful din"

BERLIN, MAY 25, 1925. "*Bis! Bis!*" shouted the audience at the Admirals-Palast — literally "Twice! Twice!" and figuratively "Encore Encore!" To Sam Wooding, and to his fellow musicians accompanying the revue *Chocolate Kiddies*, the words sounded like jeers — "Beasts! Beasts!" Wooding's saxophonists, seated nearest the exit from the orchestra pit, began to move in anticipation of a hasty retreat, stopping only when Wooding himself realized that they were hearing cries not of abuse but of approval.[1]

So began the Wooding orchestra's eight-year odyssey abroad with but a single trip home to New York in the interim. The 11 musicians had good reason to be concerned about their reception in Berlin. Six years had passed since the end of the First World War — Wooding himself had served in France with the 807th Pioneer Infantry — but Germans still felt deeply the privations and humiliations forced upon them by the Americans, French and British in the Treaty of Versailles in 1919.

On the eve of the *Chocolate Kiddies'* premiere, O.M. Seibt, Berlin correspondent to *The Billboard*, suggested that race might be a factor in the show's uncertain welcome. "Ever since the French occupied large slices of German territory with thousands of black [ie, Senegalese] soldiers, who at the moment of writing are still stationed there, the majority of the German people do not exactly crave to see colored performers, and repeated experiences with such acts turned out indifferent successes, no matter how clever the individual artiste may have been. Even on the concert platform there were outbursts of feeling when Roland Hayes, famous Negro tenor, appeared in Berlin last year."[2]

At the same time, though, Berliners had developed a taste for the exotic, and indeed the extreme, as an outlet for a cynical, if not nihilistic hedonism born of post-war despair. These were Berlin's "decadent" years, framed by the abdication of Kaiser Wilhelm in 1918 and the rise of the National Socialists in 1930 — a period of great social, economic, political and moral turmoil and, equally, of powerful cultural initiatives, including expressionism in the visual arts, theatre and the cinema, the Bauhaus in design and serialism in music.

It was also a period in which the city's nightlife and its attendant vices flourished without constraint. "There are more places of amusement in Berlin today than there were in all Germany before the war," reported *The Billboard* in 1924. "Every hole and corner and cellar has been turned into a cabaret."[3]

Bricktop, who followed *Chocolate Kiddies* to Berlin in an ill-fated attempt to open a cabaret of her own in 1927, described the city's nightlife as "the most exciting" she had ever seen. This, after working in Chicago, Los Angeles, New York and Paris. "It was like a circus," she continued. "Compared to it, Montmartre, even at two in the morning, was a sleepy little town. Friedrichstrasse, Behrenstrasse, the Jäger were so packed with nightspots — sometimes two or three in a single building — that you wondered how there could be enough customers to fill them all. But there were. At night the sounds of music and singing and laughing made a steady, joyful din, and there were so many lights that you could hardly see the sky."[4]

Naturally, American jazz was part of that joyful din, although American jazz musicians had started to work in Berlin only recently. In their absence, the German alto saxophonist and clarinet player Eric Borchard had embraced the new music with great enthusiasm, as had the pianist Julian Fuhs, each popular locally and elsewhere in central Europe with his own group. By the time the Wooding orchestra had arrived, however, at least two white American bands were working in the city.

One, drummer Harl Smith's Lido-Venice Orchestra, so-named for an Italian resort island, was appearing at the Heinroth Cafe;[5] the Belgium jazz historian Robert Goffin, himself an amateur musician, had previously heard the band in Brussels and was effusive with his praise, describing it as "the equal of any hot orchestra of its time" and noting that it "improvised to such an extent that we were sometimes surprised to find that we failed to recognize a number which we ourselves played."[6]

The other band, in residence at the Barbarina, was led by Alex Hyde, a violinist born in Germany but raised in the United States. Hyde returned twice to to Europe in 1924, the first time in January with stops through July at the Piccadilly Hotel in London, the Metropole in Berlin and the Tivoli in Hannover,[7] and the second time in November for engagements through August 1925 in several Germany cities.[8] Hyde recorded 11 titles for Vox and some 50 for Deutsche Grammophon during his visits to Berlin, many of the latter recordings valuable for the trumpet solos of Mickey Diamond or Wilbur (Wib) Kurz and the banjo work of Mike Danzi.

On the last of his Deutsche Grammophon sessions, in June and July 1925, Hyde looked to Sam Wooding's band for one of its saxophonists, Gene Sedric, and its trombonist, Herb Flemming.[9] By then, of course, the Wooding band itself was introducing Berlin to the very latest sounds from New York — in fact from the Club Alabam, a popular Times Square cabaret that had been

Wooding's home for the previous 10 months. Jazz was beginning to move in two divergent, yet complementary directions, one that favoured the individual and another that saw a developing role for the ensemble.

Soloists had been emboldened by the compelling example of Louis Armstrong, fresh from King Oliver's Creole Jazz Band and now a member of the Fletcher Henderson Orchestra at New York's Roseland Ballroom. At the same time, bands were increasing in size — Henderson, like Wooding, had 10 musicians in his employ — and arrangements accordingly were becoming more cohesive and complex as they moved away from the determined unisons and casual polyphony of earlier styles.

Wooding, who wrote his own arrangements, was already looking beyond the conventional brass and reed instruments of early jazz to the woodwinds, mellophones and cello of classical music for the "symphonic" effects that presaged his desire to be perceived in Europe as something other — and implicitly *more* — than a jazz musician.

The members of Wooding's *Chocolate Kiddies* orchestra were relatively young and thus well acquainted with the latest developments in jazz; Wooding had even tried to hire Louis Armstrong as his "punch man for the hot choruses"[10] but settled instead on Armstrong's successor with King Oliver's band, Tommy Ladnier, who turned 25 on the third day of the Admirals-Palast engagement.[11] All but two of Wooding's other musicians — "brass bass" (tuba) player John Warren and drummer George Howe — were also 25 or younger. One, Gene Sedric, was just 17, although he identified himself as being 24 on the passenger list of the *S.S. Arabic*, which carried the cast of *Chocolate Kiddies* from New York to the German port of Hamburg.[12]

The rest of the *Chocolate Kiddies* cast was similarly youthful, with singer and dancer Arthur Strut Payne, at 41, the eldest member of the entire troupe. Singer Lotte Gee and the dance team of Rufus Greenlee and Thadeus (Teddy) Drayton were in their 30s, and the rest in their 20s, notably singer Adelaide Hall, who would sing the wordless vocal on Duke Ellington's classic recording of *Creole Love Call* in New York two years hence. The revue itself, however, was caught between old and new. One of its scenes was set on a plantation, another in a Harlem cafe; some of its songs were spirituals, some were the early work of the young Ellington, who had lately moved to New York from Washington.

The Wooding orchestra accompanied the show's singers and dancers and had a spot to itself onstage for a concert of "symphonic jazz" that mixed arrangements of Tchaikovsky and Verdi, as well as Gershwin's recent *Rhapsody in Blue*, with such jazz tunes as *Shanghai Shuffle*, *Alabamy Bound*, *Tiger Rag* and

*The Memphis Blues.*[13] It also recorded two versions each — *Bis! Bis!* indeed — of *O Katharina, Shanghai Shuffle, Alabamy Bound* and *By the Waters of the Minnetonka* for Vox before it left Berlin with *Chocolate Kiddies* in late July. All eight titles were released commercially.

The recordings, like the show, mixed old with new. Wooding's arrangement of *O Katharina*, a surprisingly "hot" medley of popular German melodies, came with a whinnying clarinet that harked back to the Original Dixieland Jazz Band's barnyard effects. *Shanghai Shuffle*, on the other hand, was decidedly more ambitious in its intricacy, urgency and dynamic contouring than a version of the tune recorded in November 1924 by Fletcher Henderson in New York, even though Tommy Ladnier's chortling, muted cornet work with Wooding suffered in comparison with Louis Armstrong's contribution to the Henderson performance. *Alabamy Bound* in turn was notable for Herb Flemming's agile trombone solo but also ventured into the realm of novelty with its train effects and its slide whistle, while *By the Waters of the Minnetonka,* which had no improvised content at all, documented Wooding's symphonic pretensions, modest though they proved to be.

The recordings complete, and the Admirals-Palast engagement nearing an end, Wooding and the members of his orchestra had a decision to make. Their original contract with the show's New York producer, Arthur Lyons, and his Russian partner, one Leonidoff, called for eight guaranteed weeks of work abroad; the musicians started their ninth and last in Berlin at half salary and then, together with the rest of the cast, were asked to take a permanent salary cut — in the orchestra's case from a reported $1200 to $1050[14] — in order to continue with the show when it moved on to Hamburg for a month at the Thalia Theater, with engagements in Scandinavia expected to follow.

To a man, they agreed, despite prescient concerns about the financial stability of *Chocolate Kiddies* as a touring company. The orchestra remained together with only minor changes in personnel until it returned to New York — some 30 cities and a dozen European and South American countries later — in the summer of 1927.

# "The best terp music in all Asia"

SHANGHAI, MAY 30, 1925. Two thousand Chinese students gathered in front of the Louza police station, a stone's throw from the Nanking Road that ran west through the International Settlement from The Bund, on the banks of the Whangpoo River. There was anger in the air, fueled by the killing two weeks earlier of a Chinese worker at a Japanese-owned textile mill and further fanned by the arrests this very afternoon of several of the demonstrators themselves.

With no more than 10 seconds' warning, the police — a force of Chinese and Sikhs under the command of a harried British inspector — opened fire on the students. At least 30 were hit; 11 died. History would record the event as a turning point in the development of Chinese nationalism.

That night, the New York Singing Syncopators opened at the Hotel Plaza.[1]

While American jazz musicians in Europe found themselves unknowingly at the centre of a variety of esthetic and philosophical debates, the Singing Syncopators — violinist Andrew F. Rosemond, with saxophonist Bailey Jackson, banjo player Clinton Moorman, pianist William O. Hegamin and drummer Jack Carter — were caught up immediately in a far more fundamental conflict.

China was in the throes of a death struggle between nationalist and communist factions for political control of a country run from afar by imperialistic French, British, Japanese and American business interests and ruled from within by greater and lesser Chinese warlords and gangsters.

Shanghai nevertheless flourished in this often violent swirl of social, political and cultural tensions. The Paris of the East, it was called — certainly China's most cosmopolitan city, with its imposing foreign banks, branch offices, hotels and embassies on The Bund, its self-defining French and International (British and American) residential "settlements," its post-revolution influx of "White" (as opposed to "Red") Russian émigrés and, of course, its unrestricted nightlife and attendant pleasures.

Eleven years earlier, in May 1914, William O. Hegamin, just turned 20,[2] was working at another Plaza, this one a Chicago cabaret, at least until he was provoked into a fight by the club's drummer, Charles Gilliam, a man known for his propensity for violence. The Indianapolis *Freeman's* entertainment columnist, Sylvester Russell, who had been the victim of a previous Gilliam attack, took note of the altercation, reporting with apparent satisfaction that Hegamin, "once a prize fighter, lightweight, of Camden, New Jersey, flogged Gilliam until he was helpless."[3]

Having won the battle but lost the job, so to speak, Hegamin moved on, finding work during the next three years at mostly second-rate clubs in Chicago and Milwaukee while his wife, blues singer Lucille Hegamin, known as "The Georgia Peach," appeared more prominently on The Stroll — Chicago's State Street — with Dan Parrish, Jelly Roll Morton and Tony Jackson. Indeed, to the limited extent that the Hegamin name has survived in jazz history, it has done so through her legacy, notably the recordings that she made during the 1920s — the earliest of them for Arto with her husband at the piano. His own discography would be limited in its entirety to just two piano rolls, *Arkansas Blues* and *The Saint* [sic] *Louis Blues,* for Arto in 1921.

The Hegamins spent the better part of 1918 and 1919 working together on the West Coast, then parted company both professionally and personally around 1921 in New York. William Hegamin was thus free in July 1923 to join Andrew Rosemond, Bailey Jackson and the two other original New York Singing Syncopators, banjo player Toney Yates and drummer John (Junk) Edwards, on a train trip first from New York to Montreal and then from Montreal to Vancouver — whence they sailed on the *Empress of Australia* for Manila.

J.A. Jackson, who covered African-American show business for *The Billboard* as "The Page," acknowledged the venture with evident pride. "While several smaller contracts have preceded this one," he noted, "this is the biggest piece of business that the new orchestra has handled to date. In point of distance it is probably the longest range musical contract involving our group [ie, black musicians] from New York or any other American center."[4]

In point of fact, however, Billie Powers, an African-American pianist from San Francisco, was leading a band in Shanghai at the Del Monte Cafe, a roadhouse on the outskirts of the International Settlement, as early as 1921. He called his quintet the Del Monte Jazz Band, a name belied by the boasts that he and the band's manager, Frank Augustin, made in a letter that they wrote to *The Metronome*: "The instrumentation, violin, sax, banjo, piano and drums, lends itself very easily to the different styles of music necessary to please our patrons. We find the fox-trot (slow) to be the most favored dance, with the waltz a close second."[5]

Several white bands with some affinity for jazz had also preceded the New York Singing Syncopators to Shanghai. One, led by pianist Harry

"Sincerely Yours
Louis A. Mitchell
The 7 Spades,"
London, 1917
Mark Berresford
Collection

Mitchell's Jazz Kings, Paris or Brussels, 1920
From left: Louis Mitchell, Dan Parrish, Crickett Smith, Joe Meyers, Walter Kildare (standing), Frank Withers, James Shaw.
Mark Miller Collection

Paris *Excelsior*, 22 December 1921

Red Devils, London, 1920
From left: Creighton Thompson, Sammy Richardson, Opal Cooper, Elliot Carpenter, Roscoe Burnett. *The Dancing World*, September 1920. Mark Berresford Collection

Peyton's Jazz Kings, London, 1920
From left: Pierre de Caillaux, George Smith, Sidney Bechet, Joe Caulk, Fred Coxito, Benny Peyton. *The Dancing World*, November 1920. Mark Berresford Collection

Billy Arnold's American Novelty Jazz Band, London, 1920
From left: Billy Arnold, Harry Johnson, Henry Arnold, Charles Kleiner, Billy Trittle, Charles Moore. Mark Berresford Collection

Southern Rag-A-Jazz Band, London, 1921
From left: Gayle Grubb, Bert Reed, Edward Cressell, Donville Fairchild, Harold Peterson, A.H. Schmidt. John Hackett Collection

Original Capitol Orchestra, Hayes, Middlesex, England, 1923
Includes, from left: Vic Sells, Richard Macdonald, Les Russuck, William Sells, ? Evans, Leon van Straten, Tracy Mumma, George Byron Webb, I.V. Bud Shepherd. Richard L. Mumma Collection

Sam Wooding Orchestra, Copenhagen, 1924
From left: Willie Lewis, Gene Sedric, Garvin Bushell, John Warren, Sam Wooding, John Mitchell, George Howe, Bobby Martin, Herb Flemming, Tommy Ladnier, Maceo Edwards. Mark Berresford Collection.

Paris, 1927
Standing, from left: Bert Marshall, Crickett Smith, Billy Taylor, Henry Walton, James Smith, Glover Compton, "Kaiser" Bill Winthrop, George Archer, Walter Kildare, Jocelyn "Frisco" Bingham, Charlie Clarke, Sammy Marshall, (exteme right) Palmer Jones. Seated, from left: Frank Withers, Cyril Blake, Arthur Briggs, Eugene Bullard (at drums), Ferdie Allen, Joe Caulk, Charles Lewis, Sammy Richardson, Roscoe Burnett, Sidney Bechet, Frank "Big Boy" Goudie, Rollin Smith, Bobby Jones, Greeley Franklin, Warren Smith. Theo Zwicky Collection. Identifications from and New York *Amsterdam News*, 12 December 1928.

Members of the Leon Abbey and Sam Wooding bands, Buenos Aires, 1927
Includes Willie Lewis (extreme left), Demas Dean (extreme right), Joe Garland (crouched), Leon Abbey (rear, in bowler hat). Juan Carlos Lopes Collection

Ivy Anderson with members of Sonny Clay's *Colored Idea*, Sydney, Australia, 1928
Hood Collection, State Library of New South Wales

(From left)
"Yours jazzingly Gordon Stretton," Buenos Aires, 1929
Juan Carlos Lopes Collection

Valada Snow and Jack Carter, 1929
Calcutta *Statesman*, 2 March 1929

MISS VALADA SNOW
and Mr. Jack Carter of the
Serenaders, who will
appear at the Calcutta
Empire next week. .

Kerrey, was in residence at the Cafe Parisien in 1919;[6] Kerrey remained in the city at least through 1923, latterly with his Six Mad Wags at the New Maxim's Cafe.[7] Another band, under the direction of a San Francisco musician, Freddie Lynch, appeared at the Astor House Hotel in 1920.[8] A third, fronted by alto saxophonist and trumpeter Jimmy Lequime at the Mumm Cafe in the early 1920s, reflected Shanghai's cosmopolitanism: Lequime was a Canadian, his pianist Monia Liter a Russian, his trombonist Nick Amper (or Ampier) a Filipino, and his saxophonist and drummer — Pete Harmon and Bill Houghton, respectively — both Americans.[9]

Shanghai first saw the New York Singing Syncopators in August 1923, but only in passing; the band slipped ashore from the *Empress of Australia* for special appearances in hotels at several of the ship's ports of call in the Sea of Japan and East China Sea. "Traveling in Japan and China," noted William Hegamin in a letter written in transit to the Chicago *Defender*, "I find that they want jazz music bad in the European places, really a great field."[10]

The "European places," of course, were those establishments that catered to an international, rather than local, clientele. As in Europe itself, jazz in the Orient was a diversion for the social elite — travellers, tourists, businessmen, royalty and the idle rich. Typically, the Prince of Wales, on his royal tour of India in 1922, sought drum lessons from Dan Hopkins, a Cameron Highlander who had apparently just resigned his rank as sergeant major in Rawalpindi to join — and soon to take over — an obscure American jazz band that lost its original drummer to sunstroke.[11]

Hegamin reaffirmed the Singing Syncopators' good fortune in a follow-up letter to the *Defender* from Manila. "Our trip to the Orient has been a success and is the opening of a new field to Colored musicians and entertainers. Japan and China are jazz crazy... They opened the doors to the best hotels, cafes, etc., to us, and they are still open for Colored musicians."[12]

The Manila Hotel, which would employ the Singing Syncopators for the next 21 months, made a particular point of the musicians' race, advertising them in the Manila *Times* as "Those Kolored Kings of Jazz."[13] The *Times* itself took up the theme in a report on a luncheon given for the musicians by the local Rotary Club, quoting each musician as introducing himself to his hosts in a *faux* plantation dialect from the South.

"This yeah nigger, bein' me," the *Times* had Jackson saying, "is registered as Bailey W. Jackson, the W bein' for wailing. My trade-mark, suhs, is mah genuine non-phoney saxophone."[14]

Jackson might well have been from the South, although he was working out of Springfield, Ohio, with the Synco Septet — forerunner to the famous

McKinney's Cotton Pickers — in the months before he joined the Singing Syncopators.[15] Hegamin — "William O'Hegamin, suhs, am me" — hailed from the East Coast, however, as did Rosemond, whose putative "Yo'al is facing de one an' only king ob de violin," was in any event inconsistent with a classically trained musician who would give solo recitals in Europe after he left the band late in 1925.

By contrast, the musicians' race appears to have been of no consequence at all once they reached Shanghai in May 1925. Nothing in ads that appeared in the city's *North-China Daily News* for their appearance at the Hotel Plaza offered any intimation of their colour, black or white. Once again, they were simply the New York Singing Syncopators — Rosemond, Hegamin, Jackson and now the banjo player Clinton Moorman, who had worked with pianist Sammy Stewart in Columbus, Ohio, and the drummer Jack Carter, who had escaped Miami in 1922 with another Columbus band, Howard's ill-fated Whispering Orchestra of Gold, and subsequently joined the Carroll Dickerson Orchestra in Chicago.

In keeping with their name, which promised songs as well as instrumentals, the Singing Syncopators were praised for their versatility in a survey of Shanghai's nightlife written for *Variety* by an American businessman recently returned from several years in China. The Plaza, he wrote rather cryptically, had "a darb Negro band" that "[dished] out the best terp [terpsichorean] music in all Asia and environs."[16]

By year's end, however, the band's personnel had changed twice more, first with Rosemond's departure for Europe and then Moorman's sudden death in late December from pneumonia.[17] Rosemond solicited his own replacement in September with a letter to the Chicago *Defender*, promising that "the engagement is a very fine one, money is absolutely sure, and the hotel furnishes first-class board and lodging. It is the finest contract ever obtained in the Orient. All contract business is done at the American consulate, which makes everything absolutely safe."[18]

His successor was Darnell Howard, the first figure of some significance in jazz history to travel to the Far East. Howard, who had recorded as a violinist with W.C. Handy in 1917 and travelled to England with James P. Johnson in *Plantation Days* in 1923, was playing clarinet and saxophone with King Oliver's Dixie Syncopators at the Plantation Cafe in Chicago when he took the Plaza engagement; in later years he was associated most notably with pianist Earl Hines.

On his arrival in Shanghai, Howard affixed his signature retroactively to a contract that kept the Singing Syncopators at the Plaza through May 1926.

According to its terms, the band would receive $450 (U.S.) a week, plus "suitable board and lodging" at the hotel for its members and their wives, in return for seven nights of work from 8:30 p.m. to 2 a.m. — 3 a.m. on Saturdays and special holidays. The Plaza featured a floor show but the musicians were not required to "play for, or rehearse any Show Features or Acts (including Russian Ballet, Dancing or Singing Acts, or any extra features) other than those within their immediate orchestra."[19]

Came May 1926, however, the hotel was more interested in keeping the band on than some of the Singing Syncopators were in staying, despite the favourable working conditions. Hegamin was more than happy to remain in Shanghai; he and his second wife, a woman from Macáu, were expecting the birth of a son, the first of two, at the end of the year; by then, Hegamin himself had inaugurated The Little Club on Bubbling Well Road with a new band of American musicians that probably included the New York trumpeter Cyril Mickens.[20] The pianist remained in China with his family until 1945, save for a sojourn in Java in 1927; he worked again at The Little Club in 1928 and 1929 and took a long engagement at the Cathay Hotel on The Bund during the 1930s.

Darnell Howard and Jack Carter, meanwhile, returned in the summer of 1926 to Chicago. Howard immediately resumed his affiliation there with King Oliver's Dixie Syncopators at the Plantation Cafe. Carter set about organizing a new band to take back to the Plaza.

# "Shuffling along slow"

**PARIS, OCTOBER 2, 1925.** Sidney Bechet watched from one side of the Théâtre des Champs-Élysées stage with pianist Claude Hopkins and the five other members of Hopkins' Charleston Jazz Band as Josephine Baker and Joe Alex made their dramatic entrance for the finale of *La Revue Nègre* in this, its first public performance.

Though organized in New York by an American producer, Caroline Dudley Reagan, in collaboration with the African-American dancer Louis Douglas, the show had been refined in its Paris rehearsals for the local audience, mindful of the French fascination with African and African-American culture and particularly with the sexual subcurrent that ran through it. Baker, just 19[1] and already a veteran at home of the Sissle & Blake revue *The Chocolate Dandies*, had startled the opening night crowd with her version of the latest American dance, the Charleston; her physical contortions were ungainly to the point of grotesque. Now, against the backdrop of a Harlem nightclub, she and Alex began their *danse sauvage*.

London had witnessed *Plantation Days* and *The Plantation Revue* in 1923, and Berlin *Chocolate Kiddies* earlier in 1925. Paris, however, had seen nothing like *La Revue Nègre* before, and certainly no one like Baker. And Paris was seeing virtually *all* of her just now, as she swung down from Alex's shoulders and stood nude, save for a flamingo's feather, at centre stage. The unrestrained eroticism of the *pas de deux* that followed was more than merely a sensation, it was a *scandale*, one received with the same mixture of delight, derision, surprise and shock as the premiere of Stravinsky's *Le Sacre du printemps* on this very same stage in 1913.

Two days later, the theatre critic for the Paris edition of the New York *Herald*, R. Joviet, was circumspect about the details of the *danse sauvage* but offered this prediction: "Josephine Baker with her sleek black close-cropped hair, shining like a varnished boot, with her lithesome, supple and beautiful body, her crazy songs and still crazier costumes, with her sense of drollery, and eccentric fun, will soon be the pet of Paris."[2] As indeed Baker was, and would be for many years to come.

Sidney Bechet, who enjoyed a similarly enduring relationship with the French in the 1950s, took a role of his own in *La Revue Nègre* beyond simply accompanying Baker as a member of the Charleston Jazz Band. In the three years since he had been forced to return to New York from London, he had started his recording career with Clarence Williams, worked briefly with Duke Ellington, travelled in vaudeville and appeared in residence at two Seventh Avenue nightspots, the Rhythm Club and his own Club Basha. His fame was growing and his skill as a soloist, as well as his experience more generally as a musician, made him a valuable addition to a band that Claude Hopkins had formed only a few months earlier for an engagement — his first as a leader — in Atlantic City.[3]

Bechet joined the cast of *La Revue Nègre* just before it sailed for France in September and once in Paris was given a featured spot in a New York street scene with Louis Douglas and Douglas's wife, Marion Cook. As the Charleston Jazz Band's trumpeter Henry Goodwin later remembered, Bechet "would come out on the stage wheeling a fruit cart, with imitation fruit piled in it, and dressed in a long duster. He'd come out shuffling along slow, and then he'd leave the cart and start to play the blues."[4] Occasionally, when the unreliable Bechet went missing at showtime, Goodwin — like Josephine Baker still a teenager — took his place.

*La Revue Nègre* remained in Paris for just 11 weeks, an altogether brief run in light of the show's initial impact and of the significance that it would acquire as a pivotal event in the history of African-American performers in Paris. It stayed at the Théâtre des Champs-Élysées for seven weeks — members of the cast also made nightly appearances at the Abbaye de Thélème and the Embassy during this period — and then moved to the smaller Théâtre de l'Étoile for another four.

After a week at the Cirque Royale in Brussels, *La Revue Nègre* spent January and most of February 1926 at Nelson's Kabarett-Theater in Berlin, where it was latterly abandoned by Baker in favour of an offer from the Folies-Bergère in Paris. The show struggled on briefly without its star and, soon enough, without Bechet, who left for Russia.

# "An ideal ensemble"

MOSCOW, FEBRUARY 22, 1926. The first American jazz musicians to perform in Moscow, fittingly, had already been among the music's pioneers in London and Paris more than six years earlier — Sidney Bechet, his fellow saxophonist Fred Coxito and drummer Benny Peyton from Will Marion Cook's Southern Syncopated Orchestra at Philharmonic Hall, and pianist Dan Parrish, trumpeter Crickett Smith and trombonist Frank Withers from Mitchell's Jazz Kings at the Casino de Paris.

It was Withers, surprisingly enough, who took charge of the band when it opened its 10-week engagement at Moscow's Little Dmitrovka Cinema; he had previously shown scant interest in shouldering such responsibility, save for a brief stint at London's Portman Rooms late in 1919.[1] Like Parrish and Smith, he had remained more or less loyal to Mitchell's Jazz Kings at the Casino de Paris and its cabaret, Le Perroquet, until Mitchell's retirement from music in 1923. Withers stayed on under Smith's leadership until the Real Jazz Kings — who latterly also included Coxito and Peyton[2] — saw their association with the two Montmartre establishments come to an end during the summer of 1925.

Sidney Bechet, meanwhile, had just returned to Europe with *La Revue Nègre* after an absence of more than three years. He joined Withers and the other former Jazz Kings when they passed through Berlin en route to Moscow; the prospect of playing a dozen jazz tunes nightly with old friends was surely more appealing than his one feature per show with *La Revue Nègre* and the need to push a fruit cart out on stage as a pretense to take it. Financially, too, the Russian trip was attractive: the band would be paid $200 a night for its services by Rosfil, the state-run philharmonic society.[3]

Thus American jazz musicians appeared in Moscow not only with the sanction but in effect under the aegis of the Bolshevik cultural bureaucracy. Their presence coincided with a period in which Russia, nine years after the Communist revolution, was enjoying relative prosperity and personal freedom, the result of V.I. Lenin's New Economic Plan of 1921, which allowed elements of capitalism to flourish and — even for a time under Lenin's successor, Josef Stalin — tolerated the wave of liberalism that accompanied them.

Repression would follow soon enough, in fact in 1928 — as signalled politically by the implementation of Stalin's first "Five Year Plan," which vilified capitalism among all other things foreign, and culturally by Maxim

Gorky's widely read essay for *Pravda* about "toxic music," a fervid attack on the decadence of Western society in general and of jazz in particular.[4]

For the moment, though, the country remained open to international influence, as witness not only the arrival of Withers *et al.* but the Hollywood fare presented by the cinema in which they appeared — *Our Hospitality*, starring Buster Keaton, for the first six weeks of their engagement at the Dmitrovka and *The Love Flower*, with Richard Barthelmess, for the last four.

Indeed, the mood in Russia on the Withers band's arrival was as light as the late February air was cold. A report in *The Billboard* caught the surrealism of the occasion: "The appearance a few days ago of one of the musicians outside the Soviet Foreign Office carrying a huge saxophone excited great curiosity among the bewhiskered citizens, several of whom thought the innocent Buescher [the name of an American instrument manufacturer] was a new kind of explosive."[5]

Inasmuch as references to royalty of any sort would have been problematic in post-Czarist Russia, the Dmitrovka billed the former Jazz Kings in *Izvestiia* and *Pravda* simply as "Negro Orchestra" or "Jazz Band."[6] Its ads further identified Withers just once by name as the group's leader,[7] while singling out Bechet more frequently as a "well-known Negro touring artist,"[8] and proclaiming after the third week that attendance had reached 80,000.[9]

But what would the politically astute among those 80,000 have made of a style of music that, on one hand, was created collectively by musicians who, on the other hand, were asserting their individuality in the process? How could Marxist thought reconcile such a contradiction? The conductor Nikolai Malko juggled it carefully in a review for *Zhizn Iskusstva*, describing the band as "an ideal ensemble" to the extent that no single musician was in charge. Indeed, at least one symphony orchestra in Moscow was operating on this very same egalitarian principle.

Malko pronounced himself more impressed by the style of the band's presentation than the substance of its music, a view consistent with the current trend among many of Russia's own artists toward experimentation at the expense of content, inasmuch as content was the one element of cultural expression that the Bolshevik government monitored closely, even as it turned a blind eye to other artistic excesses.

"It is not the content but the performance of their music that counts," Malko wrote of the Americans. "Their execution truly stunned the listeners and not just with clever effects, which were few." Malko's analysis then turned slightly more specific. "A transition to new tempos and rhythms is not done according to any written music," he explained. "It is *played*, subordinated to the freely developing sense of the tunes."[10] But if the musicians showed any individuality — and surely at least one, Bechet, would have — Malko did not hear it, or could hear it only as part of the larger whole.

Bechet aside, of course, Withers and his musicians were now part of the "old guard" in jazz; they had started their careers in ragtime and adapted to newer developments — when and if they were exposed to them — as best they could. Again Bechet aside, they had also been abroad for six years at a time when jazz at home was undergoing dramatic change, as Moscow would learn on the arrival in mid-March 1926, three weeks after the Withers band, of *Chocolate Kiddies* with Sam Wooding's orchestra, by then just 10 months out of New York.

Since its departure from Germany in August 1925, *Chocolate Kiddies* had appeared in eight other European countries, from Sweden in the north to Spain in the south and west and Hungary in the east.[11] It was in Spain where the prospect of travelling to Russia, again at Rosfil's behest, was first raised.

Wooding recalled that his musicians initially baulked at the idea, having seen the Communist regime demonized by the Western press. "They were afraid that if they went into the land of the Bolsheviks they'd come back — if they came back at all — minus their ears. We were being very well paid, as it was, and we did not want to go to Russia. Consequently I kept on raising and raising the price, and [Rosfil] kept meeting our terms, until the United States Consul at Madrid, who was our adviser, thought that it would be ridiculous not to accept such enormous figures."[12]

In the end, all but one of Wooding's original musicians agreed to the trip; drummer George Howe stayed behind, at that for personal rather than political reasons. His replacement was Percy Johnson from Claude Hopkins' band in *La Revue Nègre*. "Much to our surprise," Wooding later wrote, "our Russian engagements were the best in all Europe."[13]

*Chocolate Kiddies*, billed as a "Negro Operetta,"[14] spent seven weeks at Moscow's Second State Circus and was reviewed in *Izvestiia* toward the end of the second week by Sergei Bugoslavsky, who found the Wooding band on its best behaviour — "by no means a noise orchestra," as he put it, summoning up and at once dismissing a comparison to the modernist Russian ensembles of the 1920s that used sirens, machines and other nonmusical items in concert.

Bugoslavsky found a different point of local reference more helpful. "Percussion and sound effects play in it almost the least role," he continued, "a role no more important than in our symphony orchestras. In sound, instrumentation and harmony, the negro jazz band most resembles our brass bands.

144

Even the repertoire does not stray too from the salon and 'garden' repertoire of our brass bands."

While acknowledging the music's syncopation, its incisive attack and its rich timbral colour, Bugoslavsky nevertheless suggested that its style was similar to that of — in his words — "light English or German cabaret music," a description consistent with Wooding's "symphonic" aspirations.[15]

Bugoslavsky's colleague at *Pravda*, E. Bravdo, also heard Wooding's orchestra as "an expanded brass band." It was interesting, Bravdo added, not so much for its musical content as for its sound, "at once soft and sharp," the latter quality requiring "a high level of playing, which these musicians commanded completely."[16]

In time, Wooding returned the compliments to his Russian counterparts. "On our rest days in Moscow," he wrote in 1939, "we attended the concerts of an orchestra of a hundred and ten pieces, which played without a conductor. We enjoyed Tchaikowsky, Rimsky-Korsakoff and Stravinsky immensely — particularly Stravinsky, because of the tricky rhythms."[17]

*Chocolate Kiddies* continued at the Second State Circus until early May 1926, following the Withers band out of Moscow by a week. As if to expose jazz as widely as possible in Russia, Withers' musicians and the *Kiddies* took different routes home, the former travelling south to Kharkov, Kiev and finally Odessa, and the latter — remembered Wooding, ruefully — heading slowly north to Leningrad on a train pulled by a wood-fired engine and followed by a pack of wolves.[18]

Withers' musicians were back in Paris by mid-June, when they opened — again under Crickett Smith's name — at a new club in Montmartre, the Imperial. *Chocolate Kiddies* reached Berlin at the same time after stops at the Baltic port cities of Riga, Königsberg [Kaliningrad] and Danzig [Gdansk], the last marking the end of the revue as a touring show; Wooding and his musicians, sometimes billed hereafter as the Chocolate Kiddies Orchestra, continued on their own to Hamburg, Birmingham, London, Paris, Zurich and, in the summer of 1927, Buenos Aires.

"We were sorry to leave Russia with its art loving public," Wooding later wrote. "Their politics was none of our business, but the people were."[19] Indeed, quite apart from the sympathetic hearing offered by Moscow's critics, Wooding and his musicians enjoyed a warm personal welcome from its citizens.

"They'd come to the theater after every performance and pick out different band members," saxophonist Garvin Bushell recalled. "We'd take a sleigh out to somebody's house and stay until four or five o'clock in the morning, singing songs, dancing, drinking and eating shish kebab. It was a great time."[20]

Wooding's musicians also renewed old acquaintances and made new ones with the members of the Withers band; Tommy Ladnier first met Sidney Bechet over the sale of a camera — a handy item for a visitor in Moscow to have — and struck up a friendship that flourished in New York during the 1930s when the two men formed the New Orleans Feetwarmers and ran a tailor shop together.

Vodka, of course, contributed to the general feeling of camaraderie both between the musicians themselves and between the musicians and their Russian hosts. Ladnier, who suffered from arthritis, found relief by wrapping his leg in a poultice soaked with the spirit. But vodka also took its toll, inducing Sidney Bechet, for one, to tackle a winter's night in Moscow without an overcoat, an act of bravado that led to a bout of bronchitis. Its effect was even more severe on Wooding's trombonist Herb Flemming, who — by his own account — required major stomach surgery and was hospitalized in Leningrad for three months.[21]

Nevertheless Russia made a profound impression on at least three of its African-American vistors in 1926. "Russia was the first country I'd ever been in," marvelled Bushell, "where I was accepted as a human being — a person like anybody else. In France, you were 'la Nègre.' In Germany, 'ein Schwarze.' But in Russia I was accepted as a *man*, and treated like an artist."[22]

Bechet later named Russia as the country where he'd most like to live permanently, though he would in fact settle in France.[23] Dan Parrish harboured similar aspirations. As late as 1934 — at which point the pianist had been a fixture at the Grand Écart on *rue* Fromentin in Montmartre for many years — he was quoted in the Chicago *Defender* as saying, "Russia is the greatest country in the world for the Negro and I am longing for the day to come when I will receive a good contract so as to return to my beloved Moscow."[24]

# "All the force of a revelation"

SHANGHAI, OCTOBER 1, 1926. From The Stroll to The Bund — drummer Jack Carter, 26,[1] was back at the Hotel Plaza with his new Serenaders. Clarinetist Albert Nicholas and saxophonist Billy Paige were playing with King Oliver's Dixie Syncopators at the Plantation Cafe on Chicago's South Side when Carter returned from Shanghai during the summer of 1926 to recruit musicians for the Plaza; pianist Teddy Weatherford and banjo player, guitarist and violinist Frank Etheridge had been members of Erskine Tate's orchestra at the Vendome Theatre; Valada[2] Snow was an attraction at the Sunset Cafe.

Nicholas, 26,[3] and Weatherford, a small giant of a man just days shy of 23,[4] had also appeared on record — the former as one of Richard M. Jones' Three Jazz Wizards in 1925, and the latter rather extravagantly behind Louis Armstrong with the Tate orchestra in May 1926. Weatherford's work on *Static Strut* and *Stomp off, Let's Go*, issued by Vocalion, was remarkably progressive in its departure from ragtime's formality in favour of a freer approach to improvisation that would be a particular influence on his contemporary among Chicago pianists, Earl Hines.

Indeed, Weatherford's star was rising locally during the mid-1920s. Perhaps for that reason alone he seemed to be of two minds about leaving the city, much less the country. According to Chicago orchestra leader and *Defender* columnist Dave Peyton, Weatherford said yes to Carter, then no, then yes again.[5] It was a fateful decision: the pianist would return home only once in the remaining 19 years of his life.

Frank Etheridge, on the other hand, hesitated not at all. As reported by Peyton in late August 1926, he "made his escape two weeks ago from the Windy City. Wifey was after him for several reasons."[6] Maeme Moon Etheridge, a singer, had in fact sought a court order earlier in the month to keep Etheridge in Chicago until her petition for divorce, alleging drunkenness and abusive behavior, was resolved.[7] The order was eventually served in Los Angeles, delaying Etheridge's departure for the Far East; in a countercharge, he claimed that his wife had thrown acid in his face.[8]

Peyton, meanwhile, could not hide his skepticism about the entire venture. "I wonder what Teddy Weatherford will think of China," he mused in late July. "He may like it, but they all come back."[9] Two weeks later, Peyton observed, "China may be all right, but give me the dear old U.S.A. How many Chinamen can understand American jazz?"[10] And when Billy Paige returned home early in 1927, citing his discomfort with Shanghai's weather,[11] Peyton noted with some satisfaction, "Billy says never again. The good old U.S.A. is good enough for him."[12]

On at least one count, of course, Peyton had missed the point. Whether or not jazz would find a receptive audience among the Chinese was moot; Carter's Serenaders, no less than the other American bands in Shanghai during the 1920s, were vying for the attention of the city's large foreign population.

Whitey Smith, a Danish-born American who led dance bands in Shanghai hotels and cabarets from 1922 to 1937, remembered an opening night at the Carlton ballroom: "There were beautiful women there, and important men; ambassadors, admirals, generals... Champagne corks popping all over the place. But there was this queer thing I noticed. There was someone of every nationality you could name, except the Chinese. There were Chinese waiters, but there were no Chinese customers in the whole place. I was surprised. Next day I asked [the club owner]. He said Chinese tradition kept them out. They didn't want to listen to western music or to dance."

Later, at the Astor House Hotel, Smith made a point of adapting Chinese folk songs "so that the melody was dominated a bit by the rhythm" in an effort — by his account, successful — to expand his audience. "At first [the Chinese] were stiff; they danced alone; they were dancing the jerk, way back in 1925. But now we were drawing crowds for the tea dances. I'd get the lights down and give them the 'St. Louis Blues.' They stopped jerking and started to sway. They turned out to be beautiful dancers."[13]

Carter's Serenaders, meanwhile, did well enough by the international crowd alone, with Valada Snow quickly emerging as their star attraction. At 22[14], she was probably the youngest member of the band. She was also already the most widely travelled, a veteran since childhood of vaudeville, where she sang, danced and played violin as Valada The Great with her father's Piccaninny Troubadours and as one of the Gold Dust Twins. Nor was the trip to China her first out of the country; she had ventured south with the Troubadours to Cuba some 14 years earlier[15] and north with Josephine Baker in *The Chocolate Dandies* to Canada in 1925.

Snow still sang in a sweet, girlish voice and danced with youthful abandon, but she had switched from violin in her mid-teens to trumpet, which she now played in emulation of Louis Armstrong. Such was the range of her contributions to the Serenaders that the Hotel Plaza could safely offer a $1,000 reward as a publicity stunt "to the individual who can produce any theatrical Performer now appearing in any Shanghai Cafe that can compare with the ability of Valada Snow"[16] without fear of having to pay up.

Snow's role with the Serenaders continued to expand in the course of their two years in Shanghai, particularly after the departure of Albert Nicholas and Frank Etheridge toward the end of 1927. "[Carter] wanted me for another year," Nicholas noted later, "but I had enough... one year in China was enough. I liked to travel... if I just wanted to play music I could stay in the States." The issue, notwithstanding Dave Peyton's forebodings in the Chicago *Defender*, was simply wanderlust. "We had a good job at the Plaza Hotel," Nicholas added, "good pay, no taxes... and at that time we didn't know what that was."[17]

As Nicholas and Etheridge began to work their way home together via Hong Kong, Manila, Singapore and other stops in Java, India and Egypt, Jack Carter sent Snow back to California for replacements. She returned in due course with saxophonist James Carson and two entertainers — her own, teenaged sister Lavada and the eccentric dancer Clarence (Bo Diddly) Williams.

Carson had played in Tijuana nightspots during the early 1920s and with the Los Angeles bands of Reb Spikes and Buster Wilson more recently; once in China, he — like William Hegamin before him — married locally and started a family, eventually emerging in Shanghai as a bandleader in his own right during the mid-1930s at Lafayette Gardens and the Paradise Ballroom.[18] For the moment, though, he was just one of three new saxophonists in the Serenaders, playing alongside Teddy Tapia and Philip (Shorty) Cubinar, likely members of Shanghai's growing community of Filipino musicians.

With Snow in the dual role of star and producer, the Serenaders — now eight, including Jack Carter and Teddy Weatherford — opened in December 1927 for four months with the revue *Plantation Varieties* at the Plantation, a new cabaret on Bubbling Well Road. Snow was no less prominently billed — "Jack Carter presents Valada Snow And Her Company of 5 Red Hot Masters of Syncopation" — in a second revue, *Jazz Madness*, which ran briefly at Shanghai's Carlton and Isis theatres in the fall of 1928. The show, according to a Carlton ad in the *North-China Daily News*, promised "negro spirituals, plantation melodies, the latest songs and dances, including the famous Charleston and Black Bottom, funny comedians, Hawaiian steel guitar solos, piano solos, trumpet solos, and first class jazz bandnumbers [sic] in conjunction with single, double and trio specialties and a first class Harmony Quartette."[19]

By then, however, the Serenaders' sojourn in Shanghai was almost over. After a farewell appearance on November 2, 1928 opposite Whitey Smith at the Majestic Hotel,[20] Carter, Snow, Weatherford and Bo Diddly Williams sailed for Hong Kong — the first port of call on the same, roundabout route that Albert Nicholas and Frank Etheridge had taken on their way home a year earlier.

The four Americans set out with a Filipino trombonist, Angel Jimenez, and three Hawaiian musicians identified — albeit incompletely — by the *South China Morning Post* during the Serenaders' engagement at the Star Theatre in Hong Kong as Joe Kanepuu, Pokiala (or Pokilapa) and Louis.[21] The Serenaders' stops included the Adelphi Hotel in Singapore and the Oost Java Restaurant in Batavia [Jakarta], as well as Firpo's Restaurant and the Empire Theatre in Calcutta. Snow was later reported to have also performed during this period in Bangkok, Rangoon and Colombo.[22]

At the Adelphi Hotel in late November 1928, according to the Singapore *Straits Times,* "Valada Snow was positively a riot; the audience were loath to let her leave the floor. Her songs were given with a lilt which is intriguing and her dancing brought the house down. Her 'Old Man River' number was particularly good." Bo Diddly, "that drollest of coloured comedians," was also a hit, as was the demonstration that he and Snow offered together of the Black Bottom.

"What," asked the *Straits Times* reporter rhetorically, "is the secret of these coloured artists' success? Surely it is that they are entirely un-selfconscious. While white performers may be worrying as to whether they are 'getting over,' [ie, winning favour] the originators of jazz just let themselves go."

Ironically, no sooner had "real 'coloured cabaret' reached Singapore at last," in the words of the *Straits Times'* reviewer,[23] than a second African-American troupe opened at the Victoria Theatre — even as the Serenaders were still at the Adelphi. Wilbur's Black Birds, a Los Angeles company, had left home with 18 members on a tour that took in Honolulu, Yokohama, Tokyo, Kobe, Shanghai, Hong Kong and Manila before it stopped in Singapore. By then, however, they were down to about a dozen and, as *The Straits Times* noted, "the jazz band has dwindled to one cornet."[24]

The Black Birds had four shows in their repertoire — *Plantation Days, A Minstrel Review, Variety* and *Election Time in Dixie* — and counted Buddy Brown, Lottie Brown, Buddy DeLoach and former Creole Band front man H. Morgan Prince among their performers. That lone cornet aside, musical accompaniment was provided by Frank (Dr. Jazz) Shiver, remembered in his Los Angeles days by Reb Spikes as "more of a comedy piano player than any-thing"[25] and by Alfred Levy as "a hellava good piano player... good enough to be a stage act by himself."[26]

Shiver was indeed featured on his own in the Black Birds' programs, "[making] the piano say things that never were in any text book,"[27] according to the *South China Morning Post.* The Black Birds themselves were nevertheless found to be somewhat wanting in Singapore; although no direct comparisons were made to the Serenaders, *The Straits Times* suggested "perhaps the minstrel show of former days has lost something of its appeal in this sophisticated age of jazz."

Certainly it was the relative sophistication of the Carter show, by the standards of the acts previously heard further still south in Java, including the Black Birds, that appealed to a young guitarist in Batavia, Otto Mackenzie. "At last I heard a real band, just like on the records, with all the new numbers and tricks," he remembered of the Serenaders' engagement at the Oost Java Restaurant on Koningsplein Square in what was then the city's European quarter. "But the older numbers also got played. I remember, for instance, *I Scream, You Scream,* actually a trashy number, but in their hands it just became a piece of fireworks. For that matter, almost all of their numbers were played like fireworks. [To] me their music came over as 'terrific' and especially the performances of Jimenez and Weatherford, and Carter himself... all were very dynamic and inspired... Valaida [sic] Snow was a true bred artist as well. She sang excellently, then played a solo on trumpet, on which instrument she could do all kinds of tricks and improvise tremendous breaks. After this she would give out with some more choruses of dancing..."[28]

Snow's trumpet playing also caught the ear of an Englishman, Iain Lang, during the Serenaders' month-long engagement at the turn of 1929 at Calcutta's leading restaurant, Firpo's, on Chowringhee Road. Lang had heard the Original Dixieland Jazz Band in London nine years earlier but was now as much in the dark about later developments in jazz as the vast majority of Snow's other new fans in the Far East, and thus just as impressionable.

"I spent every night at Firpo's," Lang later wrote, "and every early morning with the members of the band at the Maharani of Cooch Behar's house, in my flat or in their hotel rooms. It was the pianist, a thickset fellow named Teddy Weatherford, who ungallantly let me into Valaida's secret; her solos, which had burst upon my ears with all the force of a revelation, were in fact copied note for note from the records of Louis Armstrong."[29]

Of course Snow and Weatherford, now two-and-a-half years abroad, were also falling behind the latest developments, even if — as Lang recalled — the pianist travelled with some of Armstrong's recent recordings in his possession. In any event, Snow, at least, was not much longer for the Orient; her appearance with the Serenaders at the Empire Theatre in Calcutta in early March

1929 would have been one of her last before she made her way via Egypt to Paris, where she was first sighted in August[30] and was performing with Sam Wooding's Chocolate Kiddies Orchestra at the Embassy in October.[31]

Jack Carter either accompanied or followed Snow to Paris in 1929, making headlines there in December when he lost 200,000 francs worth of rings to hustlers;[32] the value of the jewellery would suggest that he had done very well indeed for himself in the Far East. He sailed for home in 1931 as a member of Noble Sissle's orchestra and later ran a "rib joint" in New York for many years.[33]

Weatherford, meanwhile, turned back in 1929 for Shanghai, which had continued in his absence to attract American musicians. Drummer Smilin' Ted Lewis was new at the Palais Cafe by the end of that year and erstwhile Black Bird Frank Shiver took William Hegamin's place at The Little Club early in 1930. "Shanghai's just as cosmo as 'Frisco," Shiver marvelled, writing to the Chicago *Defender* later that summer from Java, where he had gone to perform at the Cercle Artistique in Surabaya. "You can also get anything from a toothpick to a murder."[34]

Weatherford was reunited in September 1929 with James Carson at the Canidrome under the leadership of yet another American musician new to the city, trumpeter Bob Hill.[35] Taking over both the band and the engagement for himself at the turn of 1930,[36] Weatherford remained in Shanghai until 1934, then spent the rest of his life working in several of the other cities throughout the Far East that he had first visited with the Serenaders.[37]

# "A delicate and fresh thrill"

ROME, DECEMBER 11, 1926. The fire that swept through the Apollo at 12:30 a.m. left four of the cabaret's female entertainers dead — three Italians and one German, all trapped in their dressing rooms. Drummer Benny Peyton's Jazz Kings, who had just finished onstage, barely escaped, but not before one of their number, saxophonist Rudolph Dunbar, guided four other patrons to safety, then clambered out a window himself.[1]

A second Jazz King, saxophone and banjo player Greeley Franklin, later told an unlikely tale of survival graced by the supernatural. He had returned to the stage to retrieve his saxophone, reported the New York *Herald*, only to be stopped by the sound of his banjo, in unseen hands, playing *Show Me the Way to Go Home* from the wings. As he turned back abruptly, a curtain engulfed in flames crashed behind him.[2] A third member of the band, pianist George Clapham, was not so lucky; according to the *Herald*, he was "badly burned" in the blaze.[3]

The Kings Jazz, as they were billed, had been in Rome for just two weeks, playing for *thés danzantis* at the Plaza Hotel and appearing among the variety acts at the Apollo. The band included at least one musician, and likely two, who had travelled with Peyton to Moscow under Frank Withers' leadership, saxophonist Fred Coxito and possibly cornetist Crickett Smith, the latter identified improbably as "Joseph" Smith in reports published in the United States about Franklin's heroism at the Apollo.[4]

Though no doubt shaken by their ordeal, the Jazz Kings carried on at least into early January 1927 at the Plaza. There, just days after the Apollo fire, they were reunited briefly with yet another member of the Withers band from Moscow, Sidney Bechet, who was passing through the city with Louis Douglas's *Black People*, a show that took up where *La Revue Nègre* and *Chocolate Kiddies* had left off and with several of the same performers, including two of Sam Wooding's musicians, Tommy Ladnier and John Warren. Its three-night run at the Qurino in Rome followed stops in Berlin, Stockholm, Oslo, The Hague, Amsterdam, Munich, Zurich, Milan and several smaller cities.[5]

*Black People* continued on over the next few months to Prague, Vienna, Belgrade, Constantinople, Athens, Alexandria and Cairo, while Peyton's Jazz Kings entered their eighth and final year on an uncertain note. They were rumoured to appear in Vienna after Rome, but the report of their pending arrival came with the qualification to the effect that, "So far the contract has not been signed for the sole reason that the troupe asked for too much money."[6]

Indeed the Kings had started to fall from fashion. Jazz bands in Europe were growing larger, and their style smoother, as exemplified by the Wooding and Billy Arnold orchestras. Peyton, who turned 39 in 1927, made the necessary accommodations and emerged by year's end at the Embassy in Paris with a new band, the New Yorkers, and a more sophisticated sound that would bring him work in the elite social circles represented by engagements in Le Touquet during the summer of 1928 and at the Palais de Méditerranée in Nice over the following winter.

"Benny" Peyton became "Benton E." Peyton in accordance with this new sense of decorum; his business letterhead read "Blue Ribbon Orchestra — colored American musicians and entertainers playing refined syncopation."[7] Only Fred Coxito remained from the Jazz Kings when the New Yorkers, now 10 strong, moved in August 1929 from the elegant Hotel Atlanta in Brussels to the tony New York Restaurant on St. Margaret's Island in Budapest; the band, directed by violinist James Boucher, also included Jelly Roll Morton's old clarinetist from the Regent Hotel in Vancouver, Horace Eubanks, as well as saxophonist Fletcher Allen, trumpeter James Bell, trombonist Hubert Parker and sousaphonist June Cole.[8]

Peyton, loath to be forgotten at home even after a 10-year absence, forwarded to the Chicago *Defender* and the New York *Amsterdam News* awkward translations of the reviews in Hungarian that his orchestra had received in Budapest newspapers. As published in both the *Defender* and the *Amsterdam News*, they made clear the extent to which Peyton's had tempered his approach to jazz.

The *8-Araiujsag* of August 3, 1929 noted that "It was a decidedly agreeable surprise that Peyton's orchestra, differeing [sic] from other similar bands, never tried the brutal dynamic effects and [instead] offered some high-class, civilized variety of the jazz music."[9] The *Estikurir* of the same day echoed its competition, suggesting that Peyton and his musicians gave the audience at the New York Restaurant "a fresh and delicate thrill" with their "American dance hits" and "Hungarian numbers." The orchestra, it added definitively, "has nothing to do with loud, shrill jazz bands; it is rather discreet and fragile but, at the same time, can bring out [...] effects which surprises [sic] anybody who hears them."[10]

# "All the stuff from the Savoy"

BUENOS AIRES, JUNE 3, 1927. Berlin had *Chocolate Kiddies* and Paris *La Revue Nègre*, each with a jazz band among its attractions. Today, and for the next seven weeks at the Teatro Maipo, Buenos Aires was enjoying a similar, if more modest production, *La Revista Negra,* with violinist Leon Abbey and a band that had lately been a fixture at the Savoy Ballroom in Harlem.

Not all of the Savoy Bearcats, as they were known to New York dancers, chose to make the trip south; Abbey had to rehearse his new recruits on board the *S.S. Southern Cross* during its 18-day voyage from New York down the Atlantic Coast to Rio de Janeiro, Montevideo and, finally, the Argentine capital.

"When we got there," remembered one of Abbey's two trumpeters, Demas Dean, "who was setting up waiting for us but Sam Wooding! But they'd been away from the States for some time and [the] arrangements we had were from Fletcher [Henderson] and Don Redman and we'd got together on [ie, mastered] most of them."[1]

Just as Wooding musicians had arrived in Berlin in 1925 with the newest ideas in jazz from New York, eclipsing the other American bands in the German city at the time, Abbey's presence in Buenos Aires — as Dean would appear to imply — revealed Wooding's music to be two years out of date. In fact Don Redman's arrangements for Fletcher Henderson and, soon enough, McKinney's Cotton Pickers, were defining the esthetic for black American jazz orchestras in the mid-1920s; the Savoy Bearcats had themselves recorded at least two Redman charts for the Victor company in 1926, *Bearcat Stomp* and *Stampede.*

The Wooding and Abbey bands overlapped in Buenos Aires for several weeks during the summer of 1927;[2] Wooding had sailed from Marseilles in March for a month of his own at the Teatro Maipo as well as a nine-week engagement at the Ta-Ba-Ris, "The Ultra Modern Restaurant" on *avenida* Corrientes beside — or possibly even at — the address of the former Royal Pigall Dancing that had employed Gordon Stretton's Syncopated Six four years earlier.[3] Wooding also appeared for shorter periods at the Empire Theatre, the Casino and the Gran Cine Florida before leaving for Rosario, inland and northwest from Buenos Aires on the Parana River, en route circuitously back to New York. Gordon Stretton, meanwhile, was drumming and singing with his jazz band that summer at another Buenos Aires theatre, the Select Lavalle, and could also be heard regularly on radio station LOX.

Garvin Bushell, still travelling with Wooding, later described Buenos Aires in 1927 as "a fast town with a lot of activity. The guys would come in from the pampas with a lot of money and spend it all in the cabarets. They lived and drank hard."[4] While the Wooding orchestra would have been at the centre of the action at the Ta-Ba-Ris, Abbey and his musicians appeared under more orderly circumstances at the Teatro Maipo and, briefly, the Empire and the Gran Cine Florida.

The violinist, then 27,[5] was quite familiar with theatrical work; prior to his time at the Savoy Ballroom, he had spent five years travelling in vaudeville with the singer and songwriter J. Rosamond Johnson. Now, in *La Revista Negra,* he led his 10 musicians[6] through several selections of their own and accompanied the dance team of Rufus Greenlee and Teddy Drayton — who coincidentally had toured Europe with Wooding in *Chocolate Kiddies* — in the show's finale. Notable among Abbey's soloists were a clarinetist known at the time for his technical facility, Carmelito Jejo, and a saxophonist formerly in the employ of the young Duke Ellington and, like Ellington a member of early jazz "royalty," Prince Robinson. The band also included Henry (Bass) Edwards, who could play tuba and smoke a cigar at the same time — much to an audience's delight.

In an incident that echoed James Reese Europe's experience in Paris with the musicians of the French Republican Guard nearly nine years earlier, Abbey's men met with a degree of disbelief, if not disdain, from the leader of the Maipo's resident orchestra, who thought — absent any written music in their act — that they played only by ear.

"He told everyone we were coal workers and couldn't read," remembered Joe Garland, who sat with Jejo and Robinson in Abbey's reed section. "To prove his point [he] wrote some music for the new show [that] we were opening and passed the word around that he was going to embarrass the whole band." As it happened, Abbey's musicians — like Europe's — had the last laugh. "The guys went through it like it was a dose of castor oil," Garland explained, "and the whole theatre roared!"[7]

Abbey's musicians had committed more than 30 of their own charts to memory, most — though not all — of them current jazz numbers. "We had an arrangement of *Rio Rita* that was a big hit down there, naturally," noted Dean, of one exception. "[Trumpeter] John Brown had a nice voice and sang it, and we made a stage number out of it." Dean also mentioned the success of *Baby Face* and *Charleston,* as well as Redman's arrangement of *I Found a*

*New Baby* and "all the stuff from the Savoy." The Argentines, he added, "really took to it."[8]

Abbey and at least a few of his musicians, including Dean, were equally taken by the experience of playing for foreign audiences. "I didn't want to come back," the trumpeter later claimed, "and if I had been able to speak the language, I would have stayed."[9] After further appearances in Montevideo, Sao Paulo and Rio de Janeiro, however, the band followed Sam Wooding home to New York and promptly broke up.

Abbey wasted little time in lining up new musicians for another trip out of the country in December,[10] this time less exotically to the Olympia Dance Hall in London. Once again, Abbey took with him the latest sounds from New York, only to have the ballroom's manager complain that the "screaming of the horns" just wouldn't do.

Just as Benny Peyton's New Yorkers had moved toward a "rather discreet and fragile" style of jazz on the Continent, Abbey was forced to temper his music in London. "Now I had spent a lot of money on special arrangements," he explained, "but I went on the stand [at the Olympia] the following evening and I didn't pass any of them out... just concentrated on melodies and popular tunes, and after that[,] everyone was tickled to death... I never did play those arrangements again."

It was, Abbey noted later, "one of my greatest disappointments," but proved to be "the foundation of my success." Thus settled, musically, he and his musicians proceeded early in 1928 to Berlin, and from Berlin on to Paris. "We had nothing planned," Abbey remembered of their itinerary, "but one thing led to another. The boys were getting letters saying how bad things were at home, so we just carried on... and the audiences were so appreciative, not like American audiences. As things seemed to be clicking, we began to look a few months ahead... and then as if we'd be there indefinitely."[11] By the time Abbey returned to New York in 1939, his travels had encompassed much of Europe, including all of Scandinavia, and twice took him as far east as Bombay.

The Abbey orchestra had long since left for France by the time Sam Wooding began his second European sojourn in Berlin at the Palast am Zoo in June 1928. Greenlee and Drayton were again on hand, as well as blues singer Edith Wilson and eccentric dancer and erstwhile Tennessee Ten frontman U.S. (Slow Kid) Thompson.

Wooding's band, like Abbey's, had undergone changes in personnel during its nine months in New York, albeit not to the same wholesale extent; trumpeters Tommy Ladnier and Bobby Martin remained from the *Chocolate*

*Kiddies* lineup, as did banjo player John Mitchell, alto saxophonist Willie Lewis and tenor saxophonist Gene Sedric. Trumpeter Adolphus (Doc) Cheatham, trombonist Albert Wynn and pianist Freddy Johnson were among those new to the band when it resumed its travels in Europe and, came 1929, undertook another series of recordings — 31 sides altogether, 10 in Barcelona for Parlophone and the rest in Paris for Pathé, Deutsche Grammophon and Brunswick. While the band's efforts in Barcelona included *Bull Foot Stomp* and *Tiger Rag*, its repertoire for the Paris sessions was on balance American pop hits of the day, *Singin' in the Rain* and *Love for Sale* — each scarcely a year in circulation — not least among them.

By the time Wooding began his Paris sessions in October of 1929, Tommy Ladnier — one of his star soloists — had moved on to Benny Peyton's New Yorkers in Paris and was also taking engagements occasionally with Leon Abbey, a reflection of the ease with which African-American jazz musicians could now find work in Europe almost at will. Opportunities were plentiful, both in Paris and Riviera clubs and on the road with Cofie's Colored Cracks, Louis Douglas's latest show, *Louisiana*, dancer Harry Flemming's *Blue Birds* and a revue led by the mysterious singer, drummer and eccentric dancer Levy Wine.[12] Indeed, by the summer of 1930, Ladnier had also worked briefly with Douglas and Flemming before joining singer Noble Sissle's Sizzling (or, more appropriately, Sissling) Syncopators.

Sissle had twice crossed the Atlantic since his tour of duty in France with James Reese Europe and the 15th New York Infantry in 1918 — the first time in 1925 with pianist Eubie Blake and the second time in 1927 on his own, in each case working in England as a variety artist.[13] During his second visit, however, he also formed a jazz orchestra for engagements on the Continent, including several appearances at les Ambassadeurs in Paris.

Sissle looked for his Syncopators to musicians already in Paris — Sidney Bechet was a member in 1928 — and recruited others during return trips to New York. In addition to Bechet and Ladnier, the band's collective personnel between 1928 and 1931 included trumpeters Arthur Briggs, Clifton (Pike) Davis, Demas Dean and Johnny Dunn, saxophone and clarinet players Buster Bailey, Horace Eubanks, Frank (Big Boy) Goudie and Rudy Jackson, violinists Andrew Rosemond and Robert (Juice) Wilson and drummers Jesse Baltimore and Jack Carter. Davis, Dean, Bailey, Jackson, Wilson and Baltimore all arrived from New York with Sissle in May 1929, along with trumpeter James (Bubber) Miley, who immediately returned home.[14] Jackson (and Miley) had previously played with Duke Ellington, while Bailey had worked with Fletcher Henderson, and Wilson with Lloyd Scott and James P. Johnson.

The Syncopators were nevertheless not the jazz band that either their name or the background of their members might have promised, at least not as documented by the dozen recordings they made in England — eight for HMV in 1929 and four for Columbia in 1930. The tunes for the most part are pop songs, even novelties, although the finest of the Syncopators' performances, *Kansas City Kitty* for HMV, does demonstrate the band's potential: the tempo is brisk, the rhythm cleanly delineated, the arrangement challenging and the allowance for improvisation generous. Happily, Sissle assigned Wilson, at 25[15] a tart, driving soloist, to a full 32-bar solo; he also asked the violinist for a 16-bar contribution to *Miranda* on the same session. Happily, inasmuch as Wilson — who would work in obscurity from 1939 to 1954 on the Mediterranean island of Malta — never recorded commercially again.

While Wilson, like Leon Abbey, stayed on in Europe, Sissle was back in New York by the end of 1931. So, too, was Sam Wooding, along with several of his musicians. Willie Lewis, Bobby Martin and Freddy Johnson stayed behind, however, and played important roles on the European scene through the 1930s, Lewis in particular sustaining the big band tradition that Wooding, Abbey and Sissle had so firmly established.

# "The guts of it all"

BERLIN, FEBRUARY 2, 1928. Dave Tough was, as usual, hungover. So too were the other members of the New Yorkers, who arrived with their young drummer at the Tri-Ergon recording studio in suburban Mariendorf toward noon after working at the Valencia on downtown Kantstrasse until 3 a.m. and drinking away the rest of the morning en route. Tri-Ergon officials were so dismayed by the sound of the band as it began to warm up that they threatened to call the session off; only when a bottle of cognac was produced did the seven musicians return to some semblance of the form that had brought them the invitation to record in the first place.[1]

The New Yorkers were a white group, not to be confused with the Benny Peyton band that was playing during this same period at the Embassy in Paris. Ironically, their two principal figures hailed from the burgeoning *Chicago* scene — Tough, just 20, and clarinet and alto saxophone player Danny Polo, 27.[2] As such they were introducing to Europe the formative sound of the "Chicago jazz" style developed during the mid-1920s by that city's white musicians — Tough himself, cornetist Jimmy McPartland, clarinetist Frank Teschemacher and tenor saxophonist Lawrence (Bud) Freeman among them — in emulation of the New Orleans players, black and white, who had migrated north in the years around 1920.

Tough and Polo were in their seventh month abroad, first in Paris, then Ostend in Belgium and now Berlin. They had left home in the employ of a New York banjo player, George Carhart, who would take three bands to Europe between 1926 and 1928, each on what proved to be a false promise of work in Paris; when Carhart went home in December 1927 after the second of these ill-fated ventures, Polo assumed responsibility for the musicians who remained behind — Tough, trumpeter Evelyn Bazell, trombonist Herb German, saxophonists Andy Foster and Milt Allen and pianist Jack O'Brien.

"I was the leader," Polo remembered 10 years later, "but Dave was the guts of it all. He played so magnificently that the rest of us just honked along... he was the man who sent the band and everyone around."[3]

They were an unlikely pair, Tough and Polo. The drummer, travelling in the company of his wife Dorothy, was already a heavy drinker, unreliable and abusive under the influence and yet surprisingly erudite when sober. Polo, who married a German woman while in Berlin, was affable and conscientious, though not without his own indulgences; he had arrived at Le Havre with five pounds of marijuana in his possession — according to Jack O'Brien[4] — and somehow managed to smuggle it ashore.

Tough and Polo were among the finest of the many white American musicians in Europe during the late 1920s. And unlike so many of their fellow expatriates, who would fall out of step with the latest developments in jazz during travels abroad, they adapted successfully to Swing on their return to the United States, Tough in 1929 and Polo 10 years later. The drummer's influential work with the Tommy Dorsey, Benny Goodman and Woody Herman orchestras in the 1930s and 1940s even moved beyond Swing to anticipate the rhythmic advances of bebop. Indeed, Tough was the fourth significant figure in the evolution of jazz — after Willie The Lion Smith, Sidney Bechet and Eddie Lang — to spend some part of his early career in Europe.

Arriving at the Barbarina in Berlin with Carhart's New Yorkers in September 1927, Tough and Polo found several other musicians from across the Atlantic already established in local clubs and studios, most notably the Grenadian trumpeter Arthur Briggs and two members of the Alex Hyde Orchestra that had toured Germany in 1924 and 1925, trumpeter Wib Kurz and banjo player Mike Danzi.

Briggs, whose Savoy Syncops preceded the New Yorkers at the Barbarina, was in the midst of a series of recording sessions for Deutsche Grammophon, the 38 sides that resulted revealing his growing familiarity in the span of just a few short months with the style of Louis Armstrong. Danzi, meanwhile, was in residence with the British saxophonist Billy Bartholomew at the Eden Hotel in the fall of 1927,[5] and Kurz was working with a German violinist, Norbert Faconi, at the Cafe am Zoo.[6]

Bands in Berlin typically mixed musicians of various nationalities freely. African-Americans, however, remained rare. Briggs' Savoy Syncops were now all white save for the leader himself — three Frenchmen, two Germans, a Belgian, a Hungarian and, at least on their recordings, singer and guitarist Al Bowlly, who was born to Greek and Lebanese parents in Mozambique and raised in Johannesburg. Bowlly also worked in Frankfurt during this period with the German pianist Julian Fuhs in the company of two Americans, two Russians, a Czech, a Frenchman and an Italian.[7] He was on hand as well to sing on the second of the two tunes, *Hoosier Sweetheart* and *Sunny Disposish*, that the "Jazz Orchestra George Carhart's, New Yorker's" recorded in late September 1927 for the German Homocord company.

Notwithstanding Carhart's billing as leader, Danny Polo's guiding hand is evident on the session, particularly in the choice of tunes, each of which he had recorded earlier in 1927 as a member of the Jean Goldkette Orchestra in

New York; Polo adapted his arrangements for Homocord from Goldkette's recordings for Victor and added an alto saxophone solo to *Hoosier Sweetheart* (a play of words on "Who's Your Sweetheart?") that shows the clear influence, in its rakish melodic lilt and easy rhythmic bounce, of his bandmate in the Goldkette orchestra, Bix Beiderbecke.

Polo was fully in charge of the New Yorkers by the time they arrived at the Tri-Ergon recording studio — the worse for their night of heavy drinking — four months later.[8] They had moved from the Barbarina to the Valencia just days after the Homocord session and looked to their nightly repertoire there for the six tunes that they recorded at Tri-Ergon's behest, all of them obscure pop songs of the day, and just two, *My Sunday Girl* and *I'm Living in Love*, arranged to offer any evidence that the New Yorkers were at heart jazz musicians.

They returned three weeks later to the same studio, this time to find *two* bottles of cognac provided for inspiration. Accordingly, they mustered up lively versions of the Original Dixieland Jazz Band's *Ostrich Walk* and *Clarinet Marmalade*, each faithful to the spirit of Nick LaRocca and company; they also recorded two waltzes and two more pop songs in arrangements that made little if any reference to jazz at all.

By the time Tri-Ergon released its 14 "Tanz-Orchester New Yorkers" sides — the first six in March, the second eight in April[9] — the band itself had returned to Paris. It was in the middle of a six-month engagement there at the Abbaye de Thélème when George Carhart arrived in July 1928 with fresh recruits, among them Tough's old friend from Chicago, Bud Freeman, Freeman's fellow tenor saxophonist Irving (Babe) Russin, and Russin's older brother Jack, who played piano. The band was completed by trombone and trumpet player Jack Purvis, bass saxophonist Spencer Clark and drummer Vic Moore, the last a member of the Wolverines alongside Bix Beiderbecke for that band's classic Gennett recordings in 1924.

Once again, Carhart's promise of work in Paris proved worthless. Freeman left for home after only 11 days in the city, dismayed by the "terrible music" that he had heard at the Abbaye and elsewhere — "not because the musicians played it badly," he explained later, "but because it was just for acts and cabaret."[10] In other words, it wasn't jazz. In fact, the New Yorkers played less jazz in Paris, according to Jack O'Brien, than they had in Berlin.[11] At that — if their Tri-Ergon repertoire was any indication — they hadn't played all that much jazz in the German city either.

Carhart and his other young men — Babe Russin was all of 17 — stayed on undeterred, their lack of prospects offset by the lure of Paris, even as

Moore was sidelined almost immediately with a broken shoulder suffered in a *contretemps* with a taxi driver over the size of a tip. Here, as in Berlin, white American musicians could move with relative ease into local orchestras alongside their European counterparts, language differences notwithstanding. Three members of the original New Yorkers, Milt Allen, Evelyn Bazell and Herb German, had done exactly that, Bazell most notably leaving Danny Polo for Billy Arnold in the summer of 1928. A fourth, Andy Foster, had followed Bazell into the Arnold orchestra by the end of the year.

Several other Americans were working in this period at Le Perroquet with one of their own, Ludwig (Lud) Gluskin, who had stayed on in Paris after touring Europe as a percussionist with the Paul Whiteman Orchestra in 1924. Gluskin's orchestra, which recorded extensively in Paris and Berlin between 1927 and 1933, variously numbered Spencer Clark, alto saxophonist Gene Prendergast, trumpeters Johnny Dixon and Eddie Ritten and, from the Original Dixieland Jazz Band, trombonist Emile Christian, among its American members during that time.

Moreover, George Carhart's promises of work may have been unfounded, but they were certainly not unprecedented. American dance bands had for several years crossed the Atlantic to take residencies in Paris, particularly at Les Ambassadeurs, which presented Paul Whiteman in 1926, Irving Aaronson and his Commanders in 1927, and Fred Waring's Pennsylvanians and the Ted Lewis Orchestra in 1928.

Carhart — clearly a man skilled in the art of persuasion — eventually found employment in the fall of 1928 at the Casino in Aix-les-Bains and, briefly, at the Hotel Negresco in Nice. He also convinced Tough, Foster and Jack O'Brien to abandon Danny Polo for the latter engagement, thus bringing the original New Yorkers to an end. Polo responded by forming a new band that included some of the young French musicians who had been listening closely to the New Yorkers at the Abbaye de Thélème, including trumpeter Philippe Brun, pianist Stéphane Mougin and drummer Maurice Chaillou — the last something of a Tough protégé, at least to the extent that Tough was capable of serving anyone as a mentor.

By then, perhaps feeling nostalgic after Bud Freeman's brief visit to Paris, Tough had made a quick trip to New York with the ship's orchestra of the *Île de France*, spending the brief layover visiting several old friends who had moved east from Chicago in his absence. Back in France by October 1928, and in Paris by November, he spent the next four months at l'Hermitage Muscovite on *rue* Caumartin with a small band led by a Russian banjo player,

Misha Levandowski, before returning permanently to New York in late February 1929.

His decision to put Europe behind him was no doubt influenced by the professional and personal rejections that he experienced in fairly quick succession during this period, each due at least in part to his drinking. In the first instance, he failed an audition to join Lud Gluskin's band for an engagement back at the Barbarina in Berlin. In the second — just days before his departure — his wife left him for Jack O'Brien.

# "A 'very raw deal'"

It was with some combination of anger, regret and embarrassment that Sonny Clay watched from the *S.S. Sierra* as the ship moved out to sea on the 19-day voyage that would take his Plantation Band home to Los Angeles. In a very sudden and sensational turn of events, he and his nine musicians had effectively been deported after some of their number were found in a compromising situation with five young Australian women during a police raid just a few nights earlier on the band's two rent-ed flats in East Melbourne. Clay and his musicians were appearing in a revue, *Colored Idea*, at the Tivoli Theatre at the time. The women, needless to say, were white.[1]

It was an unfortunate end to what must have originally seemed to Clay like a promising venture and, whatever its risks, yet another achievement in a career that had already found the pianist at 28[2] among California's leading jazz musicians. His band, with clarinetist Leonard (Big Boy) Davidson, the New Orleans trumpeter Ernest (Nenny) Coycault and others,[3] had been a fixture at the Plantation Cafe in Los Angeles since at least 1925 and was one of the few groups on the West Coast to have recorded; its various titles for the Vocalion company trace the development of a small, loosely polyphonic sex-tet in the New Orleans style to a smoother 10-piece orchestra whose full ensembles and rhythmic lean looked forward to the coming of Swing.

Several white Californians, some with more limited inclinations toward jazz of their own, had previously taken bands to Australia for dance or theatre engagements, including pianist Frank Ellis in 1923, pianist Tom Swift in 1924 and drummer Ray Tellier in 1925; Tellier's San Francisco Orchestra was a par-ticular hit during its 18 months at the Palais de danse in Melbourne and recorded 19 titles, mostly pop songs, for the Austral and Condor labels.[4] Another white American bandleader, saxophonist Bert Ralton, arrived in 1923 via London, and stayed for more than two years, working in Sydney and Melbourne, touring in New Zealand and also recording for Austral.[5]

African-American entertainers, on the other hand, were far more rarely seen in Australia, as indeed were other "non-Europeans" in any line of endeavour. This, in accordance with the Immigration Restriction Act of 1901, which had formalized the country's exclusionary "White Australia Policy." Though initially motivated by concerns for the economic and social security of Australians in the face of successive influxes of labourers from

China and, closer to home, New Caledonia, Fiji and other Melanesian islands, the policy came to be applied more generally to all non-whites and took on deeper, more explicitly racist overtones when directed toward blacks.

One recent African-American visitor, however, sent back a glowing report of his experiences in Australia. Joe Sheftell spent the second half of 1926 with his *Southern Plantation Revue* in Sydney, Melbourne, Adelaide, Brisbane and elsewhere in the country. "We are an absolute sensation over here and the people treat us wonderfully," he wrote, in a letter published by the Chicago *Defender*. "They simply idolize us. I am more than proud; they are amazed at our intelligence."[6]

Coincidentally, Sheftell and his company subsequently took an engagement opposite Sonny Clay's band at the Plantation in Los Angeles during the summer of 1927;[7] even if Clay did not see Sheftell's letter to the *Defender* — the Chicago weekly had a national circulation — the subject of Australia may well have come up between the two men in person.

As the Clay band drew near its departure, it cut six new tunes for Vocalion, including Clay's own *Australian Stomp*.[8] The recording, however, like the trip that it anticipated, proved to be ill-fated; it was never released commercially, although legend has it that the band was playing the tune itself on the *S.S. Sierra* — the same ship that would carry them home — as it entered Sydney Harbour on January 20, 1928.[9]

The Clay band and its fellow Los Angeles acts in *Colored Idea* — singer and dancer Ivie Anderson (just three years away from joining the Duke Ellington Orchestra), master of ceremonies and dancer Dick Saunders and a "whirlwind" dance act, the Four Covans — were augmented in Sydney by the Four Harmony Emperors, who had been touring in Australia for the previous six months. The Emperors' second tenor, Eddie Caldwell, echoed Joe Sheftell's sentiments about the country in a letter that he sent to the Chicago *Defender* from Perth.

"We are proud of the esteem in which the Race artists are held in Australia and all who have been here to date have evidently striven to maintain that high standard," he boasted, before adding a prophetic qualification. "Of course there are some bad ones, but they are few and far between. Those bad ones are those who remind you of the lily white policy in Australia."[10] Ironically, Caldwell's letter — written a few weeks before the Emperors joined *Colored Idea* — did not appear in the *Defender* until the very week of the Clay band's expulsion.

The White Australia Policy was no secret; nor was the opposition voiced by the Australian Musicians Union to the presence in the country of

American bands of *any* race — opposition fueled by the refusal of the American Federation of Musicians in 1927 to authorize the Australian Commonwealth Band to take engagements in the United States after a tour of Canada.

The Australian public turned a blind eye to such matters, however, and instead received Clay and *Colored Idea* quite favourably. Business in Sydney was "big," according to *The Billboard*,[11] and local reviews were positive, if not quite effusive, both there and in Melbourne. Clay and his musicians played in support of Anderson, Saunders and the Covans and were also heard in several features of their own, notably the recent American hit *My Blue Heaven*; sheet music for the song was published in Australia with a photograph of the Plantation Band on the front cover. Clay's repertoire also included several other pop songs, as well as a waltz medley and such jazz standbys as *Tiger Rag* and *St. Louis Blues*.

The band's relatively modern style apparently caught Sydney off guard, however, an indication perhaps of Australia's isolation from recent developments in jazz. "The show as a whole scored strongly," a reviewer from the Sydney weekly *Everyones* noted, "but Sonny's jazz didn't quite conform to the Australian idea, which demands a hot finish to each number, with piano, saxes, banjos and trombones hitting on all eight, instead of the fade away that this combination [ie, the Plantation Band] effects. Personally, we prefer Sonny's style, but for the gallery [ie, audience] a switch to frenzied finishes may supply all [that] the outfit needs. Because it can certainly put syncopation across."[12]

Clay and his musicians came under far less sympathetic scrutiny from *Truth*, a weekly known for its editorial support of the White Australia Policy. After the newspaper put the band's Evelyn Street lodgings in East Melbourne under surveillance, it alerted the police to its findings and reported the details of the resulting raid in the most salacious of terms.

Clay in fact complained in an article published by *Everyones* five days after his departure on the *S.S. Sierra* that he and his musicians had been harassed from the outset of their stay in Australia, "victims of national revenge" for the fate of the Commonwealth Band in the United States. Moreover, he was also quoted as saying, "From the time the boys and I landed we were chased by women who popped up no matter where we hid. It was impossible to avoid them."[13]

While the musicians were not detained after the raid, the women, aged 19 to 23, were arrested for vagrancy, a charge quickly dropped in court two days later when all five proved to be gainfully employed. The scandalized tone of the attendant media coverage nevertheless had the effect that *Truth* and other supporters of the White Australia Policy desired: the remainder of the Plantation Band's Tivoli contract was cancelled, as were arrangements to have the musicians play at a Melbourne dance hall, the Green Mill, thus nullifying the musicians' permits to be in the country.

"In face of the tirade of criticism the management had no alternative but to send the company back to the U.S.," explained the Tivoli chain's publicist, William Maloney, in one of several letters of reference and clarification written for the musicians before they left Sydney, "but I wish to state that it is thought that Sonny Clay and his bandsmen have had a 'very raw deal' and one which we have no power to offset or rectify, however willing we may be."[14]

Word of the band's fate, and of Australia's decision henceforth to ban all African-American entertainers, was noted in newspapers as far afield as The New York *Times* and the London *Times*.[15] The Four Covans and the Harmony Emperors were allowed to complete their contracts, and several singers and dancers did in fact visit the country during the late 1930s,[16] but it would be another 26 years before another black American jazz band, Louis Armstrong's All Stars, appeared in Australia again.

# "No one in any big time way"

Glover Compton was, by his own account, simply an innocent bystander when Sidney Bechet and Mike McKendrick exchanged gunfire outside a tobacco shop on *rue* Fontaine in Montmartre. Compton took a bullet in the right leg; two women on the street, a young Australian dancer, Dolores Giblins, and an older *Parisienne*, a Madame Radureau, were also struck.[1]

Compton, 44,[2] originally from Louisville, Kentucky, was at least the ninth pianist from the Chicago scene of the 1910s to take his career outside the United States for longer or shorter periods, following William Dorsey, Jelly Roll Morton, Pierre de Caillaux, Dan Parrish, Oscar Holden, Slap Rags White, William Hegamin and Teddy Weatherford. Compton sailed for Europe in May 1926, worked briefly with the Palm Beach Six in Berne, then settled in Paris. There, in Montmartre, he played for Bricktop and by early 1927 was working with Crickett Smith at Zelli's on *rue* Fontaine.

Bechet, now 31, had returned to Paris in 1928 after travelling with Louis Douglas's revue *Black People* in Europe and the Middle East and leading his own band in Frankfurt; he spent the summer with the Noble Sissle Orchestra at les Ambassadeurs and by year's end had joined Opal Cooper and the International Five in Montmartre at Chez Florence on *rue* Blanche.

McKendrick, 24,[3] a banjo and guitar player from Chicago, had only recently arrived in Europe as a member of violinist Eddie South's Alabamians; after an engagement of roughly three months at the Embassy in Venice, the quartet opened in November 1928 at The Plantation, a block southeast of Zelli's on *rue* Notre-Dame-de-Lorette near the corner of *rue* Pigalle.

McKendrick was inclined to drink, according to the Alabamians' pianist Henry Crowder — the same Henry Crowder whose orchestra Jelly Roll Morton had taken to Canada in 1927, and the same Henry Crowder who would cause something of a scandal of his own in Paris through his tempestuous, seven-year relationship with a white woman of considerable social standing, Nancy Cunard of the Cunard shipping-line family.

"Mike had been on a spree for some days," Crowder wrote in his autobiography, *As Wonderful as All That?*, setting the stage for the shootings on *rue* Fontaine, "and though he always turned up for work he was usually in a pretty drunken condition. One night he came to work particularly drunk and expressed his intention of shooting anyone who interfered with him."[4]

Bechet, who was equally well known for his belligerence under the influence of alcohol, encountered McKendrick at a Montmartre cafe after their respective evening engagements had ended. According to Glover Compton's account in a letter that he wrote to the Chicago *Defender* following the incident, the two men argued "about music, rhythm and each one's ability as a musician and who could demand the highest salary, etc."[5] — as if Bechet should, much less would, defer to any other jazz musician in Paris on such matters.

The saxophonist himself later claimed that Compton had put McKendrick up to the argument, playing on the contempt in which "Northern" musicians were known to hold their counterparts from the South. "He wasn't no one in any big time way," Bechet wrote of Compton in his biography *Treat It Gentle*, returning the slight 22 years later, "but he was always trying to cut in as much as he could. He was always acting like he wanted to stir up trouble."[6]

Other versions of the events leading up to the *contretemps* expand on or contradict these themes. Henry Crowder remembered that Bechet had been making dismissive remarks about the members of the Alabamians, most notably about Crowder himself. A report published at the time of the incident in the Chicago *Tribune*, however, put a woman at the centre of the conflict, prompting Compton in his letter to the *Defender* to assert, "There is absolutely no truth in the statement that a blonde Belgian girl was the cause of the shooting." (In fact *Variety* identified the woman in question as the Australian dancer, although Bechet in his biography implied she was with Compton.[7]) Years later, Compton took yet another tack, suggesting that the trouble began when Bechet remarked on McKendrick's reluctance to stand a round of drinks.[8]

Whatever the truth of any or all of these motives, the initial encounter between Bechet and McKendrick ended without violence. Some three hours of drinking later, however, Bechet crossed paths again with McKendrick and Compton on *rue* Fontaine. Accounts differ as to which musician fired first — Bechet, according to Compton; McKendrick, according to Bechet. Neither adversary was hit. Both, however, were arrested immediately and, at the end of February 1929, sentenced to 15-month jail terms. Bechet, at least, was released early and in December 1929 left Paris for a year in Berlin before returning to New York late in 1930.

All of the wounded parties recovered — Madame Radureau was awarded a settlement of 10,000 francs for her injuries — and Bechet eventually

found it in his heart to make peace with McKendrick, thought not, apparently, with Compton.[9] All was forgotten, save perhaps by Bechet himself,
when he made Paris his home once again in 1950 and lived as a celebrity in
France for the last nine years of his life.

# "Shot"

PARIS, DECEMBER 7, 1929. Louis Mitchell was back in business again, this time at The Plantation.[1] In the six years since he had left his Jazz Kings in the hands of Crickett Smith at the Casino de Paris, Mitchell had been involved as an entrepreneur in at least five late-night or all-night Montmartre establishments, four of which on rue Pigalle — Mitchell's, the Music Box, Mitchell's Quick Lunch and Pile ou face. The fifth and most successful, also known as Mitchell's, operated from late 1924 through the summer of 1925[2] at 61 rue Blanche; like the first Mitchell's, coincidentally, it passed into the hands of singer Florence Jones, who renamed it Chez Florence.

By early 1929, however, Louis Mitchell's fortunes were beginning to falter. His willingness to take a risk had served him well in music but poorly at the track. Accordingly, he announced plans to open an agency that would assist African-American artists arriving in Europe[3] and introduced a new version of the Jazz Kings for what proved to be a short engagement at El Garron on rue Fontaine; in keeping with the trend toward larger ensembles, the Mitchell band now numbered 10, though likely not any of the original Jazz Kings from the Casino de Paris.

Crickett Smith, Dan Parrish and Walter Kildare were all still in Montmartre — Smith at Zelli's, Parrish at the Grand Écart and Kildare with the Crackerjacks at the Palermo. Frank Withers, meanwhile, was in his third year on the road as music director for Cofie's Colored Cracks, a nine-piece revue fronted by singer Madge Cofie and managed by drummer Harry Cofie.[4] The Cracks enjoyed particular success in Spain and had also worked at the Parisien Grill of the Royal Grand Hotel in Budapest, the Capitol Cabaret and Carlton Hotel in Paris and the Cafe Esplanade in Zurich. They were at the Esplanade when Mitchell took his new Jazz Kings into El Garron in March 1929; they had moved on to Barcelona's Eden Dancing by the time Mitchell reopened The Plantation in December.

The prospects for Mitchell's latest venture were enhanced by the recent departure from Paris of two of Montmartre's most popular attractions, the Crackerjacks and the International Five — the former for Cannes in September and the latter for New York in November. Meanwhile, Eddie South's Alabamians, who closed a seven-month engagement at the Plantation during the summer (with Sterling Conaway replacing South's incarcerated banjo and guitar player, Mike McKendrick), had just followed Benny Peyton's New Yorkers into the New York Restaurant in Budapest.

Still, Mitchell would not be without competition. Sam Wooding was in residence at the Embassy, as were the banjo player Seth Weeks at the Royal Haussman Restaurant and saxophonist Nelson Kincaid's Close Harmony Boys — in place of the International Five — at Chez Florence.

Mitchell later claimed to have spent $126,000 on the Plantation,[5] installing a new "quick lunch" at street level — complete with "a log-cabin window display" and "a real colored mammy handling pots and pans"[6] — and redecorating the cabaret upstairs. For his entertainment, Mitchell looked to the Versatile Four, still active 13 years after recording *Down Home Rag* in Hayes, Middlesex, England, although with only banjo player Tony Tuck remaining from the original lineup. It was now "a singing group mainly," according to the French pianist Alain Romans, a member during this period, "but it was also jazz because we used to take choruses — we would scat them. We did Negro spirituals and also blues."[7]

Mitchell's choice of music for the Plantation, however, was no less *passé* than his choice of decor, each perpetuating African-American popular culture in stereotypes with which Montmartre audiences were all too familiar. Moreover, his timing, which had been so very shrewd during the past dozen years in Paris, now failed him, albeit under circumstances far beyond his control.

The Plantation reopened just five weeks after the Wall Street stock market crash of October 29, 1929, an event that signalled in both symbolic and real terms the end of the Jazz Age. Its impact was immediate and international, stifling the sense of release and reckless hedonism that had followed the First World War and that flourished throughout the 1920s, swept along by the exhilarating momentum of its own extravagance.

"Paris nite life is shot," announced Abel Green bluntly in a dispatch to *Variety* just days after the Plantation opened. "What little is left is making a special play for the American and British element or, at least, [for] any and all who speak English."[8] Indeed, many members of the American "element" — in Paris and elsewhere in Europe — had watched helplessly as the investments, inheritances or remittances that allowed them to live comfortably abroad disappeared. Those same Americans had been Montmartre's — and Mitchell's — best customers.

Paris nightlife would soon recover, and American jazz musicians would continue to arrive in the city during the 1930s, but the Plantation, ill-fated from the outset, closed after only seven weeks. "I tried to keep up for a while,"

Mitchell later remembered, "but I was facing impossible odds. Ruin and jail stared me in the face, for you see, it is against French laws for a foreigner to declare bankruptcy."[9]

Mitchell spent the next eight months in Paris settling his affairs, then sailed in early October 1930 for New York.[10] There, he was back in business once again by the following summer, turning his 12 years in Paris to advantage as the manager now of the Last Stop on Seventh Avenue. It was, of course, a French restaurant.[11]

# "A pretty sad lot"

## (Epilogue)

NEW YORK BAY, OCTOBER 27, 1939. A heavy fog hung over Manhattan, a vapour so thick that the *S.S. St. John* was forced to drop anchor in the Ambrose Channel until visibility had improved enough to allow the ship to enter the Narrows between Brooklyn and Staten Island and approach its assigned dock at West 22nd Street safely.

The delay was the last of several on a trip that could not end quickly enough for the St. John's anxious passengers, among them a dozen or more musicians and entertainers who had heeded the call from the American Ambassador in Paris to leave France in light of Germany's successful invasion of Poland — the opening act of the Second World War.

After a two-week wait at Bordeaux, the *St. John* left for Cobh, in Cork Harbour, Ireland, whence she sailed westward on October 19. Her voyage was given particular urgency by the fate of two other ships that had undertaken similar transatlantic crossings in these, the early days of the war. One, the British liner *Athenia*, was sunk off the Hebrides without warning by a German submarine on September 4, the day after hostilities had been declared; more than 130 people were lost at sea, nearly a quarter of them Americans. The other, the *S.S. Iroquois*, which left Liverpool for New York on October 2, sailed under threat of German attack as she neared American waters; in fact she docked safely in New York on the 12th.

The *St. John's* 437 passengers included dancer Teddy Drayton, who had gone to Europe with *Chocolate Kiddies* 14 years earlier, violinist Leon Abbey, trumpeters Albert Barnes and Ted Brock, trombonists Emile Christian and Frank Withers, saxophonist Antonio Cosey, clarinetist Danny Polo, pianists Una Mae Carlisle, Tommy Chase, Glover Compton and Garland Wilson, guitarist Mike McKendrick, and drummers Benny Peyton, Creighton Thompson and Harvey White.[1]

White had been overseas since 1916, Withers and Peyton since 1919, Christian and Thompson since 1920. Barnes, Chase, Wilson and Carlisle were more recent arrivals, part of a new wave of musicians drawn to Paris during the 1930s. Withers, who turned 59 on the day that the *St. John* sailed from Cobh, was the oldest of the returning Americans, Carlisle at 33 the youngest.

They had left France with only the greatest reluctance. Floyd G. Snelson of the New York *Age* described the plight of "a noted Negro musician" — possibly Withers — who, after 20 years in Europe, found himself refused permission to join his British wife and their twins in England and was instead forced to sail from France without them.[2]

"We were a pretty sad lot leaving Paris, nobody wanted to go home," Emile Christian told *Swing Music* shortly after his return to New York. "[I]t was pretty awful, but once on board, we tried to pep up the rest of the folks, by getting together a jam band each nite, and it worked it... soon, the whole boat was jumping... we had enough musicians on board for a symphony, and had a revised personnel each night. You can be sure we rocked the St. John all the way in."[3]

Even as they tried to sustain some vestige of the life and times they were leaving behind in France, however, they were reminded of a reality that lay still further in their past and now loomed again in their future. The *St. John*, which was chartered by the U.S. government expressly to repatriate Americans stranded in France, had a black crew commanded by white officers. According to Floyd Snelson, "many colored men were brutally treated and placed in irons" during the voyage.[4] The New York *Times* took note more generally of "numerous brawls among the crew," three of whom completed the crossing in the ship's brig.[5]

Of course, life for those Americans who chose to remain behind in Europe was even more uncertain. Arthur Briggs, Henry Crowder and Freddy Johnson were interned by the Germans; remarkably, all survived, Briggs to spend the rest of his 92 years in France, Crowder and Johnson to return to the United States. Valada — now Valaida — Snow was detained by Danish authorities but apparently decided that being held in a Nazi concentration camp made for a more dramatic story, one that she developed for the American media after her return in 1942; she continued to perform in the United States and Canada for another 14 years.

In the Far East, William Hegamin and his two sons were confined by the Japanese to an internment camp at Chapei, near Shanghai; they too returned at the war's end to the United States, where Hegamin died in Los Angeles in 1960. His early rival in Shanghai, Teddy Weatherford, spent the war years out of harm's way in Calcutta but did not survive the cholera epidemic that swept India in 1945.

For the musicians on the *St. John*, meanwhile, repatriation proved to be as difficult as it was dramatic. Jazz had continued to evolve in their absence.

Swing was popular; bebop was in the air. The returnees found themselves both musically and culturally out of step.

"It's a new world to me, after eighteen years," marvelled Emile Christian. "It's as strange as any of the foreign countries I've visited," he added, speaking from the experience of stops throughout Europe and, with Leon Abbey, as far away as India. "[I] can't seem to get used to all the hustle and 'go,' [and I] suppose it will take some time to adjust myself to it all and get along without all that good French wine with my meals."[6]

Christian returned to New Orleans, and Glover Compton and Mike McKendrick to Chicago. Leon Abbey and Benny Peyton remained in New York. Ted Brock, who had worked in Montreal before heading to Europe in 1928, returned briefly to that city, perhaps in search of some facsimile of the Paris he had left behind. Frank Withers, meanwhile, made his way back to Los Angeles, where he served as a pall bearer at the funeral in July 1941 of Jelly Roll Morton,[7] re-establishing another link — one still lost to history — between two of the many musicians who had taken jazz to the world.

# End Notes

## NOTES

i) Unless otherwise indicated, references to the Chicago *Defender* are to its City edition. City and National editions have been microfilmed in separate series.

ii) All references to the New York *Herald* are to its Paris edition.

iii) Unless otherwise indicated, all birth and death dates have been taken from Kernfeld, Barry, ed. *The New Grove Dictionary of Jazz*. 2d ed. London: Macmillan 2002.

## NEW YORK BAY, MAY 26, 1914

1 Marvel Cooke, "Mitchell, sensation of Europe," New York *Amsterdam News*, 2 March 1940, 15.

2 Louis Mitchell was born 17 December 1885 in New York and died there 12 September 1957. A comprehensive review of his career can be found in Robert Pernet and Howard Rye's "Visiting Fireman 18: Louis Mitchell," *Storyville 2000-1*, 221-248.

3 According to documentation held in the British Public Record Office (see Pernet and Rye, "Visiting Firemen 18"), Mitchell et al. entered the country at Dover on June 8, which suggests that they may have remained with the *Vaderland* — perhaps in its employ as entertainers — for the entirety of the New-York-to-Hamburg crossing before disembarking on the return leg.

## WINNIPEG, CANADA, SEPTEMBER 21, 1914

1 Freddie Keppard was born 27 February 1890 in New Orleans and died 15 July 1933 in Chicago.

2 "News and reviews of things theatrical," Winnipeg *Tribune*, 19 September 1914, second section, 2.

3 "'Just Kids,' winner," Winnipeg *Tribune*, 22 September 1914, 3.

4 "Much cleverness seen at Pantages," Victoria *Daily Colonist*, 12 September 1916, 8.

5 The travels of African-American performers in Europe have been reviewed in detail by Rainer E. Lotz in *Black People: Entertainers of African Descent in Europe, and Germany* (Bonn: Birgit Lotz Verlag, 1997).

## LONDON, MAY 16, 1915

1 Daniel Augustus Kildare was born 13 January 1879 in Kingston, Jamaica, and died 21 June 1920 in London. He and his musicians arrived at Liverpool on 9 April 1915 and opened at Ciro's on 18 April 1915. His career has been documented in detail by Howard Rye and Tim Brooks in "Visiting Fireman 16: Dan Kildare," *Storyville 1996-7*, 30-57.

2 "N.Y. Artists in London" [Dan Kildare letter], New York *Age*, 17 June 1915, 6.

3 Marvel Cooke, "12,000 nights of entertainment," New York *Amsterdam News*, 2 March 1940, 15.

4 "Ragtime at Ciro's: Police critics of music and dancing," London *Times*, 6 December 1916, 5.

5 "Clef Club member shot self in London," New York *Age*, 16 September 1915, 1.

6 London *Times*, 6 December 1916, 5.

7 "Ciro's struck off register," London *Times*, 21 December 1916, 4.

8 Joe Jordan was born 11 February 1882 in Cincinnati and died 11 September 1971 in Tacoma, Washington. His career, including his British sojourn in 1915, has been documented by Howard Rye in "Visiting Fireman 14: Joe Jordan 1915," *Storyville*, no. 134 (June 1988). 55-58.

9 "Hip's new revue," *Variety*, 14 May 1915, 4.

10 "The effort to cheer: 'Push and Go!' at the Hippodrome," London *Daily Chronicle*, 11 May 1915, 5.

11 "Push and Go," London *Daily News and Leader*, 12 May 1915, 3.

12 New York *Age*, 17 June 1915, 6.

13 Anne Judd, "A portrait of Russell Smith," *Jazz Journal*, vol. 20, no. 4 (April 1967), 6.

14 Len Gutteridge, "The first man to bring jazz to Britain," *Melody Maker*, 14 July 1956, 6.

15 R.H.S., "Variety theatres," Manchester *Guardian*, 17 August 1915, 12.

16 Pollard was born c1892 in Chicago and died there 13 February 1926 ("Death takes Pollard," Chicago *Defender*, 20 February 1926, 6). Hughes was his mother's maiden name; references in jazz literature to "Hugh" Pollard are incorrect. The Pollard family's background is detailed by John M. Carroll in *Fritz Pollard: Pioneer in Racial Advancement* (Chicago: University of Illinois Press, 1992), 9-22.

17 See Lotz, *Black People*, for details of the careers of Belle Davis, Louis Douglas and the Four Black Diamonds in London, and Europe more generally.

18 At least one of the Versatile Four, Anthony Tuck, was a member of the Clef Club (as listed in "Clef Club plans to build," New York *Age*, 29 February 1914, 8). The status of the others vis-à-vis the Clef Club is not clear, nor is the year of the Versatile Four's arrival in London. A.A. Haston, writing in 1925, dated the quartet's debut to 6 November 1913 but did not identify the city

explicitly ("With our performers in Europe," New York *Amsterdam News*, 23 December 1925, 5). A 1918 news item, which also appears to have had a member of the group as its source, stated that the Versatile Four had "already been engaged for five years" at Murray's ("St. Dunstan's Day," Chicago *Defender*, 23 November 1918, 7). However, Billy E. Jones noted in late 1914 that "The Versatile Four sail for London from New York to fill a two and one-half year's engagement. The quartet has been working steadily in and around New York." ("New York news," Indianapolis *Freeman*, 2 January 1915, 5).

19 Ads, London *Times*, 1 October 1917, 8; London *Daily Telegraph*, 1 October 1917, 6.

20 Obituaries in the African-American press differ as to the date of William Dorsey's death. The Chicago *Defender* reported that he was born in Louisville, Kentucky, and died 29 February 1920 at "about 40 years of age" ("W.H. Dorsey dead," 13 March 1920, 7). The Indianapolis *Freeman* suggested that he had been born in Louisville "about 42 years ago" and died 9 February 1920 ("Will H. Dorsey is dead, was an exceptional musician," 20 March 1920, 2). Both newspapers agreed on the place of his demise — Yuma, Arizona.

21 Len Gutteridge, "The man who brought jazz to Britain," J. Hadfield, ed., *The Saturday Book* (London: Hutchinson, 1957), 113. In addition to interviewing Mitchell, Gutteridge appears to have had access to a scrapbook that the drummer kept of his career.

22 Ibid., 113.

23 "'Freak music at the Coliseum," London *Times*, 26 September 1916, 11.

24 "London variety stage: London Opera House," *The Stage*, 12 October 1916, 15.

25 La Belle Leonora's presence at the Alhambra in Paris was first noted in *La Presse*, 8 November 1916, 2; she was part of a bill that, according to items on other days in the same newspaper, ran from November 3 to 16.

## HAYES, MIDDLESEX, ENGLAND, FEBRUARY 3, 1916

1 Details of the Versatile Four's complete recording session have been noted by Brian Rust in *Jazz Records 1897-1942* (New Rochelle, NY: Arlington House, 1978), 1603.

## CALGARY, CANADA, SEPTEMBER 1, 1916

1 "Cabaret opening draws a crowd," Calgary *Daily Herald*, 2 September 1916, 18.

2 "A big hit," Chicago *Defender*, 30 September 1916, 3. The band was identified by the *Defender* as the Instrumental Four but advertised in the *Daily Herald*, 8 September 1916, 8, and thereafter, as the Musical Four Quartette, perhaps in view of the fact that all four instrumentalists also sang.

3 As noted on a file card, NA-625-20, in the Glenbow Archives, Calgary, accompanying a police department photograph of Lawrence B. Morgan taken 12 June 1917.

4 The activities of African-American musicians in Alberta during the 1920s have been documented by Mark Miller in *Such Melodious Racket: The Lost History of Jazz in Canada, 1914-1949* (Toronto: The Mercury Press, 1997), 47-49, 84-91.

5 Dave Peyton, "The musical bunch: Shirley Oliver in," Chicago *Defender*, 20 August 1927, 8.

## WASHINGTON, D.C., APRIL 6, 1917

1 "Scrap-Iron Jazz Band will tour American Leave-Centres in France," New York *Herald*, 24 March 1919, 2.

2 Advertisement, New York *Age*, 10 May 1917, 6.

3 Advertisement, Baltimore *Afro-American*, 3 December 1917, 5.

4 Noble Lee Sissle was born 10 July 1889 in Indianapolis, and died 17 December 1975 in Tampa.

## SOUTHSEA, ENGLAND, APRIL 9, 1917

1 The Seven Spades' British itinerary is listed in Pernet and Rye, "Visiting Firemen 18," 232. Personnel of the group is confirmed by Norris Smith, "Dear old Lunnon," Chicago *Defender*, 19 May 1917 [page number missing from microfilmed copy].

2 *The Encore*, 19 April 1917, 7.

3 Recordings by Ciro's Club Coon Orchestra are listed in Rye and Brooks, "Visiting Firemen 16," 51-54.

4 Reproduced in *The Melody Maker*, 14 July 1956, 6.

## HAMILTON, CANADA, SEPTEMBER 1, 1917

1 "Jass band," Hamilton *Spectator*, 31 August 1917, 14.

2 Advertisement, Hamilton *Spectator*, 24 August 1917, 20.

3 "Royal re-opened," Hamilton *Times*, 3 September 1917, unpaginated clipping, Hamilton Public Library.

4 "Canada," Chicago *Defender*, 24 November 1917, 7.

## WINNIPEG, CANADA, NOVEMBER 5, 1917

1 "Kid" Killaire is mentioned in "A note or two," Chicago *Defender*, 6 October 1917, 4. "Young" Killaire is among the musicians identified in the cutline to a photograph of the Tennessee Ten on the same page. The other members of the jazz band at this time — a month before its Canadian debut — were identified in the cutline as violinist Earl Walton, clarinetist Blaine Gaten and banjo player John Turner.

2 Jean and Marshall Stearns, *Jazz Dance: The Story of American Vernacular Dance* (New York: Macmillan, 1968), 178-179.

3 "Amusements," Vancouver *Daily Sun*, 20 November 1917, 7.

4 "First night at theatres: Orpheum has a great show," Winnipeg *Tribune*, 19 August 1919, 7.

5 Clever dancers on Orpheum circuit," Victoria *Daily Times*, 30 August 1919, 8.

## PARIS, NOVEMBER 16, 1917

1 Marvel Cooke, "12,000 nights of entertainment," New York *Amsterdam News*, 9 March 1940, 15.

2 Edgar A. Wiggins, "Race actors shine in Paris as bands feature in the main spotlight nightly," Chicago *Defender*, 4 May 1935, 15. Although Wiggins cites a matinee on 11 November 1917 as the date of the Seven Spades' Paris debut, the band is presumed to have closed an engagement at the Theatre Royal in Dublin that same day (Pernet and Rye, "Visiting Firemen 18," 232). Notices in the Paris daily *La Presse* announced a new program at the Alhambra for the next "quinzaine" (fortnight), beginning on the 16th, which would be consistent with time required by the Seven Spades to travel from Dublin to Paris. It is also consistent with the first published reference to the Seven Spades in Paris by name, an item — "Acts opening at Paris, Alhambra," *Variety*, 7 December 1919, 4 — which noted that they "*are* [italics added] appearing successfully at the Alhambra," then listed the acts that opened November 30 — the start of the next quinzaine — and thus implying that the Mitchell band was already in place.

3 Gutteridge, *The Saturday Book*, 114.

4 "Casino, Paris, reopens," *Variety*, 14 December 1917, 4, refers to "Murray Pilcer (with his seven banjo players)." Jean Cocteau, in *Le Rappel à l'ordre* (Paris: Stock, 1926), 23, mentions banjos and "grosse pipes de nickel" — literally, "fat nickel pipes" — which could by some stretch of the imagination be a reference to saxophones. The Pilcer group was initially identified as the Sherbo American Band or American Sherbo Band; Sherbo was a New York orchestra contractor.

5 According to Robert Pernet, "Quiproquo [sic] — Louis Mitchell ou Murray Pilcer?," *Record Memory Club Magazine*, no. 50 (March 2000), unpaginated [23], Murray Pilcer was born 10 October 1892 in New York.

6 E.G. Kendrew, "In Paris," *Variety*, 4 January 1918, 4.

7 Jean Cocteau, *Le Rappel à l'ordre*, 23. The original English translation by Rollo H. Meyers (London: Faber and Gwyer, 1926), 13, has been adjusted here.

8 Advertisement, *L'Echo de Paris*, 28 December 1917, 3.

9 Reid Badger, *A Life in Ragtime: A Biography of James Reese Europe*, (New York: Oxford University Press, 1995), 163.

10 "Paris theatrical notes," New York *Herald*, 29 January 1918, 2.

11 Advertisement, *La Presse*, 11 March 1918, 2.

12 Mistinguett, *Mistinguett: Queen of the Paris Night*, translated by Lucienne Hill (London, Elek Books, 1954), 120.

13 "American S. and S. Club," *New York Herald*, 23 November 1918, 2. A William Johnson is listed among the mandolinists in a Clef Club orchestra in 1914 (Lucien White, "Clef Club triumph," New York *Age*, 11 June 1914, 6). William Johnson, the band-leader at the Hotel Ritz, died 19 April 1929 in Paris at the age of 47 ("Colored musicians die," *Variety*, 24 April 1929, 60).

14 Michael Haggerty, "Michel Leiris: L'Autre qui apparaît chez nous," *Jazz Magazine*, no. 325 (January 1984), 34-35.

## NANTES, FRANCE, FEBRUARY 12, 1918

1 Background for this section has been drawn from Reid Badger, *A Life in Ragtime*, 140-173.

2 James Reese Europe was born in Mobile, Alabama, 22 February 1881, and died 10 May 1919 in Boston.

3 Sissle's letter was published as "Ragtime by U.S. Army band gets everyone 'over there,'" in the St. Louis *Post-Dispatch*, 10 June 1918, and as "Negro jazz music and rag variety taking Europe" in the Indianapolis *Freeman*, 24 August 1918, 7. The *Post-Dispatch* version is reprinted in Robert Kimball and William Bolcolm, *Reminiscing with Sissle and Blake* (New York: Viking Press, 1973), 67-68.

4 Europe recorded *The Memphis Blues* in New York for Pathé with many, if not all, of his 15th Infantry musicians in March 1919. The arrangement is presumably much the same, although it uses wood blocks rather than snare drums, no doubt in deference to the sensitivity of early recording processes.

5 Sissle's letter mentions *The Army Blues*; *Shim-Me-Sha-Wabble* is included in a concert program from 14 April 1918 published in The New York *Age*, 11 May 1918, 6; *Bugle Blues* was recalled by Sam Wooding in an oral history done for the Smithsonian Institute by Chris Albertson in 1975. *Shim-Me-Sha-Wabble* was recorded in 1916 by a military ensemble, the American Regimental Band, and later by many jazz bands, including the New Orleans Rhythm Kings in 1923, McKinney's Cotton Pickers in 1928 and the bands of Bud Freeman and Zutty Singleton in 1940.

6 "15th Infantry band scores 'over there,'" Baltimore *Afro-American*, 22 February 1918, 1.

7 "First American soldiers on leave reach Aix-les-Bains from trenches," New York *Herald*, 17 February 1918, 1.

8 Arthur W. Little, *From Harlem to the Rhine: The Story of New York's Colored Volunteers* (New York: Covici and Friede, 1936), 137.

9 "French find new kind of American," Baltimore *Afro-American*, 27 September 1918, 4.

## CAMP DIX, WRIGHTSTOWN, NEW JERSEY, JULY 12, 1918

1 "Granstaff and Davis straight and comedy instrumentalists," Indianapolis *Freeman*, 5 December 1914, 5.

2 According to the passenger list for the *Veednam*, sailing 6 September 1923, from Southampton, England, to New York, Earl Granstaff was born 23 July 1894 in Grand Rapids, Michigan (see www.ellisisland.org). Ivan Browning noted the recent but undated death of Eddie [sic] Granstaff, "a fine trombone player," in the south of France in "Notes of London," New York *Amsterdam News*, 20 February 1929, 8.

3 Seymour James, "Baltimore theatrical news," Indianapolis *Freeman*, 22 June 1918, 6.

4 "Doing his stuff" [Earl Granstaff letter, dated 12 July 1918], Chicago *Defender*, 20 July 1918, 6.

## PARIS, AUGUST 21, 1918

1 The original of this letter is in The Eubie Blake Collection, MS 2800, H. Furlong Baldwin Library, Maryland Historical Society; quoted with permission.

2 As evidence of his continuing relationship with the Clef Club, Europe's name still appears on lists of its "financial members" published in the New York Age during the spring of 1918 — eg, 23 March 1918, 6, and 11 May 1918, 6.

3 The entirety of this letter is reproduced in Kimball and Bolcolm, Reminiscing with Sissle and Blake, 69.

4 Mitchell's movements in the second half of 1918 can be traced in the Paris press, if in some cases only by inference. He brought together the jazz bands from Théâtre Caumartin (ie, the former Seven Spades) and the Casino de Paris for a single performance at the American Soldiers' and Sailors' Club on July 3 ("Next Wednesday will be big night at S. and S. Club," New York Herald, 30 June 1918, 4). He may have been featured in the Casino's revue Boum, as suggested by a review that noted, "The big booms in the revue are Dorville, Nina Myral and the player of the bass drum in the American orchestra" ("Paris theatrical notes," New York Herald, 11 August 1918, 2). And a band known as Mitchell's Midnight Frolic Jazz Band was advertised to appear in The Follies of 1918 at the Théâtre Marigny (New York Herald, 1 September 1918, 2). Mitchell's featured role latterly in the Casino de Paris orchestra was described by Lester Walton in "French now want colored musicians" (New York Age, 8 February 1919, 6).

5 Marvel Cooke. "12,000 nights of entertainment: Mitchell loves his baseball," New York Amsterdam News, 9 Mar 1940, 15.

## RETHONDES, COMPÈIGNE FOREST, FRANCE, NOVEMBER 11, 1918

1 "A Negro explains jazz," Literary Digest, 26 April 1919, 28-29; reprinted in Eileen Southern, Readings in Black Music, second edition (New York: W.W. Norton, 1983), 240.

2 Jasper Taylor was born 1 January 1894 in Texarkana, Texas, and died 7 November 1964 in Chicago.

3 "A Black Hun Chaser writes from France," Indianapolis Freeman, 28 September 1918, 2.

4 Willie The Lion Smith was born William Henry Joseph Bonaparte Bertholoff 25 November 1897 in Goshen, New York, and died 18 April 1973 in New York.

5 Willie The Lion Smith, with George Hoefer, Music on My Mind: The Memoirs of an American Pianist (New York: Da Capo Press, 1978), 75.

6 Ibid., 79.

7 Ibid., 75.

8 Samuel David Wooding was born 17 June 1895 in Philadelphia and died 1 August 1985 in New York.

9 Unpublished interview with Chris Albertson, 1975; Smithsonian Institution Oral History series.

10 "Making music for the army," New York Age, 4 January 1919, 6.

11 "Headquarters band of First Army gives show," New York Herald, 29 January 1919, 2.

12 Chris Goddard, Jazz Away from Home (New York: Paddington Press, 1979): 20.

## ROME, JANUARY 2, 1919

1 "An interesting letter from Italy," The Metronome, vol. 35, no. 3 (March 1919), 41.

2 In the absence of any information about their origins, the musicians of the Scrap Iron Jazz Band have sometimes been identified as black, possibly members of an African-American regimental band in France. The source of the information herein is "Scrap-Iron Jazz Band will tour American Leave-Centres in France," New York Herald, 24 March 1919, 2.

3 Personnel of the Scrap Iron Jazz Band, as given by the New York Herald, ibid., and cross-referenced with the passenger list of the S.S. Zeppelin, on which the musicians returned home (see www.ellisisland.org), is saxophonist Russel (Russell) Hanslaib (Handslaib), cornetist Clarence Koch, trombonist Albert Argellotta (Angellotta), violinists Syl Horn and Edwin or Vernon Dakin, pianist Clayton Thirkell and drummer Arshat (Arshar) Nushan.

4 "Jazz Band in gondolas delights A.E.F. troops," New York Herald, Paris edition, 19 February 1919, 2. See also John Smucker, The History of the United States Army Ambulance Service 1917-1918-1919 (Allentown, Penn.: United States Army Ambulance Service Association, 1967). Smucker identities the personnel of the USAAS band as pianist, saxophonist and singer Charles W. Hamp, singer Art Decker, violinists R.C. Mustarde and Charlie Paulik, violist Charlie Keck, banjoists Chuck Barlow and Norm Kennedy, ukulele player Allen Mattox, bassist Doc Neale and drummer Pat Emerick. Charles Hamp recorded in the late 1920s as "The California Blue Boy" for Sunset, Columbia and OKeh.

5 "Ambulance Jazz Band leaves for the Riviera," New York Herald, 5 April 1919, 2.

6 Roger Beardsley, ed. Fonotipia 1904-1939 [CD-ROM] (North Thoresby, Lincolnshire, England, 2003).

7 The departures from France of most of the USAAS Jazz Band's members are documented on passenger lists at www.ellisisland.org.

## WASHINGTON, D.C., JANUARY 29, 1919

1 "Advises U.S. bands to stay at home," The Billboard, 12 December 1925, 49.

2 Mark Berresford, "From New York to London — Eddie Gross Bart's Story," Storyville, no. 102 (August-September 1982), 211. See also "Prohibition kills cabarets at many B'way palaces," New York Clipper, 9 July 1919, 1.

3 Norris Smith, "Dear old Lunnon," Chicago Defender, 1 January 1921, 11.

4 Dave Peyton, "The musical bunch," Chicago Defender, 30 April 1927, 9.

5 Jimmy Bertrand, as told to William Russell [oral history], 1959, Hogan Jazz Archive, Tulane University, New Orleans.

6 Ragtime Billy Tucker, "Coast Dope," Chicago *Defender*, 31 July 1920, 4.

7 Ragtime Billy Tucker, "The Georgias," Chicago *Defender*, 9 April 1921, 6.


LONDON, APRIL 8, 1919

1 "Leon Errol back," *Variety*, 12 December 1919, 4. Robey himself made no reference either to the Original Dixieland Jazz Band in London or to an American tour of his own in his autobiography *Looking Back on Life* (London: Constable, 1933); he did write, with respect to an unnamed revue after *Joy Bells*, that its "music was the kind that our people have always liked... full of delightful tunes, with none of the silly jazz ideas that some people try to force on us."

2 "Charivaria," *Punch, or the London Charivari*, 16 April 1919, 293.

3 Rust, *Jazz Records*, 1229. Personnel of the Pilcer band includes Jack Rimmer (trumpet), Stanley Jones (trombone) and Arthur Combes (clarinet, alto saxophone); the other instruments are bassoon, violin, piano banjo, bass and drums.

4 Quoted in H.O. Brunn, *The Story of the Original Dixieland Jazz Band* (Baton Rouge, La., 1960), 135.

5 Ibid., 135.

6 "American act can't go over," *Variety*, 21 November 1919, 4.

7 Arnold, his brother Henry and his drummer, Charles Moore, all identified Paterson, New Jersey, as their place of birth on the passenger lists of the ships that took them back to New York — the Arnolds (for a visit) on the *Majestic* from Cherbourg, France, in October 1927, and Moore (permanently) on the *Aquitania* from Southampton, England, in December 1920. According to the passenger list for the *Majestic*, William Arnold Guldeman was born 6 or 26 January 1894, and Henry Guldeman, 7 July 1899; "Obituaries," *Variety*, 21 February 1962 , 71, notes that the former died "recently" in Paramus, New Jersey; according to the United States Social Security Death Index (see http://ssdi.geneal-ogy.rootsweb.com), the latter died in Belgium in 1967.

8 Arnold and his musicians gave 31 Tottenham Court Road — the address for Rector's — as their destination in London when they arrived 25 May 1919 on the *Baltic* in Liverpool (Public Records Office, BT26/654).

9 "Advises U.S. bands to stay at home," *The Billboard*, 12 December 1925, 49. Arnold's reference to a "short engagement" is consistent with the arrival of the ODJB at Rector's in late June 1919.

10 "In London," *Variety*, 20 February 1920, 26.

11 Berresford, "From New York to London," 212-213.


LIVERPOOL, JUNE 12, 1919

1 Howard Rye, "Visiting Firemen 15: The Southern Syncopated Orchestra (Part 1)," *Storyville*, no. 142 (June 1990), 139. This series — which continues in *Storyville*, no. 143 (September 1990) 165-178, and *Storyville*, no. 144 (December 1990), 227-234 — offers a detailed account of the SSO's travels, its many changes in personnel and its legal difficulties.

2 Will Marion Cook was born 27 January 1869 in Washington, D.C., and died 19 July 1944 in New York.

3 Billy E. Jones, "New York news," Indianapolis *Freeman*, 17 Apr 1915, 5; Cary B. Lewis, "Will Marion Cook very ill," Indianapolis *Freeman*, 1 May 1915, 1.

4 Sidney Joseph Bechet was born 14 May 1897 in New Orleans and died 14 May 1959 in Paris.

5 "Black and white at Liverpool," London *Times*, 10 June 1919, 9.

6 Arthur Briggs, as told to James Lincoln Collier, 1982, Jazz Oral History Project of the National Endowment for the Arts; held at The Rutgers Institute of Jazz Studies.

7 Southern Syncopated Orchestra program, Philharmonic Hall, London, reproduced in *Jazz Hot*, no. 250 (May 1969), 22.

8 E. Ansermet, "Sur un orchestre nègre," *La Revue Romande*, 15 Oct 1919; reprinted, together with an English translation by Walter E. Schaap, in *Jazz Hot*, no. 28 (November-December 1938), 4-7, 9.

9 Sidney Bechet, *Treat It Gentle: An Autobiography* (New York: Da Capo Press, 1978), 127.

10 Ansermet, "Sur un orchestre nègre," 9.

11 Bechet, *Treat It Gentle*, 128.

12 Rye, *Storyville*, June 1990, 137.

13 Ted Heath, *Listen to My Music* (London: F. Muller, 1957), 29-31.

14 John Chilton, *Sidney Bechet: The Wizard of Jazz* (London: Oxford University Press, 1987), 43 and 52, dates Bechet's Brussels trip to June 1920 and the Jazz Kings' Paris sojourn to the autumn of 1921. An ad in the New York *Herald*, 7 October 1921, 3, announces the re-opening of the Apollo with the Jazz Kings, the American Five and Ferrer-Filipotto's Argentine orchestra. The Jazz Kings were still at the Apollo in January 1922, according to a letter dated the 12th of that month and published under the headline "From Abroad" in the Chicago *Defender*, 4 February 1922, 7.

15 Harvey Astley. "London Jazz — 1919," *Jazz Journal*, December 1949, 22.

16 Bechet, *Treat It Gentle*, 129-132; Chilton, *Sidney Bechet*, 53-54.


PARIS, JULY 4, 1919

1 Reb Spikes, quoted in Tom Stoddard, *Jazz on the Barbary Coast* (Chigwell, Essex, England: Storyville, 1982), 54.

2 According to his death certificate, Frank Douglas Withers was born 29 October 1880 in Emporia, Kansas, and died 7 January 1952 in San Francisco.

3 Advertisement, New York *Age*, 8 Mar 1919, 6.

4 Olin Downes, "Clef Club at Wilbur," Boston *Sunday Post*, 4 August 1918, 21; reprinted as "Boston Club lauds Clef Club players," New York *Age*, 24 August 1918, 6. See also Mark Miller, "Frank Withers: a lost voice and a lost review," *Coda Magazine*, no. 310 (July-August 2003), 5-6.

5 William (Crickett) Smith was born 15 August 1883 in Nashville and is believed to have died *c*1947 in New York.

6 Robert Goffin, *Aux frontières du jazz* (Paris: Éditions du Sagittaire, 1932), 33.

7 The long history of the Musical Spillers is detailed in Rainer E. Lotz, *Black People*, 125-149; an earlier version of this chapter appears in *Storyville*, no. 152 (December 1992), 60-70.

8 According to his passport (cited in Rye and Brooks, "Visiting Firemen 16: Dan Kildare," 37), Joseph T. Meyers was born 29 September 1888 in Petersburg, Virginia.

9 Advertisement, *Le Petit Parisien*, 4 July 1919, 3.

10 Charles Méré, "Les Premières," *Excelsior*, 7 June 1919, 4. Translated by the author.

11 Quoted in Goddard, *Jazz away from Home*, 284.

12 André Ekyan, Stéphane Grappelly, Alain Romans and Ray Ventura, "Les débuts du jazz en France," *Jazz Hot*, no. 248 (March 1969), 38. Translated by the author.

13 Jean Cocteau, "Carte Blanche (19): Jazz-Band," *Paris-Midi*, 4 August 1919, 3. Translated by the author.

14 Modris Eksteins, *Rites of Spring: The Great War and the Birth of the Modern Age* (Toronto: Lester & Orpen Dennys, 1998), 16.

15 Cocteau, "Carte Blanche (19): Jazz-Band," 3.

16 Jacques Floronge, "Coulisses: Des Tziganes aux jazz-band," *Paris-Midi*, 31 July 1919, 2. Translated by the author.

17 "Still Jazzing" [letter from James Shaw], Chicago *Defender*, 10 April 1920, 8.

18 The boulevard de la Seine in Brussels is now the boulevard Émile Jacqmain.

19 Jacques Floronge, "Cure musicale," *Paris-Midi*, 15 November 1920, 2. Translated by the author.

20 Ch. M. [probably Charles Méré], "Les Premières," *Excelsior*, 7 October 1920, 4. Translated by the author.

21 "Boys' camp opened near Aix-les-Bains," New York *Herald*, 26 July 1922, 5.

22 A detailed discography prepared by Robert Pernet, in Pernet and Rye, "Visiting Firemen 18: Louis Mitchell," 246-248, suggests that Adolf Crawford, Edmund Thornton Jenkins, Fred Coxito and Sidney Bechet may have variously taken the second saxophone chair. It also identifies the violinist as Ralph (Shrimp) Jones and the trombonist as, possibly, Léo Vauchant, a young French musician who befriended — or was befriended by — members of Mitchell's Jazz Kings.

## PARIS, FEBRUARY 13, 1920

1 Advertisement, *Paris-Midi*, 5 July 1919, 2.

2 Advertisement, *Excelsior*, 11 February 1920, 5.

3 Elliot Carpenter was born 28 December 1894 in Philadelphia, according to the passenger list for the *S.S. Lafayette*, which took him back to New York in July 1923. He died 12 February 1982 in Los Angeles.

4 James Shaw of Mitchell's Jazz Kings noted Seth Weeks' presence at the Apollo with Carpenter et al., in "Still Jazzing," 8. Opal Cooper later identified Weeks as the band's leader in an interview with Bertrand Demeusy ("Musical career of Opal Cooper," *Record Research*, no. 90, May 1968, 3). However, in 1976, Elliot Carpenter told Chris Goddard (*Jazz away from Home*, 299) about an overture that he received from a London promoter, who asked about the band's contractual arrangements in Paris. "'Contract,' [Carpenter] said. 'We don't have no contract. Mr. Wickes [sic] over in New York, he's probably got the contract.'"

5 "American Legion gives members dance to-night," New York *Herald*, 23 Feb 1920, 2.

6 "American Legion gives jazz night to its members," New York *Herald*, 18 February 1920, 2.

7 Columbus Bragg, "On and off The Stroll," Chicago *Defender*, 28 March 1914, 6.

8 Advertisement, *Excelsior*, 25 April 1920, 5.

9 The members of Seth Weeks' band then at the Casino in Trouville were identified as "Mr. and Mrs. James [Adolf] Crawford, saxophones, and Herrera of New York, piano and flute; Grundy, drums; [Albert] Smith, banjo, and Fernandez, violin" in "News from abroad," Chicago *Defender*, 22 October 1921, 6.

10 "At Morgan's," New York *Herald*, 15 May 1920, 2.

11 Goddard, *Jazz away from Home*, 300.

12 "Merry Melody Makers create rage with Rag-time at Rector's," *The Dancing World*, September 1920, 12.

13 The other members of the Southern Rag-A-Jazz Band were Edward Cressell (violin), Gayle Grubb (piano), Donville Fairchild (banjo), and A.H. Schmidt (drums), as listed in "Musical musings," *The Billboard*, 8 Jul 1922, 40, which noted that the band had returned by then to Lincoln, Nebraska. Cressell, Grubb and Peterson were again in England toward the end of 1922 with trumpeter Robert LeRoy, trombonist Leo Daugherty and drummer Floyd Schultz; the circumstances of this second trip remain unknown. LeRoy worked in France with Billy Arnold later in the 1920s.

14 Goddard, *Jazz away from Home*, 300.

15 Wilson worked as a drummer in Paris from 1920 to 1926. Some later accounts incorrectly identify him as the leader of the Red Devils. See, for example, Dorothy Kilgallen, "Here Comes Mr. Dooley," *Collier's*, 12 February 1944, 68.

16 Advertisement, *Excelsior*, 1 June 1923, 2.

17 Aljean Harmetz, *Round up the Usual Suspects: The Making of Casablanca — Bogart, Bergman and World War II* (New York: Hyperion, 1992), 128.

## QUEBEC CITY, AUGUST 30, 1920

1 "Bands and orchestras of Shreveport, La.," Indianapolis *Freeman*, 15 August 1914, 5.

2 *Popular Songs of Today Magazine*, September 1928, 8; see also John Gilmore, *Who's Who of Jazz in Montreal: Ragtime to 1970* (Montreal: Véhicule Press, 1989), 282.

3 Sylvester Russell, "Gossip of the stage," Indianapolis *Freeman*, 25 August 1917, 5.

4 According to advertisements in the Montreal *Star*, a Famous Chicago Jazz Band appeared at Montreal's Palais de danse between mid-December 1918 and mid-January 1919.

5 The FCNO's programs were often advertised in Quebec City newspapers – eg, *Le Soleil*, 22 October 1921, 17, which promised *Get Hot* and *Spread Your [sic] Stuff*, as well as *Fantaisie Hongroise*, *My Daddy* and the waltz *Silver Strand*. Ads for other weeks promised no jazz-related material at all.

6 Advertisement, *La Presse*, 2 September 1922, 12.

7 "Le radio de La Presse," *La Presse*, 14 June 1923, 8.

8 The Famous Chicago Novelty Orchestra appeared at Luna Park in Hull, Quebec, during the summer of 1926 (advertisement, Ottawa *Citizen*, 21 May 1926, 16). Millard Thomas's next known engagement was at the Royal Knickerbocker in New York with his "syncosymphonists" in October 1929 ("Here and there," *Variety*, 2 October 1929, 89).

9 John Gilmore, *Swinging in Paradise: The Story of Jazz in Montreal* (Montreal: Véhicule Press, 1988), 29.

10 *The International Musician*, September 1920, 14, notes that J. White, R. Jackson, Wm. E. Hutt, C.E. Miller and two others had deposited their American Federation of Musicians transfers with Montreal local 406.

11 "Montreal Canada," Indianapolis *Freeman*, 27 November 1920, 2. The other members of the band were cornetist Eugene Hutt and saxophonist Elmer Smith. "Collerette" may have been a misprint for "Colored."

12 A certificate in the Alex Robertson Collection, Concordia University Archives, Montreal, notes the death 15 June 1933 of a James White, age 43. It is signed by White's wife, Rose Gushen, and by Vera Teasly; an African-American musician named Wiley Teasley (spelled with the second "e") was active in Montreal at this time.

13 Sylvester Russell, "Gossip of the stage," Indianapolis *Freeman*, 25 September 1915, 5.

14 Sylvester Russell, "Gossip of the stage," Indianapolis *Freeman*, 26 February 1916, 5.

15 Rainer Lotz, "Johnny Dixon — Trumpet," *Storyville*, no. 99 (February-March 1982), 102-111; Murray Pilcer's band appeared at the Folies-Bergère in the spring of 1918. Dixon was back in Paris by 1926 and worked there, in Berlin and elsewhere on the Continent until 1937, when he returned to the United States.

16 As reported in *The International Musician*, March 1921, 22, Mole, Napoleon and Signorelli, as well as trumpeter Nat Natoli and clarinetist Johnny Costello, deposited transfers with Montreal local 406 of the American Federation of Musicians.

## VANCOUVER, DECEMBER 16-17, 1920

1 As registered in the dues ledgers of the Vancouver Musicians' Association, local 145 of the American Federation of Musicians. See also *The International Musician*, February 1921, 18.

2 "A note or two," Chicago *Defender*, 1 January 1921, 11.

3 Ferdinand (Jelly Roll) Morton's date of birth in New Orleans is generally given as 20 October 1890; he died 10 July 1941 in Los Angeles.

4 Alan Lomax, *Mister Jelly Roll: The Fortunes of Jelly Roll Morton, New Orleans Creole and "Inventor of Jazz"* (Berkeley, Calif.: University of California Press, 1973), 170.

5 Padio is spelled Paddio, Patio and Paddeo in other sources, where his given name is variously Harold and Albert.

6 Lomax, *Mister Jelly Roll*, 170.

7 Ibid., 170.

8 References to Holden as the bandleader at the Patricia Cafe include items as early as "Gossip of the stage," Indianapolis *Freeman*, 23 August 1919, 5, and as late as "Herbert's Minstrels," Chicago *Defender*, 2 July 1921, 9.

9 "A note from Vancouver," Indianapolis *Freeman*, 27 December 1919, 5.

10 Oscar Holden was born in 1887 in Nashville and died in 1969 in Seattle. See Paul de Barros, *Jackson Street After Hours: The Roots of Jazz in Seattle* (Seattle: Sasquatch Books, 1993), 13-15.

11 "Brick-Top Smith," Chicago *Defender*, 14 February 1920, 8.

12 John Szwed, *So What: The Life of Miles Davis* (New York: Simon & Schuster, 2002), 16.

13 Lomax, *Mister Jelly Roll*, 170.

14 *The International Musician*, March 1921, 12, reported that Henry Starr and W.H. Henderson had deposited transfers with local 145; Henderson's presence in Vancouver during the summer of 1921 with his "Maple Leaf" orchestra was noted in "Herbert's Minstrels," 9.

15 "Crowder's Letter," Chicago *Defender*, 20 August 1927, 8; see also Miller, *Such Melodious Racket*, 131-132.

## KRISTIANIA, NORWAY, JANUARY 25, 1921

1 Briggs was born 9 April 1899 in St. George's, Grenada, and died 15 July 1991 in Chantilly, France. As perpetuated by Briggs himself, there has been considerable confusion over his birthplace, which has also been cited as St. George's, Canada, and as Charleston, South Carolina. However, the passenger list for the

*S.S. Maraval*, which arrived in New York from St. George, Grenada, on November 14, 1917 (see www.ellisisland.org), includes a James Arthur Briggs, who is described as a black musician and identified as 18 years and 6 months in age, which corresponds exactly with the aforementioned birth date. His place of birth is given as St. George's, Grenada, which is also consistent with the fact that Briggs travelled to Europe on a British passport as a member of the Southern Syncopated Orchestra; Grenada at the time was a British colony.

2 Briggs identified Russell, Patrick, Clapham and Hines as his band mates at the Palais de danse in an oral history taken by James Lincoln Collier in 1982 as part of Jazz Oral History Project of the National Endowment for the Arts and held at The Rutgers Institute of Jazz Studies in Newark, N.J.

3 The name Jean Paul Clinton appears in Bjørn Stendahl, *Jazz, Hot & Swing: Jazz i Norge 1920-1940* (Oslo: Norsk Jazzarkiv, 1987), 25. Bert Salnave, who was working in London at the time, refers to a clarinetist in a band there with George Hines as Roger Jean Paul. See Bertrand Demeusy, "The Bertin Depestre Salnave Musical Story," *Storyville*, no. 78 (August 1978), 215.

3 Excerpts from reports in *Aftenposten, Ørebladet, Nationen, Verdens Gang* and *Dagbladet* are included in Stendahl, *Hot & Swing*, 25-27.

4 In addition to Harris and Garrett the Premier Syncopated Five comprised saxophonist Albert Turner, violinist Alfred Tabor and drummer Jack Dixon. Ibid., 28.

5 "Can't we talk it over?" [Robert Pernet letter], *Storyville*, no. 106 (April-May 1983), 150.

6 "No early curfew at Basque resort," New York *Herald*, 4 September 1921, 5.

7 Collier, Jazz Oral History Project.

8 Goddard, *Jazz away From Home*, 284.

9 An ad in the New York *Herald*, 3 November 1922, 3, announced the opening of Mistinguett with Earl Leslie and "his famous jazz band" at the Alhambra in Paris; an item in the Chicago *Defender* ("Letters," 9 December 1922, 8), noted that "Renard and Pollard's" band had gone with Leslie into the Alhambra. Renard was likely the French trumpeter Alex Renard. The Alhambra engagement continued until 30 November 1922.

10 Robert Goffin, *Jazz: From the Congo to the Metropolitan* (New York: Da Capo Press, 1975), 76.

11 Robert Pernet, "Some notes on Arthur Briggs," *Storyville*, no. 84 (August 1979), 205-209, identifies Briggs' musicians and outlines his movements in this period. See also Demeusy, "The Bertin Depestre Salnave Musical Story," 207-219.

12 See Lester Walton, "Sang and played his way through Paris art course," Pittsburgh *Courier*, 21 April 1928, second section, 3.

13 Goddard, *Jazz away From Home*, 287.

14 Ibid., 293-294.

## SAN DIEGO, OCTOBER 7, 1921

1 Reproduced in Phil Pastras, *Dead Man Blues: Jelly Roll Morton Way out West* (Berkeley, Calif.: University of California Press, 2001), 113.

2 Lomax, *Mister Jelly Roll*, 173. Morton also composed *The Pearls* for "a pretty little waitress" at the Kansas City Bar.

3 John Bentley, "Sonny Clay: A veritable giant (Part 1)," *Jazz Report*, November-December 1962, 8.

4 "Jelly Roll," Chicago *Defender*, 12 November 1921, 7.

5 Ragtime Billy Tucker, "Coast dope," Chicago *Defender*, 11 February 1922, 8.

6 Ragtime Billy Tucker, "Coast dope," Chicago *Defender*, 10 June 1922, 8.

7 Ragtime Billy Tucker, "Coast dope," Chicago *Defender*, 24 June 1922, 8.

8 Other African-American musicians in Sylvester Stewart's employ between 1921 and 1925, as variously identified by Ragtime Billy Tucker in the Chicago *Defender*, included cornetists Audley Smith and Oscar Hurst, trombonist Baron Morehead, saxophonist and flutist Gerald Wells, pianists Billy Bentley, Charles Jackson and Homer Jones, and drummers Ernest Powell and Jesse Stansell. Tucker himself played drums with Hurst and Frank Shiver at the Chicago Bar in 1924.

9 Buddy Brown, "Coast dope," Chicago *Defender*, 24 September 1927, 8.

## PARIS, OCTOBER 14, 1921

1 Mazie Mullins was born c1888, possibly in Denver. She worked early in her career as Mazie Mullins Moore in California, before travelling east — to Chicago in 1911 and New York in 1912 — with Frank Withers, whom she eventually married. See "Mullins and Withers," Indianapolis *Freeman*, 12 April 1912, 4.

2 H. Lawrence Freeman, "A review of two leading New York orchestras — the Lafayette and New Lincoln," Indianapolis *Freeman*, 20 January 1917, 4.

3 "Paris court's fine of ex-Jazz King reveals tragi-comedy of Montmartre," New York *Herald*, 22 October 1922, 1. See also "Montmartre scene of dramatic raid on gambling club," New York *Herald*, 1 May 1922, 6.

4 Frank A. Dennie, "News from abroad," Chicago *Defender*, 22 October 1921, 6.

5 Philippe Soupault, *Terpsichore*, ed. Émile Hazan for *Les Neuf Muses*, no. 1 (Paris 1928); republished in *Jazz Magazine*, no. 325, (January 1984) 56. Translated by the author.

6 "Mazie Mullen [sic] dead," New York *Age*, 5 November 1921, 6; "Mazie dead," Chicago *Defender*, 12 November 1921, 7.

7 New York *Herald*, 22 October 1922, 1.

## PARIS, DECEMBER 6, 1921

1 Darius Milhaud, *Notes without Music*, translated by Donald Evans (London: Dobson, 1952), 103.

2 Morten Clausen, "Thompson's Jazz Band in Copenhagen 1923-1925: The story of the first black jazz band in Denmark," *Storyville 1998-9*, 139.

3 Milhaud, *Notes without Music*, 103-104.

4 Darius Milhaud, "Development of the Jazz Band, and North American Negro Music," translated by Alice Mattullath, *The Metronome*, 15 December 1925, 15. This essay was originally published as "Jazz-Band et instruments mécaniques — Les resources nouvelles de la musique," *Esprit nouveau* (July 1924); it was reprinted in Denis-Constant Martin and Olivier Roueff, eds, *La France du Jazz: Musique, modernité et identité dans la première moitié de XXe siècle* (Marseille: Édition Parenthèses, 2002), 178-181.

5 Milhaud, *Notes without Music*, 111.

6 "Billy Arnold now famous in France," *Variety*, 20 August 1924, 36.

7 A photo taken of the band sans instruments in Cannes, published in the New York *Herald*, 10 March 1923, 5, identifies the musicians as the Billy and Henry Arnold, Victor Abbs, Charles Kleiner, Chris Lee and Billy Trittle.

8 Advertisement, New York *Herald*, 16 May 1925, 5.

9 Advertisement, New York *Herald*, 20 May 1927, 12.

## CAIRO, JANUARY 1, 1922

1 Billy Brooks and George Duncan, "A letter from Egypt," Chicago *Defender*, 11 March 1922, 7.

2 Billy Brooks and George Duncan, "A letter from Egypt," Chicago *Defender*, 16 July 1921, 6.

3 "Cairo animated in social world," New York *Herald*, 9 January 1921, 5.

4 Brooks and Duncan, "A letter from Egypt," 11 March 1922, 7.

5 Both Shepheard's and the Semiramis Hotel were later destroyed and and still later rebuilt.

6 Billy Brooks and George Duncan, "A letter from Egypt," Chicago *Defender*, 15 July 1922, 7.

7 Brooks and Duncan, "A letter from Egypt," 11 March 1922, 7; the "palace" may have been the Bijou, to which they refer in a letter to the *Defender*, 10 May 1924, section 2, 1.

8 Brooks and Duncan, "A letter from Egypt," 15 July 1922.

9 Billy Brooks and George Duncan, "A letter from Egypt," Chicago *Defender*, 18 March 1922, 7.

10 "Many tourists arrive in Cairo," New York *Herald*, 4 December 1923, 5.

11 Billy Brooks and George Duncan, "A letter from Cairo, Egypt," Chicago *Defender*, 13 September 1924, section 2, 1. Written

between 15 December 1923 and 9 January 1924, the letter was serialized weekly by the *Defender* from 10 May 1924 and 13 September 1924.

12 Billy Brooks, "Billy's pal dead," Chicago *Defender*, 26 July 1924, 7.

13 "Roger Richard talks to.... Albert Nicholas," *Storyville*, no. 57 (February 1975), 91.

## MIAMI, JANUARY 25, 1922

1 "6 lured away to flogging party," Miami *Herald*, 25 January 1922, 1.

2 "White musicians were cause of Miami flogging," Chicago *Defender*, 4 February 1922, [page number missing on microfilmed copy].

3 Ibid.

4 "Flogged Negroes hasten departure," Miami *Herald*, 26 January 1922, 8.

5 Leon Cornick, "Florida mob's atrocities put 'Huns' to shame," Chicago *Defender*, 25 February 1922, part two, 3.

## BUENOS AIRES, JUNE 7, 1923

1 Wyer is identified as being 29 years of age on the passenger list of the *S.S. Northland*, which took members of the Southern Syncopated Orchestra to Liverpool in June 1919. See Rye, "Visiting Firemen 15: The Southern Syncopated Orchestra (Part 2)," 140.

2 Lomax, *Mr. Jelly Roll*, 131.

3 Ibid., 129.

4 E-mail from Kathleen Wyer Lane, New York, 6 March 2002.

5 Robert Burns de Reeau, "London letter," Chicago Defender, 11 June 1921, 7.

6 In interviews done in Buenos Aires in 1978 and 1987, Stretton offered differing accounts of the Syncopated Six's personnel on record. Paul Wyer, Sadie Crawford and George Clapham were consistent to both, but Stretton identified John Forrester the first time and Jacob Patrick the second as his trombonist and in the latter interview also added "Arthur" [Adolf] Crawford to the band and noted that Crickett Smith played trumpet on some of the tunes, Bobby Jones on the rest. Stretton did not identify the band's banjo player. (Letter from Juan Carlos Lopez, Buenos Aires, 20 May 2002; e-mail from Dr. Rainer Lotz, Bonn, 16 April 2004.)

7 "Musician says Argentina is land of opportunities," Chicago *Defender*, 30 August 1930, 5.

8 "Paul Wyer," Chicago *Defender*, 16 June 1923, 7.

9 Advertisement, Buenos Aires *Standard*, 10 June 1923, 9.

10 H.G., "Round the mulberry bush," Buenos Aires *Herald*, 24 June 1923, 3.

11 "Montevideo letter," Buenos Aires *Herald*, 25 June 1923, 9.

12 The troupe's presence at the Lyric Theatre in Rio is noted in *O Estado de Sao Paulo*, 30 August 1923, 2.

13 E-mail from Kathleen Wyer Lane, 6 March 2002.

14 Garvin Bushell, *Jazz from the Beginning* (New York: Da Capo Press 1998), 70.


## COPENHAGEN, DECEMBER 18, 1923

1 The details of E.E. Thompson's visits to Copenhagen have been drawn from Morten Clausen's "Thompson's jazz band in Copenhagen 1923-1925: The story of the first black jazz band in Denmark," *Storyville 1998-9*, 136-155.

2 Ibid., 138, 140.

3 Translated from *B.T.*, 3 February 1924, and quoted in Clausen, 141.

4 Excerpts of articles from *Folkets Avis* appear in Clausen, 145-149.

5 Translated from *Københaven*, 1 March 1924, and quoted in Clausen, 144.

6 Letter, Randall Lockhart to Jeffrey P. Green, quoted in Green's *Edmund Thornton Jenkins: The life and times of an American Black Composer, 1894-1926* (Westport, Conn. Greenwood Press, 1982), 164.

7 "Jazz player slain in Paris, wife held," New York *Herald*, 27 February 1926, 3. The operetta *L'École de Gigolos* was performed at the Théâtre Albert-1er in Paris in March 1928.

8 Green, Edmund Thornton Jenkins, 158.

9 Quoted in Goddard, *Jazz away from Home*, 26.

10 According to Clausen, "Thompson's Jazz Band in Copenhagen 1923-1925," 137 and 154, Egbert E. Thompson was born 27 January 1883 in Sierra Leone, and died 22 or 23 August 1927 in Paris.

11 Clausen, "Thompson's jazz band," 154; Theodore Wolfram, "Paris," *The Billboard*, 19 October 1929, 44.

12 Percival Outram, "Activities among union musicians," New York *Age*, 10 August 1929, 7.


## PARIS, FEBRUARY 9, 1924

1 "Kiley renames Volstead Café," New York *Herald*, 11 February 1924, 3.

2 Bricktop, with James Haskins, *Bricktop* (New York: Atheneum, 1983), 85.

3 Ibid., 85.

4 Advertisement, New York *Herald*, 1 October 1924, 5. Gilmore was still at the Grand Duc in December 1925; see "Leeds gets drum, gives house, lot," New York *Herald*, 17 December 1925, 4.

5 Ada Smith was born 14 August 1894 in Alderson, West Virginia (see Eileen Southern, *Biographical Dictionary of Afro-American*

and African Musicians: Westport, Conn., 1982, 342) and died 31 January 1984 in New York (see "Obituaries," *Variety*, 8 Feb 1984, 192).

6 Jolo., "One night in Paris," *Variety*, 22 October 1924, 2.

7 Advertisement, New York *Herald*, 3 Jan 1925, 5.

8 "Test case to be brought in Paris after Montmartre 'color-line' row," New York *Herald*, 8 August 1923, 1; "Color-line café loses license," New York *Herald*, 10 August 1923, 1; "Black princes barred; French dance hall is closed by police," New York *Age*, 22 September 1923, 1; "Condemn assault on colored prince," New York *Herald*, 19 October 1923, 5.

9 Bricktop, *Bricktop*, 127.

10 "Shooting at us" [Eugene Bullard letter], Chicago *Defender*, National edition, 4 April 1925, 7

11 "'Florences' [sic] in Paris popular with society," Baltimore *Afro-American*, 18 July 1925, 5.

12 According to the passenger list for the *S.S. Mauretania*, which took Florence and Palmer Jones back to New York in 1927, she was born 16 December 1892 in Bridgeport, Connecticut, and he was born 28 September 1888 in Mobile, Alabama. He died 29 August 1928 in Paris; see Dave Peyton, "The musical bunch," Chicago *Defender*, 15 September 1928, 10.

13 Other members of the International Five during the 1920s, as noted in contemporary sources, included saxophonists Edmund T. Jenkins, Roscoe Burnett and Sidney Bechet, trombonist Earl Granstaff, trumpeters Arthur Briggs and Henry Walton, and pianists Charles Lewis and Irving (Kid Sneeze) Williams. See, for example, advertisement, New York *Herald*, 3 Jul 1924, 5.

14 Bertrand Demeusy, "Musical career of Opal Cooper," *Record Research*, no. 90 (May 1968), 3-4.

15 Other members of the Crackerjacks during the 1920s, as mentioned in contemporary sources, included trombonist Earl Granstaff, bassist Walter Kildare and saxophonists Adolf Crawford and Rudolph Dunbar. See, for example, "Cuban jazz band," Baltimore *Afro-American*, 19 October 1929, 9.

16 "Genuine American jazz on air here," New York *Herald*, 2 December 1927, 3.

17 Members of the Palm Beach Five/Seven at various points in its three-year history, as documented by contemporary sources, included pianists Leon Crutcher, Leslie Hutchinson and Al Hughes, violinist Louis Vaughan Jones, saxophonists James Shaw and Rollin Smith, the saxophonist and banjo player Greeley Franklin, trombonist Earl Granstaff, a cornetist named Green, bassist Brom Desverney and drummers George Evans and Creighton Thompson. Hutchinson, Smith, Shaw, Green, Franklin, Desverney and Thompson appeared in Constantinople. See, for example, "Paris letter," Chicago *Defender*, 7 June 1924, 7, and "Doings in Gay Paree," Chicago *Defender*, National edition, 15 January 1927, 7.

18 Charlotte Breese, *Hutch* (London: Bloomsbury Publishing, 1999), 30-31.

19 "Sultan of jazz dies in poverty," New York *Amsterdam News*, 25 July 1928, 7.

20 "Colored band refused," *Variety*, 10 November 1926, 2.

## PARIS, MAY 10, 1924

1 "Jazz teams asks to enter league," New York *Herald*, 23 March 1924, 8.

2 "Baseball season opens here to-day," New York *Herald*, 10 May 1924, 6. Rayford Logan was in the last year of a five-year exile in Paris, where he was centrally involved in the Pan-African movement; he later wrote *The Negro in American Life and Thought* and other books.

3 "American Students defeat Clef Club," New York *Herald*, 11 May 1924, 8.

4 "Some European news," *The Billboard*, 20 June 1925, 49.

## LONDON, APRIL 13, 1925

1 This date is taken from "Hits in cabaret," *Variety*, 15 April 1925, 3, and confirmed by an advertisement in the London *Times*, 13 April 1925, 8. Many sources erroneously place the Mound City Blue Blowers' arrival in London in 1924. Ads in the *Times* for the band's appearances at the Piccadilly continue until 6 June 1925.

2 Personnel of Art Hickman's New York London Five were Harry Grancey (trumpet), Arthur Pitman (trombone), Jack Howard (saxophone), George Fishberg (piano) and George Klein (drums); see Rust, *Jazz Records*, 748.

3 Bernard Tipping, "Looking back," *Rhythm*, October 1930, 48; Tipping refers to Grancey as Clarence, Pitman as Keith and George Klein as George Clynes.

4 Ibid., 47.

5 "Jazzers' importation gets into Parliament," *Variety*, 24 November 1922, 2.

6 Howard Rye, "Visiting Firemen 13: 'The Plantation Revues,'" *Storyville*, no. 133 (March 1988), 4-15.

7 "Paul Specht gives details of treatment by English," *Variety*, 6 August 1924, 37. See also Giuseppe Barazetta, "Frank Guarante: a forgotten pioneer," *Jazz Monthly*, vol, 12, no. 10 (December 1966), 4.

8 "Paul Specht and his musicians finally allowed to land," *Variety*, 23 July 1924, 2. Personnel of the Carolina Club Orchestra were Hal Kemp (tenor saxophone, clarinet), Charles (Red) Honeycutt and Alex (Monk) Buie (trumpets), William (Buck) Weaver (trombone), Ben Williams and Joe Gillespie (saxophones), James (Slatz) Randall (piano), William Waugh or Vaught (banjo) Billy Wolfe (tuba) and Jimmy Brooks (drums). According to www.ellisisland.org (from which several of the musicians' full names here have been drawn), the band left England 23 August 1924 on the *S.S. Berengaria*.

9 Richard M. Sudhalter, Philip R. Evans, with William Dean Myatt, *Bix: Man and Legend* (New York: Schirmer Books, 1974), 56-7.

10 "Musical musings," *The Billboard*, 6 January 1923, 45.

11 Tracy Keith Mumma was born 16 April 1899 in Moline, Illinois, and died 1 January 1979 in Clearmont, Wyoming. Source: Richard L. Mumma (son).

12 Advertisement, *Excelsior*, 26 March 1924, 4.

13 Contract between George Webb and Tracy Mumma, courtesy Richard L. Mumma.

14 "Local musicians leave tomorrow to play in Paris," unsourced newspaper clipping, courtesy Richard L. Mumma.

15 Advertisement, New York *Herald*, 2 November 1924, 5.

16 Goddard, *Jazz away from Home*, 73.

17 William McKenzie was born 14 October 1899 in St. Louis, and died 7 February 1948 in New York.

18 Eddie Lang was born Salvatore Massaro, 25 October 1902, in Philadelphia, and died 26 March 1933 in New York.

19 Lait., "New acts this week," *Variety*, 20 August 1924, 40.

20 Jack Bland, "As I knew Eddie Lang," *Selections from the Gutter: Jazz Portraits from 'The Jazz Record,'* Art Hodes and Chadwick Hansen, eds (Berkeley, Calif.: University of California Press, 1977), 146.

21 "Hits in cabaret," *Variety*, 15 April 1925, 3.

22 Jolo., "Piccadilly Cabaret," *Variety*, 29 April 1925, 42.

## BERLIN, MAY 25, 1925

1 This story is told by both Wooding and Garvin Bushell; see, for example, Samuel Wooding, "Eight years abroad with a jazz band," *The Etude*, April 1939, 233, and Bushell, *Jazz from the Beginning*, 55.

2 O.M. Seibt, "Berlin News Letter," *The Billboard*, 30 May 1925, 46.

3 "From London Town," *The Billboard*, 22 March 1924, 58.

4 Bricktop, *Bricktop*, 134.

5 "Musical Musings," *The Billboard*, 18 April 1925, 39; "Berlin now dancing nightly; ban lifted," *Variety*, 6 May 1925, 50.

6 Goffin, *Jazz: From the Congo to the Metropolitan*, 80-81. In addition to Harl Smith, members of the Lido-Venice Orchestra have been identified as violinist, saxophonist and guitarist Henry Nathan, cornetist Joe Rose, saxophonist and clarinetist Freddy Morrow, trombonist Barney Russell, pianist William Haid and banjo player John Evert Davidson. See Rainer E. Lotz, "Alex Hyde's Hot Dance Recordings for Deutsche Grammophon Gesellschaft," *Storyville*, no. 74 (December 1977), 55-57.

7 "Hyde's band in London," *Variety*, 17 January 1924, 2; O.M. Seibt, "Berlin News Letter," *The Billboard*, 10 May 1924, 46; 7 June 1924, 37.

8 "Sailings," *The Billboard*, 22 November 1924, 9; O.M. Seibt, "Berlin News Letter," *The Billboard*, 30 May 1925, 46.

9 Lotz, "Alex Hyde," 50-66; by some accounts, the trombonist on at least some of these final recordings was not Herb Flemming but Earl Granstaff.

10 Art Napoleon, "A pioneer looks back: Sam Wooding 1967," *Storyville*, no. 9 (February 1967), 3.

11 Thomas Ladnier was born 28 May 1900 in Florenceville, Louisiana, and died 4 June 1939 in New York.

12 The passenger list is reproduced in Berhard H. Behncke, "Sam Wooding and the Chocolate Kiddies at the Thalia-Theater in Hamburg 28 July, 1925 to 24 August, 1925," *Storyville* no. 60 (August 1975), 215. In addition to Howe, Warren, Sedric and Herb Flemming, the Wooding orchestra comprised saxophonists Garvin Bushell and Willie Lewis, trumpeters Maceo Edwards, Tommy Ladnier and Bobby Martin and banjo player John Mitchell.

13 As remembered by Herb Flemming; see E. Biagioni, *Herb Flemming: A jazz pioneer around the world* (Alphen aan de Rijn, Holland, undated), 21.

14 "Colored show over Europe," *Variety*, 19 August 1925, 3.

## SHANGHAI, MAY 30, 1925

1 This date is recorded in "From Shanghai, China" [Andrew F. Rosemond letter], Chicago *Defender*, 3 October 1925, 8.

2 William Oscar Hegamin was born 1 April 1894 in Camden, New Jersey, and died 4 March 1960 in Pasadena, California. Sources: Robert Hegamin (son) and California Death Index (http://vitals.rootsweb/ca/death/search.cgi).

3 Sylvester Russell, "Chicago weekly review," Indianapolis *Freeman*, 23 May 1914, 5.

4 J.A. Jackson, "Band to Manila," *The Billboard*, 4 August 1923, 82.

5 "An interesting letter from Shanghai," *The Metronome*, vol. 38, no. 3 (March 1922), 89.

6 "Cafe Parisien Orchestra, Shanghai, China," *The Metronome*, vol. 35, no. 12 (December 1919), 75; "Kerrey's jazz band in China," *The Metronome*, vol. 36, no. 1 (January 1920), 69.

7 Advertisement, Shanghai *North-China Daily News*, 24 November 1923, 15; "Harry Kerrey's orchestra at New Maxim's Cafe, Shanghai, China," *The Metronome*, vol. 40, no. 1 (January 1924), 88.

8 "China," *Variety*, 19 March 1920, 17.

9 Henry A. Stonor, "They played at Raffles," *Storyville*, no. 42 (August 1972), 223. Lequime recorded in 1926 for HMV in Calcutta and later that year appeared at Raffles Hotel in Singapore.

10 "To the Orient" [William O. Hegamin letter], Chicago *Defender*, 6 October 1923, 6.

11 Sid Colin and Tony Staveacre, *Al Bowlly* (London: Elm Tree Books, 1979), 6. See also Stonor, "They played at Raffles," 219.

12 "In Manila" [William O. Hegamin letter], Chicago *Defender*, 22 December 1923, 6.

13 Advertisement, Manila *Times*, 23 August 1923, 1.

14 "Jazz babies meet Rotarians," Manila *Times*, 23 August 1923, 2.

15 "Combine concert and dance," *The Billboard*, 29 July 1922, 64; "M'Kinney's Syncos," Chicago *Defender*, 5 September 1925, 8.

16 Mark A. Hanna, "Nightlife of the world: Shanghai," *Variety*, 11 November 1925, 5.

17 Dave Peyton, "The musical bunch," Chicago *Defender*, 2 January 1926, 7; "Widow returns to America with ashes of musician," Chicago *Defender*, 13 February 1926, 8.

18 Rosemond, "From Shanghai, China," 8.

19 Contract in the possession of Robert Hegamin (son of William O. Hegamin).

20 "Back from China," New York *Amsterdam News*, 17 August 1927, 11.

## PARIS, OCTOBER 2, 1925

1 Josephine Baker was born 3 June 1906 in East St. Louis and died 12 April 1975 in Paris; see Southern, *Biographical Dictionary of Afro-American and African Musicians*, 24.

2 R. Joviet, "The Theatre," New York *Herald*, 4 October 1925, 5.

3 Hopkins, Bechet and Goodwin aside, the members of the Charleston Jazz Band were saxophonist Joe Hayman, trombonist Daniel Doy, drummer Percy Johnson and possibly tuba player Ernie (Bass) Hill.

4 Henry Goodwin, "Music is my business," Hodes and Hansen, eds., *Selections from the Gutter*, 218.

## MOSCOW, FEBRUARY 22, 1926

1 Norris Smith, "Dear old Lunnon," Chicago *Defender*, 2 January 1920, 7.

2 Bullard, "Shooting at us," Chicago *Defender*, National edition, 4 April 1924, 7, identifies the members of Crickett's Jazz Kings in March 1925 as Smith, Coxito, Parrish, Peyton, Withers, Walter Kildare and Joe Meyers.

3 "Jazz band in Russia," Baltimore *Afro-American*, 20 February 1926, 6.

4 *Pravda*, 18 April 1928, 2.

5 "Jazz for the Soviets," *The Billboard*, 27 February 1926, 22.

6 Advertisement, *Izvestiia*, 21 February 1926, 7.

7 Advertisement, *Izvestiia*, 26 March 1926, 6.

8 Advertisement, *Izvestiia*, 12 March 1926, 6.

9 Advertisement, *Izvestiia*, 18 March 1926, 6.

10 As translated and quoted in S. Frederick Starr, *Red & Hot: The Fate of Jazz in the Soviet Union* (New York: Limelight Editions, 1983), 63-64.

11 Wooding's itinerary from 1925 through 1927 is listed in Horst J.P. Bergmeier, "Sam Wooding recapitulated," *Storyville*, no. 74 (December 1977), 45.

12 Wooding, "Eight years abroad with a jazz band," 234.

13 Ibid., 234.

14 Advertisement, *Izvestiia*, 16 March 1926, 6.

15 "Theatre-Music-Cinema," *Izvestiia*, 27 March 1926, 5. Translated by Kat Tancock.

16 "Negro operetta tour," *Pravda*, 20 March 1926, 6. Translated by Kat Tancock.

17 Wooding, "Eight years abroad with a jazz band," 234.

18 Art Napoleon, "A pioneer looks back: part 2," *Storyville*, no. 10 (April 1967), 7.

19 Wooding, "Eight years abroad with a jazz band," 234.

20 Bushell, *Jazz from the Beginning*, 65-66.

21 E. Biagioni, *Herb Flemming*, 29.

22 Bushell, *Jazz from the Beginning*, 66.

23 John Chilton, *Sidney Bechet*, 77.

24 The Street-Wolf of Paris, "Montmartre," Chicago *Defender*, National edition, 3 February 1934, 10.

## SHANGHAI, OCTOBER 1, 1926

1 Melvin Jerome (Jack) Carter was born c1900 in Nashville and died 28 August 1953 in Oak Bluffs, Massachusetts; see "Musician Jack Carter dies of heart attack," New York *Age*, 5 Sep 1953, 1-2.

2 Snow spelled her given name Valada until about 1930, at which time she changed it, at least for professional purposes, to Valaida.

3 Albert Nicholas was born 27 May 1900 in New Orleans and died 3 September 1973 in Basel, Switzerland.

4 Teddy Weatherford was born 11 October 1903 in Pocahontas, Virginia, and died 25 April 1945 in Calcutta.

5 Dave Peyton, "The musical bunch," Chicago *Defender*, 31 July 1926, 6; 14 August 1926, 6; 4 September 1926, 6.

6 Dave Peyton, "The musical bunch," Chicago *Defender*, 28 August 1926, 7.

7 "Divorce suit keeps hubby from China," Chicago *Defender*, 14 August 1926, 4.

8 "Musician jailed," Baltimore *Afro-American*, 11 September 1926, 5.

9 Dave Peyton, "The musical bunch," 31 July 1926, 7.

10 Dave Peyton, "The musical bunch," Chicago *Defender*, 14 August 1926, 7.

11 Dave Peyton, "The musical bunch," Chicago *Defender*, 29 January 1927, 6;

12 Dave Peyton, "The musical bunch," Chicago *Defender*, 19 March 1927, 9.

13 As quoted from *Asia*, 3 October 1971, in Edward S. Walker, "Shanghai Shuffle," *Jazz and Blues*, May 1972, 27.

14 Valada Snow was born on June 2, 1904, in Chattanooga, Tennessee, and died 30 May 1956 in New York.

15 According to "Piccaninny Troubadours," Indianapolis *Freeman*, 19 April 1913, 6, Valada the Great had been a sensation in Cuba "two seasons ago."

16 Advertisement, North-China *Daily News*, 27 September 1926, 20.

17 Richard, "Roger Richards talks to.... Albert Nicholas," 91.

18 References to James Carson include "Fulton's letter," Chicago *Defender*, 27 June 1925, 8; "Jazzland," *Variety*, 3 November 1926, 52; Harry Levette, "The Drinkards score in Shanghai; Talk of others," Chicago *Defender*, 28 April 1934, 9; S. James Staley, "Is it true what they say about China?" *The Metronome*, vol. 52, no. 12 (December 1936), 17.

19 Advertisement, Shanghai *North-China Daily News*, 18 September 1928, 14.

20 Advertisement, Shanghai *North-China Daily News*, 2 November 1928, 17.

21 "The Serenaders," Hong Kong *South China Morning Post*, 7 November 1928, 7; "Jazz madness," Hong Kong *South China Morning Post*, 8 November 1928, 13.

22 "Toot your own horn!," Pittsburgh *Courier*, 16 November 1929, section 1, 2.

23 "Adelphi Hotel Cabaret," Singapore *Straits Times*, 30 November 1928, 10.

24 "Wilbur's Black Birds," Singapore *Straits Times*, 4 December 1928, 10.

25 Stoddard, *Jazz on the Barbary Coast*, 71.

26 Ibid., 86.

27 "The Blackbirds," Hong Kong *South China Morning Post*, 11 October 1928, 11.

28 Allard J. Mollar, "A Jazz Odyssey: Jack Carter's Orchestra," *Storyville*, no. 63 (February-March 1976), 102.

29 Iain Lang, "A pilgrim's progress," Ken Williamson ed., *This is Jazz* (London: Newnes, 1960), 126.

30 Ivan H. Browning, "Our performers in Europe," New York *Amsterdam News*, 14 August 1929, 8.

31 Advertisement, New York *Herald*, 8 October 1928, 9.

32 "Montmartre singer," New York *Herald*, 11 December 1929, 5.

33 Floyd G. Snelson, "Harlem," New York *Age*, 5 August 1939, 7; "'Brick Top' feted at Jack Carter's Spot," Chicago *Defender*, National edition, 16 December 1939, 21.

34 "Performer tells of his travels and thrills of Oriental climes" [Frank Shiver letter], Chicago *Defender*, 23 August 1930, 9.

35 Advertisement, Shanghai *North-China Daily News*, 26 September 1929, 18; other members of Bob Hill's Syncopators included singer Joe Martin, trombonist Johnny Rosario and steel guitarist Mandez Louis.

36 Advertisement, Shanghai *North-China Daily News*, 4 January 1930, 18.

37 See Peter Darke and Ralph Gulliver, "Teddy Weatherford," *Storyville*, no. 65 (June 1976), 175-190, for an account of Weatherford's post-Shanghai career, which included a return visit to the United States in March 1934 to recruit a new band — trumpeter Buck Clayton's Fourteen Gentlemen from Harlem — for the Canidrome.

## ROME, DECEMBER 10, 1926

1 See "Lo 'jazz band' che tace," *Il Giornale d'Italia*, 12 December 1926, 5; "Rome theatre burns: 4 dead," New York *Herald*, 12 December 1926, 1; "European and American notes," New York *Amsterdam News*, 5 January 1927, 10.

2 "Banjo twanging alone on table saves musician," New York *Herald*, 4 February 1927, 2.

3 New York *Herald*, 12 December 1926, 1.

4 Smith is identified as "Joseph" by the New York *Amsterdam News* ("European and American notes," 5 January 1927, 10), which appears to be the source of subsequent reports in *The Billboard*, ("Paris," 8 January 1927, 35) and the Chicago *Defender* ("Doings in Gay Paree," National edition, 15 January 1927, 7). However, Joseph Smith, a well-known trumpeter of the day, was working and recording with Fletcher Henderson in New York during the period in which Peyton's Jazz Kings were in Rome.

5 Lotz, *Black People*, 321-331.

6 Rudolf Happrich, *Der Artist*, 11 February 1927, quoted in Lotz, *Black People*, 331.

7 Frank Driggs and Harris Levine, *Black Beauty, White Heat: A Pictorial History of Classic Jazz, 1920-1950* (New York: Da Capo Press, 1982), 213.

8 Collective personnel of the New Yorkers during the late 1920s, as noted in various contemporary sources, included banjo players Maceo Jefferson and Henry Saparo, pianist Lou Henley, saxophonist Sidney Bechet, trumpeter Tommy Ladnier, trombonists John Forrester and George Brasheer, and violinist Will Tyler. See, for example, "The Robert Abbotts hear New York band," Chicago *Defender*, 31 Aug 1929, 9.

9 "A jazz premier," New York *Amsterdam News*, 4 September 1929, 9.

10 "Peyton's jazz," New York *Amsterdam News*, 11 September 1929, 9.

## BUENOS AIRES, JUNE 8, 1927

1 Ralph Gulliver, "Leon Abbey," *Storyville*, no. 73 (October 1977), 8.

2 Willie Lewis, one of Wooding's saxophonists on the South American trip, identified the day of Leon Abbey's arrival in Buenos Aires as May 25 and dated the end of Wooding's stay to July 10; see "Lewis with Sam Wooding Band in South America,"

New York *Age*, 2 July 1927, 6. *La Revista Negra* opened on June 3; see advertisement, *La Nacion*, 3 June 1927, 10.

3 Advertisement, Buenos Aires *Standard*, 1 May 1927, 5; the Ta-Ba-Ris was located at 829 Corrientes; the Royal Pigall Dancing had previously operated at 825 Corrientes.

4 Bushell, *Jazz from the Beginning*, 70.

5 Leon (Alexander) Abbey was born 7 May 1900 in Minneapolis and died there 15 September 1975.

6 Abbey's musicians on his South American trip were trumpeters Demas Dean and John Brown, trombonist Robert Horton, saxophonists Joe Garland, Carmelo Jejo and Prince Robinson, pianist Earl Fraser, a banjo player named P. Franklin Blackburn, bassist Henry (Bass) Edwards and drummer Willie Lynch. See Gulliver, "Leon Abbey," 10.

7 Gulliver, "Leon Abbey," 10.

8 Ibid., 9.

9 Ibid., 10. See also "Travellin' Man: The story of Demas Dean as told to Peter Carr," *Storyville*, no. 72 (August 1977), 212.

10 Abbey's new band initially comprised trumpeters Charlie Johnson and Harry Cooper, trombonist Jake Green, reed players Fletcher Allen, Peter Duconge and Ralph James, pianist William Caine, banjo player Harry Stevens, tuba player John Warren and drummer Oliver Tines. See Howard Rye, "Visiting Firemen — 8: a) Leon Abbey and his Orchestra," *Storyville*, no. 108 (August-September 1983), 207.

11 Gulliver, "Leon Abbey," 11.

12 Wine claimed to be an Abyssinian ("A letter from abroad," Chicago *Defender*, 19 May 1928, 10) but publicity photos reportedly describe him as a Canadian from Montreal ("Can't we talk it over?" [letter from Norman Jenkinson], *Storyville*, no. 75 [February 1978], 88-89).

13 Howard Rye, "Visiting Firemen 7: Eubie Blake & Noble Sissle," *Storyville*, no. 105 (February-March 1983), 88-93.

14 Alex Boswell, "Juice Wilson," *Storyville*, no. 75 (February 1978), 92.

15 Robert Edward (Juice) Wilson was born 21 January 1904 in St. Louis; see Boswell, "Juice Wilson," 90-94.

## BERLIN, FEBRUARY 2, 1928

1 Principal sources for this section are Horst J.P. Bergmeier, "The New Yorkers," *Storyville*, no. 145 (March 1991), 11-27; Harold S. Kaye, "Dave Tough with the New Yorkers in Europe, 1927-1929," *Storyville 1998-9*, 5-79. Details of the Tri-Ergon session are drawn from the latter piece.

2 Dave Tough was born 26 April 1907 in Oak Park, Illinois, and died 9 December 1948 in Newark, New Jersey; Danny Polo was born 22 December 1901 in Toluca, Illinois, and died 11 July 1949 in Chicago.

3 Leonard Feather, "Those were the days! Danny Polo tells the story of his work with the pioneers," *The Melody Maker*, 29 May 1937, 7.

4 Kaye, "Dave Tough with the New Yorkers in Europe," 15.

5 Rainer E. Lotz, "Howard Osmond McFarlane — trumpet," *Storyville*, no. 81 (February 1979), 95.

6 Rainer E. Lotz, "Wilbur 'Wib' Kurz — his early career in Europe," *Storyville*, no. 77 (June 1978), 173.

7 "International jazz," *Variety*, 26 October 1927, 3.

8 Personnel for the New Yorkers' Tri-Ergon sessions was Polo, Tough, Evelyn Bazell, Andy Foster, Jack O'Brien, trombonist Eddie Norman and banjo and guitar player Tony Morello. See Kaye, "Dave Tough and the New Yorkers in Europe," 41-43.

9 Kaye, "Dave Tough and the New Yorkers in Europe," 43.

10 Goddard, *Jazz away from Home*, 221.

11 Ibid., 221.

## SYDNEY, MARCH 31, 1928

1 Sources for this section include "No labour permit on Colored pros," *Variety*, 2 May 1928, 1; Jack Mitchell, "Colored ideas," *Storyville*, no. 61 (October 1975), 19-23; Mike Sutcliffe, "Sonny Clay and the Colored Idea," *Australian Record and Music Review*, no. 35 (October 1997), 3-13; Richard Hall, "White Australia's darkest days," *Jazzline*, vol 30, no. 2 (Winter 1997), 12-18.

2 William Rogers Campbell (Sonny) Clay was born 15 May 1899 in Chapel Hill, Texas, and died 13 April 1973 in Los Angeles.

3 Personnel of the Plantation Band on record in late 1927 was Clay, Coycault, Davidson, trumpeter Archie Lancaster, trombonist Luther Craven, saxophonists Louis Dodd and William Griffin, banjo player Rupert Jordan, tubaist Herman Hoy and drummer David Lewis (see Rust, *Jazz Records*, 318). Davidson did not travel to Australia; John Black and Leo Davis were identified as musicians on the *S.S. Sierra*'s passenger list (Sutcliffe, "Sonny Clay and the Colored Idea," 4). Black, Davis, Dodd and Jordan (identified as Dick Jordan) were among those rousted by the Melbourne police (Ibid., 11).

4 Mike Sutcliffe, "Ray Tellier's San Francisco Orchestra," *Australian Music and Record Review*, no. 50 (July 2001), 16-18.

5 Bert Ralton, "The Original Havana Band," *The Melody Maker*, February 1926, 29-32; Mike Sutcliffe, "Bert Ralton in Australia," *Australian Music and Record Review*, no. 20 (January 1994), 12-16.

6 "Joe Sheftell writes," Chicago *Defender*, 9 October 1926, 6.

7 "Sheftell's revue in cafe," *Variety*, 22 June 1927, 58.

8 Clay's recording session for Vocalion has been dated to 12 January 1928 (Rust, *Jazz Records*, 318). However, Clay and his musicians arrived in Sydney on the 20th after a Pacific crossing that typically took 19 days. The recordings, therefore, could have been made no later than the end of December 1927.

9 Hall, "White Australia's darkest days," 13.

10 "From Australia" [Eddie Caldwell letter], Chicago *Defender*, 10 March 1928, 9.

11 Martin C. Brennan, "Australia," *The Billboard*, 17 March 1928, 38.

12 "Sonny Clay looks good for a long run at Sydney Tivoli," *Everyones*, 25 January 1928, 41.

13 "'You took revenge on me because U.S. excluded Commonwealth Band,'" *Everyones*, 4 Apr 1928, 6.

14 Maloney's letter is excerpted by Buddy Brown in a letter written in turn to Dave Peyton and included by Peyton in "The musical bunch," Chicago *Defender*, 5 May 1928, 10.

15 "Cry of 'White Australia' raised by Ex-Premier; American Negroes deported for misconduct," New York *Times*, 29 March 1928, 18; "Negro entertainers in Australia," London *Times*, 29 March 1928, 16.

16 Michael Quinn and Mike Sutcliffe, "Visiting artists to Australia 1835-1945," *Australian Record and Music Review*, no. 30 (July 1996), 17-18. Singer Nina Mae McKinney and dancer U.S. Thompson appeared in Australia in 1937, dancer Peg Leg Bates in 1938 and singers Ada Brown and the Mills Brothers in 1939.

## PARIS, DECEMBER 22, 1928

1 "Onlookers hit when Negroes exchange fire," New York *Herald*, 23 December 1928, 3. The newspaper reported that the incident took place at about 8 a.m. "yesterday morning."

2 According to the United States Social Security Death Index, Glover Compton was born 6 January 1884 in Harrodsburg, Kentucky, and died in 1964, probably in Chicago. His year of birth was listed as 1894 on the passenger list of the *S.S. St. John*, which took him back to New York in 1939, but in 1910 he was already "one of the best piano players from Louisville" (Cary B. Lewis, "Stage Notes," Indianapolis *Freeman*, 17 September 1910, 5) and in the employ of one of Chicago's leading cabarets, the Elite — hardly the accomplishments of a 16-year-old musician.

3 Mike McKendrick was born 18 July 1904 in Paducah, Kentucky, according to the passenger list for the same *S.S. St. John*, on which he — like Compton — returned to New York in 1939. John Chilton, *Who's Who of Jazz* (New York: Da Capo Press, 1985), 216, puts McKendrick's death in Chicago in 1961.

4 Henry Crowder, with Hugo Speck, *As Wonderful as All That?* (Navarro, Calif.: Wild Trees Press, 1987), 78.

5 "Chicago musician brands tale in American papers," Chicago *Defender*, 9 February 1929, 7.

6 Bechet, *Treat It Gentle*, 150-152.

7 "2 Colored Am. musicians in shooting over white," *Variety*, 26 December 1928, 3; Bechet, *Treat It Gentle*, 153.

8 Oral History, 30 June 1959, held by the Tulane Jazz Archives.

9 Chilton, *Sidney Bechet*, 84.

## PARIS, DECEMBER 7, 1929

1 Thomas Wolfram, "Paris," *The Billboard*, 28 December 1929, 43; Wolfram's column, datelined December 11, states that the

Plantation reopened "Saturday night," the 7th; the first ads for the Plantation in the New York *Herald* did not appear until the 12th.

2 As dated by ads in the New York *Herald*, 23 November 1924, 5; 7 October 1925, 8.

3 "Louie Mitchell," Baltimore *Afro-American*, 6 April 1929, 28.

4 Cofie's Colored Cracks in 1929 comprised the Cofies, Withers, saxophonists Angelo Fernandez, Maxwell Philpott and Wilson Townes, trumpeter Titus D. Triplett, pianist Abram Henderson and banjo player Gilbert Roberts. See "'Cofie's Cracks' wake echoes in 'Ole Madrid,'" Chicago *Defender*, National edition, 17 August 1929, 6; "Cofie's Colored Cracks playing in Barcelona," New York *Age*, 26 October 1929, 7.

5 Marvel Cooke, "Mitchell closes Paris nightclub; returns," New York *Amsterdam News*, 23 March 1940, 5.

6 *The Billboard*, 28 December 1929, 43.

7 Goddard, *Jazz away from Home*, 278; Romans identified the other members of the Versatile Four in this period as drummer Charlie Clarke and saxophonist Bobby Jones. The timeframe for this reference is dated approximately by Romans' recollection that Valada Snow "later" appeared with the group; Snow and the Versatile Four were at Chez Victor in August 1929 (Theodore Wolfram, "Paris," *The Billboard*, 24 August 1929, 40).

8 Abel Green, "Paris night clubs," *Variety*, 25 December 1929, 44.

9 Cooke, "Mitchell closes Paris nightclub; returns," 5.

10 Theodore Wolfram, "Paris," The *Billboard*, 25 October 1930, 44; in a dispatch dated October 8, Wolfram noted that Mitchell "left for New York last Saturday," the 4th.

11 Clifford W. Mackay, "Going backstage with the scribe," Chicago *Defender*, National edition, 6 June 1931, 5; Mitchell later claimed that he returned to New York to open a night club at the behest of gangster Legs Diamond but that Diamond was murdered "on the Sunday I arrived." (Cooke, *Amsterdam News*, 23 March 1940, 5) Diamond, however, died in 1931.

## NEW YORK HARBOUR, OCTOBER 27, 1939 (EPILOGUE)

1 As identified from the passenger list for the *S.S. St. John*, included in "U.S. Department of Justice, Immigration and Naturalization Service, Manifest Volume 13806, October 27-30, 1939."

2 Floyd G. Snelson, "Harlem," New York *Age*, 4 November 1939, 4.

3 "Christian finds New World," *Swing Music*, December 1939, 5.

4 Snelson, "Harlem," 4.

5 "Only 437 brought by refugee liner," New York *Times*, 28 October 1939, 4.

6 "Christian finds New World," 5.

7 "Bury Jelly Roll Morton on coast," *Down Beat*, 1 August 1941, 13.

# BIBLIOGRAPHY

## NOTE

Citations are to the editions used by the author; in some cases, earlier or later editions also exist. The original year of publication, if earlier than the one cited, is noted in square brackets as follows:

Bechet, Sidney. *Treat It Gentle: An Autobiography.* New York: Da Capo Press, 1978 [1960].

## HISTORY

Bisset, Andrew. *Black Roots White Flowers: A History of Jazz in Australia.* Sydney: Australian Broadcasting Corporation, 1987 [1979].

Brierre, Jean Dominique. *Le Jazz français de 1900 à aujourd'hui.* Paris: Éditions Hors Collection, 2000.

Charters, Samuel B., and Leonard Kunstadt. *Jazz: A History of The New York Scene.* Garden City, New York: Doubleday, 1962.

John Chilton. *Who's Who of Jazz.* 4th ed. New York: Da Capo Press, 1985.

de Barros, Paul. *Jackson Street after Hours: The Roots of Jazz in Seattle.* Seattle: Sasquatch Books, 1993.

Driggs, Frank, and Harris Levine. *Black Beauty, White Heat: A Pictorial History of Classic Jazz, 1920-1950.* New York: Da Capo Press, 1996 [1982].

Duclos-Arkilovitch, Jonathan. *Jazzin' Riviera: 70 ans de jazz sur la Côte d'Azur.* Nice: ROM Éditions 1997.

Fletcher, Tom. *100 years of the Negro in Show Business.* New York: Da Capo Press, 1984 [1954].

Gilmore, John. *Swinging in Paradise: The Story of Jazz in Montreal.* Montreal: Véhicule Press, 1988.

— *Who's Who of Jazz in Montreal: Ragtime to 1970.* Montreal: Véhicule Press, 1989.

Godbolt, Jim. *A History of Jazz in Britain 1919-50.* London: Paladin Books, 1986.

Goddard, Chris. *Jazz away from Home.* New York: Paddington Press Ltd., 1979.

Goffin, Robert. *Aux frontières du jazz.* Paris: Éditions du Sagittaire, 1932.

— *Jazz: From the Congo to the Metropolitan.* New York: Da Capo Press, 1975 [1944].

Hodes, Art, and Chadwick Hansen, eds. *Selections from the Gutter.* Berkeley, Calif.: University of California Press, 1977.

Jackson, Jeffrey H. *Making Jazz French: Music and Modern Life in Interwar Paris.* Durham, N.C.: Duke University Press, 2003.

Kernfeld, Barry, ed. *The New Grove Dictionary of Jazz.* 2nd ed. London: Macmillan 2002.

Lotz, Rainer E. *Black People: Entertainers of African Descent in Europe and Germany.* Bonn: Birgit Lotz Verlag, 1997.

— and Ian Pegg, ed. *Under the Imperial Carpet: Essays in Black History 1780-1950.* Crawley, England: Rabbit Press, 1986.

Martin, Denis-Constant, and Olivier Roueff, eds. *La France du Jazz: Musique, modernité et identité dans la première moitié de XXe siècle.* Marseille: Éditions Parenthèses, 2002.

Mazzoletti, Adriano. *Il jazz in Italia: Dalle origini al dopoguerra.* Roma-Bari: Laterza, 1983.

Miller, Mark. *Such Melodious Racket: The Lost History of Jazz in Canada, 1914-1949.* Toronto: The Mercury Press, 1997.

Pernet, Robert. *Jazz in Little Belguim.* Brussels: Éditions Sigma, 1966.

Pujol, Sergio Alejandro. *Jazz el sur: la música negra en la Argentina.* Buenos Aires: Emec, 1992.

Rust, Brian. *Jazz Records 1898-1942.* New Rochelle, New York: Arlington House, 1978.

Shack, William A. *Harlem in Montmartre: A Paris jazz story between the Great Wars.* Berkeley, Calif.: University of California Press, 2001.

Southern, Eileen. *Biographical Dictionary of Afro-American and African Musicians.* Westport, Conn.: Greenwood Press, 1982.

Starr, S. Frederick. *Red & Hot: The Fate of Jazz in the Soviet Union.* New York: Limelight Editions, 1985 [1983].

Stendahl, Bjørn. *Jazz, Hot & Swing: Jazz i Norge 1920-1940.* Oslo: Norsk Jazzarkiv, 1987.

Stearns, Jean and Marshall. *Jazz Dance: The Story of American Vernacular Dance.* New York: Macmillan, 1968.

Stoddard, Tom. *Jazz on the Barbary Coast.* Chigwell, Essex, England: Storyville, 1982.

Tournès, Ludovic. *New Orleans sur Seine: Histoire du jazz en France.* Paris: Editions Fayard, 1999.

Wiedemann, Erik. *Jazz i Danmark — i tyverne, trediverne og fyrrerne: en musikkulturel undersøgelse.* Copenhagen: Gyldendal, 1982.

Wright, Laurie, ed. *Storyville 1996-7.* Chigwell, Essex, England: L. Wright, 1997.

— *Storyville 1998-9.* Chigwell, Essex, England: L. Wright, 1999.

— *Storyville 2000-1.* Chigwell, Essex, England: L. Wright, 2001.

— *Storyville 2003-3.* Chigwell, Essex, England: L. Wright, 2003.

## AUTOBIOGRAPHY

Bechet, Sidney. *Treat It Gentle: An Autobiography.* New York: Da Capo Press, 1978 [1960].

Bricktop. *Bricktop.* With James Haskins. New York: Atheneum, 1983.

Bushell, Garvin. *Jazz from the Beginning.* With Mark Tucker. New York: Da Capo Press, 1998 [c 1988].

Crowder, Henry. *As Wonderful as All That? Henry Crowder's memoir of His Affair with Nancy Cunard, 1928-1935.* With Hugo Speck. Navarro, Calif.: Wild Trees Press, 1987.

Danzi, Mike. *American Musician in Germany 1924-1939: Memoirs of the jazz, entertainment, and movie world of Berlin during the Weimar Republic and the nazi era, and in the United States.* With Rainer E. Lotz. Schmitten, Germany: Norbert Ruecker, 1986.

Mezzrow, Mezz. *Really the Blues.* With Bernard Wolfe. London: Transworld, 1961 [1946].

Milhaud, Darius. *Notes without Music: An Autobiography.* Rollo H. Myers ed. Trans. Donald Evans. London: Dobson, 1952.

Mistinguett. *Mistinguett: Queen of the Paris Night.* Trans. Lucienne Hill. London: Elek Books, 1954.

Smith, Willie The Lion. *Music on My Mind: The Memoirs of an American Pianist.* With George Hoefer. New York: Da Capo Press, 1978 [1964].

## BIOGRAPHY

Badger, Reid. *A Life in Ragtime: A Biography of James Reese Europe.* New York: Oxford University Press, 1995.

Biagioni, E. *Herb Flemming: A jazz pioneer around the world.* Alphen aan de Rijn, Holland: Micography, 1977.

Breese, Charlotte. *Hutch.* London: Bloomsbury Publishing, 1999.

Brunn, H.O. *The Story of the Original Dixieland Jazz Band.* Baton Rouge: Louisiana State University Press, 1960.

Carroll, John M. *Fritz Pollard: Pioneer in Racial Advancement.* Chicago: University of Illinois Press, 1992.

Chilton, John. *Sidney Bechet: The Wizard of Jazz.* New York: Oxford University Press, 1987.

Colin, Sid and Tony Staveacre. *Al Bowlly.* London: Elm Tree Books, 1979.

Green, Jeffrey P. *Edmund Thornton Jenkins: The life and times of an American Black Composer, 1894-1926.* Westport, Conn.: Greenwood Press, 1982.

Kimball, Robert, and William Bolcolm. *Reminiscing with Sissle and Blake.* New York: Viking Press, 1973.

LLoyd, Craig. *Eugene Bullard: Black Expatriate in Jazz-Age Paris.* Athens, Georgia: University of Georgia Press, 2000.

Lomax, Alan. *Mister Jelly Roll: The Fortunes of Jelly Roll Morton, New Orleans Creole and "Inventor of Jazz."* Berkeley and Los Angeles: University of California Press, 1973.

Pastras, Phil. *Dead Man Blues: Jelly Roll Morton Way out West.* Berkeley and Los Angeles: University of California Press, 2001.

Vaché, Warren W. Sr. *Crazy Fingers: Claude Hopkins' Life in Music.* Washington, D.C.: Smithsonian Institution Press, 1992.

## GENERAL BACKGROUND

Archer-Straw, Petrine. *Negrophilia: Avant-Garde Paris and Black Culture in the 1920s.* New York: Thames & Hudson, 2000.

Cantor, Norman F. *The American Century: Varieties in Culture in Modern Times.* New York: Harper Collins, 1997.

Clifford, Nicholas R. Shanghai 1925: *Urban Nationalism and the Defense of Foreign Privilege.* Ann Arbor, Mich.: Centre for Chinese Studies, 1979.

Cocteau, Jean. *A Call to Order.* Trans. Rollo Myers. London: Faber and Gwyer, 1926.

Eksteins, Modris. *Rites of Spring: The Great War and the Birth of the Modern Age.* Toronto: Lester & Orpen Dennys, 1989.

Stovall, Tyler. *Paris Noir: African Americans in the City of Light.* Boston: Houghton Mifflin, 1996.

## MAJOR ARTICLES

Ansermet, E. "Sur un orchestre nègre." *La Revue Romande*, 15 Oct 1919. Reprinted, together with an English translation by Walter E. Schaap, *Jazz Hot*, no. 28 (November-December 1938): 4-7, 9.

Averty, Jean-Christophe. "Sidney Bechet 1919-1922." *Jazz Hot*, no. 250 (May 1969): 22-23.

Barazzetta, Guiseppe. "Frank Guarante: a forgotten pioneer." *Jazz Monthly*, vol. 12, no. 2 (December 1966): 2-6.

Behncke, Berhard H. "Sam Wooding and the Chocolate Kiddies at the Thalia-Theater in Hamburg 28 July, 1925 to 24 August, 1925." *Storyville*, no. 60 (August 1975): 214-221.

Bergmeier, Horst J.P. "Sam Wooding recapitulated." *Storyville*, no. 74 (December 1977): 44-47.

—— "The New Yorkers." *Storyville*, no. 145 (March 1991): 11-27.

Berresford, Mark. "From New York to London — Eddie Gross Bart's Story." *Storyville*, no. 102 (August-September 1982): 209-229.

Carr, Peter. "Travellin' Man: The story of Demas Dean as told to Peter Carr." *Storyville*, no. 72 (August 1977): 207-217.

Clausen, Morten. "Thompson's jazz band in Copenhagen 1923-1925: The story of the first black jazz band in Denmark." *Storyville 1998-9*, Laurie Wright, ed. Chigwell, Essex, England: L. Wright, 1999: 136-155.

Cooke, Marvel. "Step up Louis Mitchell." New York *Amsterdam News*, 24 Feb 1940: 15.

—— "12,000 nights of entertainment: Mitchell, sensation of Europe." New York *Amsterdam News*, 2 Mar 1940: 15.

—— "12,000 nights of entertainment: Mitchell loves his baseball." New York *Amsterdam News*, 9 Mar 1940: 15.

—— "12,000 nights of entertainment: Mitchell, American boy host to Prince." New York *Amsterdam News*, 16 Mar 1940: 13.

—— "Mitchell closes Paris nightclub; returns." New York *Amsterdam News*, 23 Mar 1940: 5.

Conte, Gérard, "Les Mitchell's Jazz Kings." *Jazz Hot*, November 1968, 34-36.

Darke, Peter, and Ralph Gulliver. "Teddy Weatherford." *Storyville*, no. 65 (June 1976): 175-190.

Demeusy, Bertrand. "The Bertin Depestre Salnave Musical Story." Trans. Howard Rye. *Storyville*, no. 78 (August 1978): 207-219.

Deputier, Ivan. "Le jazz en France." *Jazz Hot*, no. 246 (January 1969): 35-37.

Ekyan, André, and Stéphane Grappelly, Alain Romains and Ray Ventura. "Les débuts du jazz en France." *Jazz Hot*, 248 (March 1969): 38-39, 41.

Englund, Björn. "Chocolate Kiddies: The show that brought jazz to Europe and Russia in 1925." *Storyville*, no. 62 (December 1975): 44-50.

Gulliver, Ralph. "Leon Abbey." *Storyville*, no. 73 (October 1977): 4-28.

Gushee, Lawrence. "A preliminary chronology of the early career of Ferd "Jelly Roll" Morton." *American Music*, vol. 3, no. 4 (Winter 1985): 389-412.

—— "How the Creole Band came to be." *Black Music Research Journal*, vol. 8, no. 1 (1988): 83-100.

Gutteridge, Len. "The first man to bring jazz to Britain." *The Melody Maker*, 14 Jul 1956: 6.

—— "The man who brought jazz to Britain." *The Saturday Book*. J. Hadfield, ed. London: Hutchinson, 1957: 108-116.

Hall, Richard. "White Australia's darkest days." *Jazzline*, vol. 30, no. 2 (Winter 1997): 12-18.

Kaye, Harold S. "Dave Tough with the New Yorkers in Europe, 1927-1929." *Storyville 1998-9*, Laurie Wright, ed. Chigwell, Essex, England: L. Wright, 1999: 5-79.

Larsen, John, and Hans Larsen. "The Chocolate Kiddies in Copenhagen." *Record Research*, no. 67 (April 1965): 3-5, 14.

Lotz, Rainer E. "Alex Hyde's Hot Dance Recordings for Deutsche Grammophon Gesellschaft." *Storyville*, no. 74 (December 1977): 50-62.

—— "Wilbur 'Wib' Kurz — his early career in Europe." *Storyville*, no. 77 (June 1978): 171-176.

—— "Nick Casti — trumpet." *Storyville*, no. 93 (February 1981): 103-111.

—— "Johnny Dixon — trumpet." *Storyville*, no. 99 (February-March 1982): 102-111.

Miller, Mark. "Frank Withers: a lost voice and a lost review." *Coda Magazine*, no. 310 (July-August 2003): 5-6.

Mitchell, Jack. "Colored ideas." *Storyville*, no. 61 (October 1975): 19-23.

Moller, Allard J. "A jazz odyssey: Jack Carter's Orchestra." *Storyville*, no. 63 (February-March 1976): 97-103.

Napoleon, Art. "A pioneer looks back: Sam Wooding 1967." *Storyville*, no. 9 (February 1967): 3-8, 37-39.

—— "A pioneer looks back: part 2." *Storyville*, no. 10 (April 1967): 4-8.

Pernet, Robert. "Some notes on Arthur Briggs." *Storyville*, no. 84 (August 1979): 205-209.

—— "Quiproquo [sic] — Louis Mitchell ou Murray Pilcer?" *Record Memory Club Magazine*, no. 50 (March 2000): unpaginated (21-31).

—— and Howard Rye. "Visiting Firemen 18: Louis Mitchell." *Storyville 2000-1*. Laurie Wright, ed. Chigwell, Essex, England: L. Wright, 2001: 221-248.

Richard, Roger. "Roger Richard talks to.... Albert Nicholas." *Storyville*, no. 57 (February 1975): 86-96.

Rye, Howard. "Visiting Firemen — 8: a) Leon Abbey and his Orchestra." *Storyville*, no. 108 (August-September 1983): 207-208.

—— "Visiting Firemen 9: The Blackbirds and their orchestras." *Storyville*, no. 112 (April-May 1984): 133-147.

—— "Visiting Firemen 13: 'The Plantation Revues.'" *Storyville*, no. 133 (March 1988): 4-15.

—— "Visiting Firemen 14: Joe Jordan 1915." *Storyville*, no. 134 (June 1988): 55-58.

—— "Visiting Firemen 15: The Southern Syncopated Orchestra (Part 1)." *Storyville*, no. 142 (June 1990): 137-146.

—— "Visiting Firemen 15: The Southern Syncopated Orchestra (Part 2)." *Storyville*, no. 143 (September 1990): 164-178.

—— "Visiting Firemen 15: The Southern Syncopated Orchestra (Concluded)." *Storyville*, no. 144 (December 1990): 227-234.

—— "Rudolph Dunbar: The jazz years: a chronology." *Storyville 2002-3*. Laurie Wright, ed. Chigwell, Essex, England: L. Wright, 1999: 102-116.

—— and Jeffrey Green. "Black Musical Internationalism in England in the 1920s." *Black Music Research Journal*, vol. 15, no. 1 (Spring 1985): 93-107.

—— and Tim Brooks. "Visiting Firemen 16: Dan Kildare." *Storyville 1996-7*, Laurie Wright, ed. Chigwell, Essex, England: L. Wright, 1997: 30-57.

Shenck, John T. "The colorful saga of Darnell Howard." *The Jazz Session*, March-April 1945: 2-3, 8-9, 16-17.

Shiver, Frank. "Performer tells of his travels and thrills of Oriental climes." Chicago *Defender*, 23 Aug 1930: 15.

Specht, Paul. "L'histoire des Georgians." *Jazz Hot*, no. 59 (October 1951): 15, 21.

Stonor, Henry A. "They played at Raffles." *Storyville*, no. 42 (August 1972): 217-229.

Sutcliffe, Mike. "Sonny Clay and the Colored Idea." *Australian Record and Music Review*. no. 35 (October 1997): 3-13.

—— "Ray Tellier's San Francisco Orchestra." *Australian Music and Record Review*, no. 50 (July 2001), 16-18.

Walker, Edward T. "Shanghai Shuffle." *Jazz and Blues*, May 1972: 26-27.

Woessner, Hans Peter. "The (unknown) Kalophon recordings of Frank Guarante's World Known Georgians in Switzerland." *Storyville*, no. 147 (September 1991): 97-104.

Wooding, Samuel. "Eight years abroad with a jazz band." *The Etude*, April 1939: 233-234, 282.

## NEWSPAPERS

The following titles have been reviewed closely for the years noted:

Baltimore *Afro-American*. 1917-18, 1925-9.

Chicago *Defender*. 1914-1940.

Indianapolis *Freeman*. 1908-1920.

*Metronome*. 1917-1930.

New York *Age*. 1911-1921.

New York *Amsterdam News*. 1926-8.

New York *Herald*. Paris edition. 1917-1930.

North China *Daily News*. 1923-1929.

*Variety*. 1917-30.

*The Billboard*. 1917-1930.

*The Melody Maker*. 1924-1930.

Other newspapers — eg, Buenos Aires *Standard*, *The Statesman* (Calcutta), *Izvestiia* (Moscow), London *Times*, Manila *Times*, *Paris-Midi*, Singapore *Straits Times* — have been consulted, as cited, with respect to specific events.

## WEBSITES

www.ellisisland.org [passenger lists for ships arriving in New York, 1892-1924].

http://ssdi.genealogy.rootsweb.com [United States Social Security Death Index].

http://vitals.rootsweb/ca/death/search.cgi [California Death Records].

# Index

Brown, Lottie, 150
Brun, Philippe, 163
Brunswick (record label), 158
Brymn, Tim, 32, 52
Buckingham Palace (London), 61, 68
Buenos Aires *Herald*, 106
Buffalos, 32, 109
*Bugle Blues* (*Bugle Call Rag*), 45, 54
Bugoslavsky, Sergei, 144-145
Buie, Alex (Monk), 189a
Bullard, Eugene, 113, *134*
*Bull Foot Stomp*, 158
Bumford, Earl, 25
Burnett, Roscoe, *77*, 79, 88, *131*, *134*, 188b
Bushell, Garvin, 107, *133*, 145, 146, 156, 190a
*Bye Bye Blackbird*, 114

Cabaret Garden (Calgary), 30
Caddo Orchestra, 81
de Caillaux, Pierre, 69, *131*, 169
Caine, William, 192b
Caldwell, Eddie, 166
California Blue Boy, 182b — see also Charles W. Hamp
California Ramblers, 84
Canaro, Francisco "Pirincho," 77
*Caramel Mou* (Milhaud), 96
Carhart, George, 160, 161, 162-163
Carlisle, Una Mae, 175
Carlos-Arolas (tango orchestra), 79
Carolina Club Orchestra, 120, 122
Carpenter, Elliot, 55, *77*, 78, 79-80, 88, *131*, 184b
Carson, James, 2, 92, 149, 152
Carter, Benny, 12
Carter, Jack, 11, 104, 127, *136*, 138, 139, 147, 148, 149-150, 151, 152, 158, 191a
Jack Carter's Serenaders, 147-150, 151-152
*Casablanca*, 79
Casino de Paris, 40, 41, 43, 49, 50, 58, 71, 72, 73, 74, 75, 76, 111, 142, 172, 182a
Casino Jazz Band, 49
Castle, Irene, 20
Castle, Vernon, 20
Caulk, Joe, 69, 70, 111, 114, *131*, *134*
*C'est la Miss...!* (revue), 106
Chaillou, Maurice, 163
Chambers, Elmer, 53

*Characteristic Blues*, 67, 68
*Charleston*, 156
Charleston Jazz Band, 140-141, 190b
*Charlestonia* (Jenkins), 156
Chase, Tommy, 175
Chateau Dupère (Montreal), 83
Cheatham, Adolphus (Doc), 90, 158
Chevalier, Maurice, 41, 74, 96
Chez Florence (Paris), 113, 114, 169, 172, 173
Chicago *Defender*, 26, 36, 37, 39, 47-48, 59, 60, 74, 86, 91, 92, 100, 101, 102, 103, 106, 113, 137, 146, 147, 149, 152, 154, 166, 170
Chicago Hot Spots, 121
Chicago *Tribune*, 170
*The Chocolate Dandies* (revue), 140, 148
*Chocolate Kiddies* (revue), 123, 124, 125, 126, 140, 144, 145, 153, 155, 156, 157-158, 175
Chocolate Kiddies Orchestra, 34, 145, 152
Christian, Emile, 61, 62, 163, 175, 176, 177
Ciro's (London), 22-23, 25, 26, 30, 34, 35, 59, 72, 75, 93
Ciro's Club Coon Orchestra, 35
Clair, René, 96
Clapham, George, 87, 105, 153, 187b
*Clarinet Marmalade*, 162
Clark, H. Quali, 37
Clark, Spencer, 162, 163
Clarke, Charlie, *134*, 194a
Clay, Sonny, 11, 91, 165, 166, 167-168, 193a
Clayton, Buck, 12, 192a
Clef Club (baseball team), 116-117
Clef Club of New York, 11, 13, 20-21, 22, 24, 26, 36, 49, 55, 62, 71, 77-78, 179a, 182a
Clinton, Jean Paul, 87, 186a
Close Harmony Boys, 173
Cocteau, Jean, 40, 73, 96, 181a
Cofie, Harry, 172, 194a
Cofie, Madge, 172, 194a
Cofie's Colored Cracks, 34, 158, 172, 194a
Cole, Bob, 15, 20
Cole, June, 154
Cole, William (Kid), 111
*Colored Idea* (revue), *135*, 165, 166, 167-168

Columbia (record label), 35, 63, 64, 70, 98, 120, 159
Combes, Arthur, 183a
Compo (record company), 82
Compton, Glover, *134*, 169, 170, 171, 175, 177, 193b
Conaway, Sterling, 172
Condor (record label), 165
Cook, Charles (Doc), 31
Cook, Marion, 141
Cook, Will Marion, 12, 66, 67, 68, 69, 71, 87, 94, 105, 108, 142, 183b
Cooper, Harry, 192b
Cooper, Opal, 54, 55, *77*, 78, 79, 114, *131*, 169
de Corville, Albert, 61, 65
Cosey, Antonio, 175
Costello, Johnny, 185b
Coxito, Ferdinand (Fred), 69, 76, *131*, 142, 153, 154, 184a, 190b
Coycault, Ernest (Nenny), 165, 193a
Crackerjacks, 111, 114, 115, 172, 188b
Craven, Luther, 193a
Crawford, Adolf, 93, 184b, 187b, 188b
Crawford, Sadie, 93, 105, 184b, 187b
*Le Création du Monde* (Milhaud), 96
Creole Band (New Orleans Creole Ragtime Band), 17, 18, 19, 25, 37, 62, 150
Creole Five, 89
*Creole Love Call*, 125
Cressell, Edward, *132*, 184b
*Crickett Rag*, 75
Crowder, Henry, 86, 169, 170, 176
Crutcher, Leon, 109, 110, 188b
Cubinar, Philip (Shorty), 149
Cunard, Nancy, 169

Dabney, Ford, 72
Dakin, Edwin (Vernon), 182b
Dan and Harvey's Jazz Band, 93
*Dancing News*, 63
*The Dancing World*, 78, 120
Arthur Daniels, 30
Danzi, Mike, 124, 161
*Darktown Jingles* (show), 26
*Darktown Strutters' Ball*, 56, 58
Daugherty, Leo, 184b
Davidson, John Evert, 189b
Davidson, Leonard (Big Boy), 165, 193a
Davis, Belle, 26, 34